# Billy Connolly's Route 66

## The Big Yin on the Ultimate American Road Trip

## Billy Connolly

*with* Robert Uhlig

ISIS
LARGE PRINT
Oxford

Copyright © Billy Connolly, 2011


First published in Great Britain 2011
by
Sphere
An imprint of Little, Brown Book Group


Published in Large Print 2012 by ISIS Publishing Ltd.,
7 Centremead, Osney Mead, Oxford OX2 0ES
by arrangement with
Little, Brown Book Group
An Hachette UK Company

**British Library Cataloguing in Publication Data**
Connolly, Billy.
    Billy Connolly's Route 66.
    1. Connolly, Billy - - Travel - - United States
    Highway 66.
    2. United States - - Description and travel.
    3. United States Highway 66.
    4. Large type books.
    I. Title II. Route 66
    917.3'04932–dc23


    ISBN 978–0–7531–5312–3 (hb)
    ISBN 978–0–7531–5313–0 (pb)


Printed and bound in Great Britain by
T. J. International Ltd., Padstow, Cornwall

# BILLY CONNOLLY'S ROUTE 66

AnC
7/13

**Blackpool Council**
BUILDING A BETTER COMMUNITY FOR ALL

1 SEP 2014

WITHDRAWN

Please return/renew this item
by the last date shown.
Books may also be renewed by
phone or the Internet.

**Tel: 01253 478070**
**www.blackpool.gov.uk**

# Contents

# CHAPTER
# ONE

## Get Your Kicks

It was a moment I'll remember for the rest of my life. I'd been travelling along Route 66 for a few days, and I couldn't resist a quick detour to Arthur, a small community nearly two hundred miles south of Chicago. "Population 800", it said on the sign at the edge of town. Beside it, another sign warned drivers that the roads might be busy with horse-drawn carriages. And with good reason: this was Amish country.

I didn't know what to expect. I'd always quite liked Amish folk; although, to be honest, I knew very little about them. It was just something about the look — the horse-drawn carriages, the hats, the plain, modest clothing, the way they carried themselves — that always led me to think they were really rather nice people.

I parked my trike outside a simple house that backed on to a large workshop. Waiting inside was a furniture-maker with the best haircut I'd ever seen — like Rowan Atkinson's pudding bowl in the first series of *Blackadder*. Beneath the mop of hair was Mervin, a man with a thick beard, no moustache and a slow, soft grin.

Mervin makes the most outstandingly great furniture: the kind of stuff that will last for ever; the antiques of tomorrow. He showed me around his workshop, then we stood in his office while he answered every question I asked with total honesty. I could tell immediately that this delightful, decent man was being absolutely straight with me. He had nothing to hide. Men like Mervin have a ring of truth about them.

"Why do you all grow beards and you don't grow moustaches?" I said.

"Well, I wouldn't want to grow a moustache when everybody just had a beard and no moustache," said Mervin. "We like to be the same and share and be equal."

How humane. In this age of individualism, what a delight to find a community of people who strive for equality and lead their lives according to whatever is best for everyone. We talked some more and Mervin explained the rules of the community, although the way he told it, those rules didn't seem like restrictions but simple guidelines for a better, more harmonious way of living. With no sign of frustration about what he wasn't allowed to do, Mervin totally accepted the boundaries of his life. Then he asked me if I wanted to go for a ride on his buggy.

You know those black Amish buggies? I'd always fancied a ride on one of them, but first we had to get Mervin's horse out of the stable and hitch it to the front of the wagon. Now, I'm a wee bit frightened of horses — not terrified, just a wee bit wary. So I lurked behind Mervin until he'd got the beast out of the stable, then I led it to the buggy and Mervin showed me how to hitch it up. We climbed into the buggy and off we went. After about two minutes Mervin said, "Here . . ." and handed me the reins. I was in charge. I was in seventh heaven. Riding along in an Amish buggy, with an Amish guy, waving to Amish people. It was a wonderful moment. It might sound ludicrously inconsequential — and I suppose it was — but it pleased me so, so much.

Once we'd ridden in the buggy for a while, Mervin invited me and the whole film crew back to his farm for something to eat. And we're not talking a bag of crisps here. An amazing meal was prepared by Mervin's wife and mother, dressed in traditional long dresses, while a group of little girls, so beautiful in their bonnets, sang wee songs to themselves, completely oblivious to us.

Not everything that I experienced with Mervin was quite so idyllic, though. While we were in the buggy, he told me about a family tragedy that was so distressing it took my breath away. I'll not tell you any more about it until we come to that part of the story. All I'll say now is that it broke my heart. Yet Mervin had a stoicism about him that had kept him sane in the face of a terrible event. If something similar had happened to me, it would have haunted me for the rest of my life, and it might have changed me for the worse. But Mervin had an acceptance that allowed him to remain a lovely, honest, happy man.

Without any doubt, the time I spent with Mervin was one of the highlights of my life. I'll remember that afternoon clip-clopping through Arthur, Illinois, for ever. There wasn't much to it, but I think of my life as a series of moments and I've found that the great moments often don't have too much to them. They're not huge, complicated events; they're just magical wee moments when somebody says "I love you" or "You're really good at what you do" or simply "You're a good person". I had one that day with Mervin, the Amish furniture-maker.

The peace and simplicity of Mervin's little community stood in stark contrast to what I'd seen over the past few days along Route 66 — that mythical highway forever associated with rock'n'roll, classic Americana and the great open road. Most people, including me, would think of wisecracking waitresses and surly short-order cooks in classic fifties diners. Grease monkeys with dirty rags and tyre wrenches. Gas-pump jockeys and highway patrolmen. Oklahoma hillbillies in overalls and work boots. Stetson-wearing Texan ranch owners and cowboys at a rodeo. Idealistic hitch-hikers following in the footsteps of Jack Kerouac. Eccentric owners of Route 66-themed tourist haunts. Native Americans in the Navajo and Apache reservations of New Mexico and Arizona. Maybe even a few surfers, hippies or internet entrepreneurs in California.

I'd already met a few of them, but when I'd set out from Chicago a few days earlier, my greatest hope had been to make a connection with someone just like Mervin. I'd thought back to similar trips I'd made in the past, like my tour of Britain and my journey across Australia. Every journey had involved visits to historic sites, explorations of beautiful landscapes, and planned

4

meetings with locals and various dignitaries. The itinerary had always been tightly scheduled, as it has to be when shooting a television series. But in every case the best moments had resulted from an unexpected encounter with an interesting character — like the time ten years earlier when I'd made a television series called *Billy Connolly's World Tour of England, Ireland and Wales*.

I met dozens of fascinating people and visited scores of locations between Dublin and Plymouth, but the highlight came when I visited the grave of Mary Shelley, author of *Frankenstein*, at the parish church of St Peter in Bournemouth. I suppose you could say I'm a bit freaky, because I've always been fond of graveyards. Many people think of them as morbid, sad places, but to me they're monuments to great lives lived and they provide a connection to our ancestors and heritage. They're full of stories about people. And the story of Mary and her fantastically talented husband, the poet Percy Bysshe Shelley, is as good as they come. Which was why, one sunny day, I was standing beside her grave with a television camera and a furry microphone pointing at me.

Just as I was telling the tragic story of how Percy Shelley drowned in Italy, a stooped figure appeared in the graveyard. Dressed in black, clutching a can of strong cider, and with a dirty green sleeping bag draped around his shoulders, he approached us with an admirable disdain for the conventions of television productions. Oblivious of the tramp's approach, I continued to talk to the camera, relating the story of

Shelley's cremation on a beach. I'd just mentioned that Shelley's friend Edward John Trelawny snatched the poet's heart from the funeral pyre and passed it on to Mary, who then kept it in a velvet bag around her neck for thirty years, when the old fella stopped beside me and pointed at the grave.

"*Frankenstein*, wasn't it?" he interrupted.

For a moment I didn't know what to say. Then I caught on. "That's right," I said. "Mary Shelley."

"Her husband was a poet, wasn't he? Shelley . . ."

"Yeah, Percy Bysshe Shelley."

Climbing on to the grave, the wino sat cross-legged on top of it and swigged from his can.

"Do you like Shelley?" I asked. "Or have you just chosen to sit there?"

"I studied him at school."

It was soon obvious that this was a bright guy who had fallen on hard times. We rabbited away about Shelley and Shakespeare — if you give people a chance, they shine — and then he told me he came from the Midlands.

"The Black Country?"

"Nearer Birmingham . . . You haven't got a cigarette on you, do you?"

"I don't. I don't smoke cigarettes."

I liked this man. He was very straightforward. So I offered to get him some. "What do you smoke?"

"Just ten. Ten cigarettes," he said.

So I walked off to a nearby shop and bought him a packet. When I got back we had a long chat. He was pleased with the fags and I was tickled to have made

**6**

contact with such a lovely, open man. It was another of those wee unexpected moments that I'll always remember.

Something similar happened in 2009 when, during the making of *Journey to the Edge of the World* — my voyage through the North West Passage, deep within the Arctic Circle — I met Brian Pearson, the local undertaker, cinema owner and bed-and-breakfast proprietor. A former dishwasher, lord mayor and taxi driver, Brian was a complicated man who reminded me of plenty of people I'd known as a kid. He was well read, self-educated, but had a kind of grumpiness because he could see things turning to shit all around him. And his mood wasn't helped by the fact that nobody tended to listen to him. Sat behind the wheel of his hearse, he drove me around the streets of his small town, relating stories about what really went on in his community. I spend a lot of time on my own — even when I'm with people I often feel like I'm alone because I think differently to most of them — so I'm always thrilled when I manage to connect with another human being. That afternoon, I felt a real connection with Brian, an interesting and interested man.

So when I was preparing to spend six weeks travelling across the heartland of America, from Chicago to Santa Monica, I told myself that if I had one encounter that equalled the tramp at Mary Shelley's graveside or Brian Pearson, then the trip would have been more than worthwhile. Less than a week into my journey, I'd met Mervin, and everything I'd hoped for had come true.

My journey along Route 66 began long before the first wheel turned on tarmac beneath me. About a year after making *Journey to the Edge of the World*, various television companies approached me with a load of ideas about where I could go next. None of their suggestions appealed, but then I mentioned to one of the producers at Maverick Television that I had always wanted to travel along Route 66. They leapt at it — after all, Route 66 is the most famous road in the world. Everyone's heard of it. My interest in it goes back to when I first heard Chuck Berry belting out one of the best rock'n'roll records of all time: "(Get Your Kicks on) Route 66". Ever since, I've wanted to travel the length of Route 66 — just for my own enjoyment, without a film crew in tow, as a holiday. It's the grooviest road in the world.

Of course, many other roads have been made famous by songs. There's the road to the Isles and the road back home. There's Abbey Road and the Yellow Brick Road. And, as a Scotsman, I know all about taking the high road or the low road. But that song's all about being dead. (I don't mean to insult Scotland here, but it's true. In "Loch Lomond", a dying soldier is talking to one of his comrades. The "high road", travelled by the healthy soldier, will be slower than the "low road" that the dying man's spirit will be able to take.) "Route 66" is about being alive. It *is* rock'n'roll. From Nat King Cole and Chuck Berry to the Rolling Stones, Dr Feelgood, Depeche Mode and even Dean Martin, it's a classic. And because of the song, Route 66 has become one of those magical places that you've always longed to see if you've got any interest at all in rock'n'roll music and being alive.

None of the other songs urged people to hit the road simply for the pleasure of getting their kicks from watching the miles go by. With its exhortation to travel from Chicago through St Louis, Joplin, Oklahoma City, Amarillo, Gallup, Flagstaff, Winona, Kingman, Barstow and San Bernadino to Los Angeles, the song is an open invitation to anyone seeking adventure to find their thrills and spills on a California road trip. Who could resist? Not me, that's for sure.

But it's more than just the song. Route 66 is special for many reasons. In America, all other routes, north — south and east — west, are pronounced "rowt". It's rowt this and rowt that. But thanks to the song, Route 66 has remained *Root* 66. And it's steeped in a potent mix of histories — of America as a nation and of rock'n'roll as a cultural force. So it is perhaps not surprising that Route 66 appeals to everyone. Americans, Europeans, Australians, Japanese and Southeast Asians, you'll meet them all along its 2,278 miles. It attracts car enthusiasts, motorcyclists, guitar players, people with long hair, silly people and dreamers. I hadn't quite realised the extent of this popular appeal until a few days after it was announced that I was going to ride its full length. From then on, people started telling me that they'd always longed to do the same thing. "My wife and I have been saving up for five years to do Route 66," wrote one guy. "I hope you have a good trip," wrote another. "For me, it was the trip of a lifetime."

Like the Silk Road or the salt and spice roads through Africa, the Pan-American Highway or the Trans-African Highway, Route 66 is one of those wonderful trails that will always exist. It's been called a road of dreamers and ramblers, drifters and writers. Well, I want to be part of that. I want to sit on my bike and ride Route 66. I want to go to Santa Fe and New Mexico. And I want to sing the song as I head down through the plains of Illinois and Missouri, the Oklahoma and Kansas prairies, the Texas Panhandle, the deserts and mountains of New Mexico, Arizona and California. I want to sing along with Chuck Berry, the Rolling Stones, Nat King Cole and all the other guys who have recorded Bobby Troup's fabulous song. And when I do it, I want to be singing at the top of my lungs as the miles pass beneath my wheels.

More than anything, I want to reconnect with old small-town America. Like a lot of Britain, much of it has been smothered under a beige blanket of franchised coffee shops, fast-food palaces, faceless shopping malls and edge-of-town superstores with uninspiring, unimaginative corporate brand names above their doors. That's not real America. It's the creation of blue-suited marketing and advertising executives. Real America is to be found in all those small towns that have been bypassed by the freeways. That's where I hope to find the fragments of thirties, forties and fifties Americana that I love. Funky neon signs enticing travellers to pull in at motels and diners. Or the giant oranges that used to lurk along the highways of California, selling ice-cold, freshly squeezed juice to thirsty motorists. At one time there was a chain of them across the state and they did a roaring trade. In the days before air-conditioned cars and express freeways, a single stand could easily go through six thousand oranges in a week. Now there's just one left on Route 66 — and I want to see it before it's too late.

Representing freedom, migration and the empty loneliness of the American heartland, Route 66 is one of the essential icons of America — not just for Americans, but for anyone who, like me, is fascinated by the United States. Snaking across eight states, its concrete and asphalt was a ribbon that tied the nation together and enticed millions of Americans with a romantic ideal of adventure and an exodus to a better life.

To some, it's the "Mother Road" immortalised by John Steinbeck in *The Grapes of Wrath* — an escape route for thousands of farmers and poverty-stricken families fleeing the barren dust bowl of Oklahoma and Kansas for the promised land of California during the Great Depression. To others — me included — just the mention of its name always evokes the birth of rock'n'roll and Chuck Berry urging us to "get our kicks". To the beatniks and hipsters, it epitomises the great American open road eulogised by Jack Kerouac in *On the Road*. To the generation of baby-boom Americans that I know, it will always be associated with a 1960s television series, called *Route 66*, in which two young men travelled across America, seeking adventure and getting caught up in the struggles of the people they met. And, like my grandson, many of today's youngsters know it from *Cars*, the Pixar animated film that was conceived as a way of making a documentary about the road and which features several businesses and residents along the route.

When I thought about it, it struck me that in many ways, roads like Route 66 are as significant to American culture and social history as cathedrals and palaces are to European history. For a young nation founded on exploration and migration west, these great arteries of transportation became a major agent of social transformation. They did more than just move people; they changed America. Among all those highways, Route 66 was the everyman's road that connected Middle America with southern California, a strip of hardtop that led to the birth of those icons of Americana I like so much: diners, motels and road food. Route 66's 2,278 meandering miles inspired thousands of cross-country road trips. And what fun it must have been to travel its length. Taking its travellers from Chicago on Lake Michigan to Santa Monica on the Pacific Ocean (and vice versa), it traversed prairie, open plains, desert, mountains, valleys and countless rivers and creeks. What a trip.

Now that much of it has been bypassed by faster, cleaner and more sterile interstate highways, the Mother Road has become, for me and countless others, a historically significant relic of America's past. To those of us for whom it was once small-town America's Main Street, Route 66 represents a simpler time when family businesses, not corporate franchises, dominated the landscape and neon motel signs were icons of a mobile nation on the road.

One of the things that fascinates me is that by following the rutted paths of Native American trails in some parts, Route 66 could even be said to pre-date the arrival of white colonists in the New World. And the road as we know it today can trace its origins to the great migration west beyond the Mississippi in the nineteenth century. When I set off from Chicago, I'd be riding along a route with a pre-history that began in 1853, when the American government commissioned a survey to build a transcontinental railway for military and civilian use. But when the survey was complete, rather than investing in steel tracks, the wise guys in Washington chose to construct a network of wagon trails. Even in those days, it seems to me that the American instinct was to empower the individual to make his or her own way in life. In 1857 a wagon trail costing $200,000 was extended from the New Mexico — Arizona border along a line close to the 35th parallel as far as the Colorado River and linked into other trails to create a route between the Arkansas River in Missouri and the furthest reaches of American expansion into the southwest of the country.

Fifty years later, when the first motor cars started to chug along American dirt tracks, the Washington wise guys' attention turned to creating a hard-surfaced road right across the United States. At that time, the main coast-to-coast road was the ramshackle Lincoln Highway, which followed a northerly route from New York to San Francisco, but few people made the trip and even fewer could afford a car. In 1912 the federal government started building a road from Washington, DC to St Louis along the Cumberland Road, an old wagon trail. From St Louis, it was extended along a path following the old Santa Fe Trail to Albuquerque in New Mexico before veering southwards to Flagstaff in Arizona. Called the Grand Canyon Route, the road then passed through Ashfork and Seligman to Topock on the Colorado River, where cars were loaded on to railway trucks and transported to Needles in California. The last section of road ran through the Mojave Desert to San Bernardino before heading due south to San Diego.

Except for a few minor diversions, all of that route from St Louis to San Bernardino followed what would later become part of Route 66. Then in 1914, Henry Ford, that genius of mass-manufacture, applied the methods he'd seen in the Colt Revolver factory to making cars. Within a decade of Henry Ford inventing his Model-T, the number of registered vehicles on American roads had leapt from 180,000 to more than 17 million, and motoring had become a means of transportation for the masses. For American families and businesses, the automobile promised unprecedented freedom and mobility. By the early 1920s, they were demanding a reliable road network on which to drive their newly acquired vehicles. In response, the federal government pledged to link small-town USA with all of the metropolitan capitals.

At last Route 66's hour had come. In the summer of 1926 the first interstate highway connecting Chicago to the West Coast was finally authorised. Officially designated Route 66, it ran from Chicago to Los Angeles, linking the isolated, rural West to the densely populated, urban Midwest and Northeast. Chicago had long served as a central meeting and distribution point for goods and people moving to the West, so it made sense for it to be the starting point. A large part of the new highway followed the old Santa Fe Trail and Grand Canyon Route. Cobbled together from existing roads and designed to connect the Main Streets of remote local communities, much of it was in poor condition. Speeds above 20 m.p.h. were rarely possible in Oklahoma, Texas, New Mexico and Arizona, where the road was often little more than a dirt track cleared of the largest boulders. Nevertheless, by running south to avoid the high passes of the Rocky Mountains, Route 66 was the first road from the Midwest to the Pacific that was passable all year round.

By 1929, the whole of the Illinois and Kansas sections, two-thirds of the Missouri section and a quarter of the road in Oklahoma had been paved. Even bikers like me would have been happy with that. But across all of Texas, New Mexico, Arizona and non-metropolitan California only sixty-four miles had been surfaced. Nevertheless, businesses in the numerous small towns along the route prospered as local entrepreneurs built service stations, restaurants, motels, campgrounds and entertainment attractions.

When the Great Depression gripped America in the early 1930s, more than 200,000 people escaped from the dust bowl states of Kansas and Oklahoma.

Strapping their belongings on to their flatbed trucks, they set off along Route 66 with dreams of a better life in the promised land of California. President Roosevelt's New Deal programme increasingly eased their way, as thousands of unemployed men were set to work on the road as part of a nationwide investment in public works. By 1938, all of the Mother Road was surfaced with concrete or tarmac, making it America's first transcontinental paved route.

The highway experienced its heyday over the next two decades. As soon as America entered the Second World War in December 1941, Route 66 became the primary transport route for millions of GIs and mile-long convoys of military supplies, and a string of new military bases soon sprang up along its length, particularly in New Mexico, Arizona and California. Meanwhile, an unprecedented movement of people began as several million more Americans headed west to work in weapons and munitions plants, with the vast majority of them making the journey along the Mother Road.

After the war, the road remained as busy as ever. Millions of Americans, among them thousands of soldiers and airmen who had done their military training out west, exchanged the harsh climate of the "snowbelt" for the easy living of the "sunbelt". With more leisure time on their hands, millions of others spent their vacations on road trips and sightseeing. Catering to the holiday traffic and migrating masses, the motels, campsites, cabins, diners, petrol stations, mechanics, tyre dealerships and souvenir shops

multiplied. The most iconic Route 66 landmarks —
those neon-lit diners, gas stations and motels that I love
— all date from this period.

However, the Mother Road's huge popularity sowed
the seeds of its own downfall. Like many of the roads
that were constructed in the 1920s and 1930s, it was
too narrow and structurally antiquated for the fin-tailed
gas guzzlers and vast "humping to please" trucks of the
1950s. President Eisenhower had been impressed by
the German autobahn network he'd glimpsed during
the war and his government decided that the nation
needed a similar network of multi-lane highways, as
much for military purposes (this was the height of the
Cold War) as for use by commercial freight and private
vehicles. So, starting in the late 1950s, sections of
Route 66 were replaced by four-lane interstate
highways until, by 1970, travellers could drive the
entire distance from Chicago to Los Angeles along
Interstates 55, 44 and 40 without ever coming into
contact with small-town America. In fact, the
interstates made it possible to drive coast to coast
without even speaking to another human being. Stop,
swipe your credit card, pump some gas, buy a snack,
then floor the pedal to the metal until the next stop.

Life was slipping out of the Mother Road and in
1979 the Route 66 designation started to be removed
from the hodge-podge of Main Streets, farm-to-market
roads and rural highways that had once linked the two
seaboards of America. Thousands of businesses that
had relied on it withered and died. Some entire towns
ceased to exist. The death knell for Route 66 itself

finally sounded in 1985, when the Mother Road was officially decommissioned.

Yet Route 66 refused to die. Realising its social significance in America's short history, a band of enthusiasts kept interest in the road alive. In 1990 the US Congress passed a law that recognised Route 66 as a "symbol of the American people's heritage of travel and their legacy of seeking a better life". A few years later an official preservation programme was enacted by the National Park Service, turning Route 66 into a de facto national monument.

Now it was my turn to set out on the legendary Mother Road and fulfil the dream of a lifetime. As I packed my bags and left home, my only hope was that I would experience proper emptiness — that sense of being the only human alive for tens or even hundreds of miles around. I wanted to be in the middle of nowhere, totally on my own, enveloped by silence, like those scenes in the movies when you see the homeward-bound GI step off the Greyhound bus into a vast empty plain beneath a big blue sky.

I had made it clear to Nicky Taylor, the show's producer, that although I would obviously have a documentary crew in tow, I was determined to travel with no preconceptions about what was lying ahead of me. I told Nicky I wanted to keep the experience as pure as possible. Even if it drove the crew doolally, I wouldn't allow myself to be barracked into visiting places that didn't interest me. There was no way I was going to take part in stunts or make detours simply because they'd look good on television. I didn't want set-up meetings with weirdos and professional eccentrics, the kind of people whose entire existence depended on promoting Route 66.

I wanted this to be a personal journey of discovery. I wanted to experience every mile as it came upon me. When I woke each morning, I didn't want to know what I would be doing that afternoon, let alone the next day. What would happen would happen. The serendipitous nature of the trip was everything to me. Planning ahead would kill the adventure and the excitement. If that happened, there would be no point leaving home.

A few days later, I was standing on a fishing boat on Lake Michigan in front of a spectacular view of Chicago. Spread out across the horizon were the Willis Tower (still known by most people as the Sears Tower), the Hancock Center, with its two pointy spires, and dozens of other skyscrapers. You might wonder what I was doing on that boat. Well, I was there to have a good look at Chicago before setting off — like getting the target in my sights. It wasn't my idea and, to be honest, I found it a wee bit pointless. But these things have to be tried. Nothing ventured, nothing gained.

Personally, I am not a boaty man. The rising and falling on the swell, the false horizon and the diesel fumes combine to do me no good at all. They make me bitchy. And on that windy, overcast afternoon in late April, I was even bitchier than usual because, for some reason, I was pissing like a racehorse. I'd gone about twelve times by the time I had to shoot the first segment for the programme, introducing Chicago. But in the midst of all this, I heard something that made me forget my foul mood. The skipper told me he'd recently caught twenty-nine salmon in a single day. In Lake Michigan, of all places! I'd always thought that the lake was so polluted that nothing could possibly live in it.

To an ageing hippy like me, the skipper's news was a bolt of joy. Then he told me that commercial fishing has been banned on the lake. Another wonderful thing. Sometimes old idealistic eco-heads like me can get kind of depressed when we switch on the television and are confronted by programmes about people killing crabs or hauling in swordfish or hoovering the bottom of the sea in Alaska. Those fishermen tend to be portrayed as macho heroes who do a very brave and wonderful job, but to my mind they are vandals. So when I heard that they are no longer allowed on such a vast expanse of water as Lake Michigan, my heart sang a wee song. After all, it wasn't so long ago that Lake Erie, another of the Great Lakes, was officially declared dead; and the Cuyahoga River, which flowed into it, was declared a fire hazard. Can you imagine anything more ridiculous than a river being a fire hazard? But it happened because they poured tons of shit — logs, oil, old tyres, paint, flammable chemicals and, literally, shit — into it. The muck decomposed and created methane and other flammable gases. Then, in June 1969, the inevitable happened and the Cuyahoga did indeed catch fire, devouring two bridges in Cleveland — a city that people started to call the "Mistake by the Lake". What in the name of God were we doing to ourselves?

**20**

Fortunately, the fire sparked so much public indignation that a legal framework for protecting watercourses and lakes — the Clean Water Act — was passed three years later. And now salmon were back in Lake Michigan, which would never have happened without that piece of legislation. We have our arses kicked on a daily basis by people who don't know what they are talking about, so it's lovely to hear something that makes me feel a wee bit proud to be a member of the human race.

By the time we were heading back towards shore, I'd totally shaken off my grouchy mood. It was still choppy on the lake, but now I was feeling good about the world and excited about the journey ahead. I was going to have lots of fun. Meet lots of people. See lots of things. And tell you all about it. So come with me. Join me on Route 66. We'll get our kicks together on the Mother Road. Come on, I dare you.

# CHAPTER
# TWO

# Winding from Chicago

First things first. If I was going to travel the length of Route 66, I needed the right kind of transportation. A sleek saloon car would have been too dull; a 4×4 too plush. In many people's eyes Route 66 requires either a convertible or a fat Harley-Davidson. But neither seemed right for me.

I did my time on bikes in my youth, but I felt that like most other things of joy, the motorbike had become lifestyled and corporatised, a packaged form of rebellion of which I wanted no part. So, with the Chicago skyline looming in the distance, in a dirty backstreet squeezed between semi-derelict buildings and empty spaces strewn with boulders and rubbish, I met my steed. One hundred horsepower of mean, throbbing heavenliness: a Boom Lowrider LR8 Muscle. Officially, it was a trike, but for some reason I'd never been able to say that word. I'd always said "bike". Whatever I called it, though, it was a thing of absolute beauty.

Water-cooled and fuel-injected, it had a 1.6-litre, four-cylinder Ford Zetec engine and it rode like a dream. Most of it was fairly standard, but I'd removed the leg guards and some tan-coloured panels along the side of the black seats, added a pair of extra headlights and adjustable suspension, and replaced some parts with chrome or polished stainless-steel equivalents. It looked the business.

Now the thing about trikes — especially a modern, low-slung one like the LR8 — is that my arse is only about eighteen inches off the tarmac. I reckon it's partly for this reason that they have such a profound effect on people in their nice, safe, grey cars. I'd watch them as they drew alongside me, gawping, mouthing, "Shit, look at that!" and wishing they were me. It happened countless times every day. Sometimes they lowered their side windows and leant out. Then the questions start.

"Oh, *man*, where did you get that thing?"

"What kind of engine does it have?"

"*Jeez-sus!* What's that thing you're riding?"

I just make shit up. When they ask, "How many cylinders?", I say, "Eight," then smile when they shout, "Wow! No way, man!" (It only has four.) But the trike is so outlandish to most people that I could make almost anyone believe almost anything. Compared with anything else on the road, it looks like a three-wheel Batmobile. It's a joy, it's funky and it's designed for showing off. A total poser's machine. Some people mightn't like that, but I don't give a shit what they say, because I love it.

My trike was like a cross between a hot-rod car and a chopper bike, but in fact it had all the disadvantages of a motorbike and none of the advantages of a car. I couldn't squit through a static line of traffic like a motorcycle — I was stuck in the queue with the cars. But while I was sitting there, waiting, I couldn't listen to Radio 4. There was no heater, so I'd freeze my bum off; and if it rained, my crotch would get soaking wet. But that was also the great delight of a trike — I'd be at one with nature, out in the fresh air, smelling and feeling and hearing my surroundings, immersed in the landscape. A motorbike offered the same sensation, but on a trike I could enjoy all that *and* lean back and relax. Maybe that's why bikers hate them so much, particularly those Harley-riding weekend bikers (which, incidentally, is another reason why trikes appeal to me).

One final thing I had to make clear from the very beginning of the trip was that a bike was like a horse. It's *my* bike. The production company might have bought it at enormous expense, and the film crew might be filming me on it, but it wasn't *our* bike. And it certainly wasn't *their* bike. It was *my* fucking bike. So, if anyone fancied sitting on it, they had to ask me fucking nice. And if they dared to swing their leg over *my* bike without asking permission, they would get a very old-fashioned look from me. At one point in the trip one of the girls in the crew climbed aboard to turn off the lights and my immediate thought was: *Fuck! She never asked me!*

But you should see the looks I got from people when I parked it. They gazed at it enviously and I knew what they were thinking: Oh, I can picture myself rattling along Route 66 on that thing, headphones on, singing along to ZZ Top's "Sharp Dressed Man" or the

opening line from "Born to be Wild" by Steppenwolf —
"*Get your motor running . . .*" The trike brings out that
in all of us, which is no bad thing. Forget Viagra, get
yourself a trike!

Before I took the beast out for the first time, I did
something I'd never done before. I strapped on a
helmet. That's right, I bought myself a crash helmet. I'd
always thought I was the last person on earth who
would do something like that. I didn't know whether it
was my age or the age we lived in, but before I left
home, I'd done a bit of serious thinking. Now, some
American states allowed bikers to ride without a lid
while others didn't, but I wasn't going to go splitting
hairs over it. It wasn't like I wanted to be on some kind
of bloody crusade. I'd always enjoyed the freedom of
wearing only a wee leather hat. After all, I had three
wheels, so it wasn't like I was going to fall off. But then
I started thinking that somebody might thump into me.
Don't be a bloody penny pincher, I thought. Just wear a
helmet. Then my wife said, "Wear a helmet," and that
sealed it.

I'll repeat that. I *thought*, Wear a helmet. My wife
*said* "Wear a helmet." So I did.

Actually, that's a complete lie. I didn't even consult
Pamela about it this time. But she'd always thought I
should wear a helmet, even on my own trike in
Scotland. So I decided all by myself: Cut out the crap,
Billy. Get a helmet.

Then I thought of two more good reasons for
wearing a helmet.

Gary. And Busey.

In 1978, Gary Busey was nominated for an Oscar for his portrayal of Buddy Holly in *The Buddy Holly Story*. He also appeared in *A Star is Born*, *Top Gun* and *Lethal Weapon*. But in December 1988 he had a bike accident. He fractured his skull and suffered permanent brain damage because he was not wearing a helmet. In time, he recovered, but life was never the same for Gary.

So, I found myself in a Chicago motorbike store, looking for a helmet. The choice was overwhelming. First up was a whole-face helmet, like the ones that assassins wear. It was easy to decide against one of those because the camera crew and viewers needed to see my face when I was riding my bike. But that still left hundreds of open-face helmets. I asked someone in the store for advice.

"Does this look okay to you?" I said. "Is it the right fit?"

"Yeah," said the guy.

Then I realised he was carrying a bag of groceries and didn't have a clue what I was talking about. He'd just wandered in on his way back from the supermarket.

Eventually I found someone who actually worked there and was instantly reminded that most Americans are brilliant salesmen. Not only did this guy sell us a helmet; he ran out and bought cheeseburgers and soft drinks for all the crew, told jokes, had a laugh and made us all feel absolutely welcome. A great representative of an extraordinary country.

I'm one of those guys who looks slightly odd in a helmet, so I had to be careful about exactly which model I chose. I tried on one that was very popular with American bikers — it looked a bit like a Third Reich helmet. I was relieved when it didn't fit, because I thought the Nazi look was much better left under the bed. In the end I settled on a black open-faced number with a visor. And to my surprise, having bought it, I didn't feel any less cool. I was even looking forward to wearing it. It was fitted up electronically so I could hear music on the trike, which was brilliant, like having a jukebox wrapped around my head. And it was rather comfortable, as long as I didn't put the visor up. If I did that, it caught the wind, so I decided that I'd either have to remove the visor or keep it down at all times. No visor, I suspected, was going to win, and I'd wear the helmet with my fishing glasses. "Wait till you see them," I told the crew as I tried them on with the helmet. "They will blow you away. They're yellow, kind of amber, polarised lenses with silver sides."

I checked myself in the mirror to see how the helmet looked with the glasses. Pretty groovy, I thought. Windswept, interesting and much better than I'd expected. The salesman tried to sell me a pair of motorcycle gloves, but I'd already decided I'd go to a cowboy shop. Cowboys do much better gloves than motorcyclists. The problem with most motorcycle gloves is they do this thing, the go-fast look. Well, I don't like it. I prefer it more casual, because a trike's different from a bike. Bikes are for going fast, making a lot of noise and all that. A trike's kind of laid back. As

I've said, it's a posing machine. And I knew exactly what I wanted to wear on my hands while I posed: tan-coloured, deer-hide cowboy gloves. Oh yes.

Sorted with helmet and gloves, it was time to christen the trike. I'd been looking forward to this moment, but taking the beast out for its virgin ride was a nightmare. It had a different gearbox from mine back home, so I couldn't find the gears instinctively. But once I'd studied a diagram and learned how to go through the gears, it became a joy; although, for some reason, I still needed to know Serbo-Croat yoga to get it into reverse. I liked to think the soul of the bike didn't want to have a reverse gear. It just wasn't right — bikes shouldn't go backwards. So I thought the bike was fighting it all the way. But once I'd worked it out, I was as happy as a clam. And, as you know, clams are very happy things.

With the camera crew ahead of me in a car, we did a big tour around the outskirts of Chicago so that I could get used to the trike. It was fantastic to see the city looming up all around me, like in a science-fiction movie. Then I rode into town and it was just great. The trike ran like a cuckoo clock.

The only downside was the weather. It was a dodgy-looking day, with the weather neither one thing or the other. One of those greyish, yellowy, funky, funny days. Every time I phoned someone in Scotland, they told me they were in the middle of a searing heatwave and I seethed with envy. That morning, I'd seen a weather report from Britain. It was mid-April and seventy-five degrees Fahrenheit, and everyone was

28

running around in their underwear. I love the British fervour for throwing off our clothes. And the first people to disrobe are always the ones with the grubbiest underwear, like the guys I knew in the shipyards who put on long johns in September and took them off in May. Meanwhile, we were freezing our balls off in Chicago.

As I rode through downtown Chicago, past the famous water tower, I tried out the communication link with the director, Mike. It worked like a dream, and it was great to show him that I could talk straight to the camera from the bike. It meant that I didn't need to stop at a location before explaining it to viewers. I was dead against television that spoon-fed information to people. If I said, "There's a water tower over there," as I drove past, I could then talk about it later, knowing that the viewers would remember it. I didn't have to stop, lean against it, point and labour the point that I was talking about a water tower. We shot a piece about the city from the bike as we drove along with all the other traffic flying around us, before eventually arriving at the shiny black monolith that dominates the Chicago skyline.

For twenty-five years, the Sears Tower in Chicago was the tallest building in the world. But it was overtaken in 1998 by those cheeky upstarts in Malaysia with their twin skyscrapers, the Petronas Towers. So these days it was just the tallest building in America, but that was more than good enough for me when I visited it. Built as the headquarters of Sears Roebuck and Co., the tower used nine exterior frame tubes of different lengths, from 50 to 110 storeys, bundled together to provide strength and flexibility, avoiding the need for interior supports. It was said that the architect conceived this technologically innovative building when he watched someone shake cigarettes out of a packet.

Officially, the building was rechristened the Willis Tower in 2009, but it would always be the Sears Tower to me. Willis, a London-based insurance broker, leased three of the tower's 110 floors and gained the naming rights to the whole shebang until 2024. The name-change was not a popular move. *Time* magazine said it was one of the top ten worst corporate rebrandings, while CNN reported that many Chicagoans were refusing to acknowledge the new title.

Whatever its name, though, the tower was a beauty and I loved it. Riding up in the lift — or, more appropriately, the elevator — a recorded message reeled off some very impressive statistics about this 1,450-foot "modern marvel". In just seventy seconds we shot past the height of the Great Pyramid, the Seattle Space Needle, the Gateway Arch in St Louis, Moscow State University, the Eiffel Tower and so on until we emerged 103 floors above ground level. There were still another five storeys above me, but this was the viewing floor, which has the most spectacular views, if you like that kind of thing. All of Chicago, a large chunk of Lake Michigan and a fair bit of the State of Illinois were spread out around the tower. It was stunning.

Much of what made the view so spectacular was there because of the events of four days in 1871, when Chicago was devastated by a massive fire. At that time, the entire city centre, stretching over four square miles, was built of wood. Eighteen thousand properties were destroyed, 300 people died and 90,000 were made homeless. Only the water tower that I'd ridden past earlier in the day was left standing. It was remarkable to think that all of central Chicago was rebuilt around that tower. Nowadays, it served as a monument to the Great Fire of Chicago. (Incidentally, on the same day that the fire broke out, not far from Chicago, a forest fire killed even more people, but few people ever mentioned or remembered it.)

Once the fire had burned itself out, Chicago's mayor, a guy called Roswell Mason, sent out an all-points bulletin. He said: "Tomorrow, one hundred thousand people will be without food and shelter. Can you help?" It worked like magic. People responded unbelievably well. Millions of dollars flooded in, and the cash enabled the city authorities to rebuild Chicago from scratch, something that had never been done on such a large scale. Architects, builders and anyone else with a good idea flooded in from all over the world. There was no rule book in 1871, no health and safety officers or building regulation inspectors, so the rebuilding of Chicago was fast and furious.

But possibly the most significant factor in the whole process was that seventeen years earlier, a bedstead maker in New York — Elisha Otis — had designed a hoist for lifting heavy equipment around his factory. Otis's device had ratchets fitted to the sides of the hoist. These ratchets, which allowed a platform to move up and down smoothly, also snapped into action at any sudden downward movement, preventing a lethal plunge. Otis immediately realised that he had something special on his hands, so he urged the bed company to market his invention. At an impressive public display at New York's Crystal Palace in 1854, Otis ascended on his hoist to the height of a house, then ordered someone to cut the rope with an axe. The audience gasped as the ratchets sprang into action and Otis remained suspended in mid-air. Everyone was very impressed.

Three years later, Otis turned his invention into the first "safety elevator", which was installed for passenger use in a New York department store. Of course, it was more than just a gimmick. By transporting people rapidly and effortlessly upwards, it made multi-storey buildings practical and safe for the first time. Thanks to Otis, no one needed to fear the vertical abyss opening up beneath their feet as they ascended a skyscraper like the Sears Tower in a high-speed lift. If the steel cables hoisting up the cart snapped, they'd feel nothing more than a slight wobble as the ratchets sprang into action. The lift would stay put, suspended in mid-air until help arrived.

So, when Chicago's leaders started rebuilding the city centre after the devastating fire, they had the opportunity to build bigger, better and especially higher. Land was expensive and scarce, so developers went upwards not outwards. The Home Insurance Company Building, a ten-storey office block completed in Chicago in 1885, was regarded as the first true modern skyscraper. It was the first to use steel girders, which were stronger than iron, and the first to hang an outer masonry curtain wall on the load-bearing steel skeleton. Sadly, it doesn't exist any more, but there is a wee plaque commemorating it on Route 66. Of course, at only ten storeys high, it would be considered a dwarf in comparison with today's skyscrapers, but after it was built it was clear that the only way the city could go was up. In Chicago, the sky was the limit.

Standing in the Sears Tower, there was a real sense of where Mr Otis's invention had taken us, particularly when I stepped into the wee glass cubicle that jutted out of the side of the building, more than a thousand feet above the ground. It was like a high version of the Pope-mobile, and stepping into it was a real nerve-tickler, the creepiest feeling I'd ever experienced. Looking between my feet straight down to the street, something inside me insisted I shouldn't be standing there. I felt my heart pumping, my nerves tingling and my body shouting, "Don't do this. Please don't do this. This is wrong. This does not compute. Go back. *Go back*." I didn't know what anyone hoped to achieve by offering visitors the chance to walk into that glass box, except for a celebration that they weren't dead.

Like anyone who had ever stepped into that wee glass box, I really had to fight the urge not to do it. And that fitted with something that had always amused and amazed me about human beings. If you go up to a baby and roar at it, the baby will show signs of being frightened and will close its eyes. But then it'll open its eyes and want you to do it again. Well, it was the same thing with the glass box. The floor was going "roar" and

**33**

I was going, "Again, again!" for the same reason that people freefall parachute. So, even though something kept nagging at me to get out of the wee glass box right away, I stuck at it, not least because the view was so remarkable.

Far beneath me, I spotted a line of yellow taxis turning into Adams Street. Although it was just a regular Chicago street, it was also the start of Route 66, from where I'd soon be heading out west. But before I turned my trike towards California, I had to visit a few places in the Windy City. Incidentally, the Windy City nickname is believed to have come either from the propensity of Chicago's politicians to make long-winded speeches or from a New York newspaper editor's accusation that Chicagoans tended to boast about their hometown. It was apparently not a comment on the notoriously nippy winds that blasted from the plains and Lake Michigan through Chicago's concrete canyons. Chicago was not significantly windier than any other American city, such as New York or Boston, although when the Arctic wind came off the lake and blew down Michigan Avenue, it could cut you in half.

Before leaving the Sears Tower, I made it up the final five floors from the glass bubble to the roof. Standing on the very top of the building, I stood like a dooley while a helicopter swooped from a great distance and filmed me pointing to the west. Easy enough, but the highlight of the roof visit was the story I was told of a guy who was painting the antenna and was microwaved. It's said that he cooked himself, losing the use of his legs because of the sheer power of the transmitter. It had the ring of an urban legend about it, but it still amused me.

One of the best things about the Sears Tower was that whenever I saw the building again, I'd know I'd been on top of it. Having already stood on top of lots of things, it added to the collection, which included Sydney's Opera House and Harbour Bridge. Both of them reminded me of my daughter, who once said the nicest thing. She was on the back of my Harley trike as we were coming over the Harbour Bridge, driving towards the Opera House, where I was performing a gig.

"God I love it here," she said. "I love being here."

"What do you mean?" I said.

"When you're here, you know exactly where you are on the planet."

I thought, Oh my goodness, so you do. It was absolutely true. Since then, I've become more and more aware of how iconic landmarks could do that to you — let you know exactly where you were on earth. The Taj Mahal did it. The Empire State Building did it. The Houses of Parliament and the Eiffel Tower did it. And so did the Sears Tower. Most of the time we didn't know precisely where we were, but those buildings made us totally aware of our place in the world. It was no big deal, just a wee jolly, but it pleased me no end.

Before leaving the tower, I looked out one last time from the roof and gazed southwest. Seeing my journey laid out in front of me got me thinking of what lay further along the road — Illinois, Missouri, Kansas,

Oklahoma, Texas, New Mexico, Arizona and California, then the Pacific. Far below, I could see the thick artery of eight lanes of Interstate 55 snaking through the conurbation — the most popular way out of Chicago. Since the mid-1960s, it had been the official replacement for Route 66. As I mused about starting the journey, I heard the whine of a train horn in the distance. The loneliest sound in the world, but also one of the most romantic, it beckoned me to venture out into the vast plains of America and explore what lay along the mythical highway. But first I wanted to go on another quick spin around central Chicago, one of my favourite cities.

Whenever I'm in Chicago, I make a point of visiting Fort Dearborn. Nowadays it's just some brass plates on the road and pavement outside Fanny Mae's sweet shop on the corner of two city centre streets. I always stop in the shop to buy a few sweeties. They do a lovely plain chocolate caramel. If I could force one through the pages of this book, I'd give you one. Those brass plates mark the point where Fort Dearborn used to be located. For some unfathomable reason, I've always had a romantic image of the fort, which I used to think was the site of the last Indian battle on American soil. But I recently discovered that it was actually the site of a massacre of French pioneers conducted by Native Americans, supported by the British.

In the 1670s, French pioneers were the first Europeans to travel along the Chicago River. They settled near its mouth and claimed a large surrounding territory for France. About thirty years later, they were driven out by Fox Indians during the Fox Wars, which continued until the 1730s. At the end of the French and Indian War (the North American portion of the Seven Years War between Britain and France) in 1763, the area was ceded to Britain, which in turn lost it to the United States at the end of the American War of Independence. As a result, in 1776 the mouth of the Chicago River was resettled by a new wave of pioneers. Among them was Jean Baptiste Point du Sable, a Haitian farmer and trader who, as the first permanent resident of Chicago, is regarded as the founder of the city. (In case you were wondering, the city takes its name from *shikaakwa*, the Miami-Illinois Indian word for the stinky, leek-like vegetables that can still be found rotting along the banks of the Chicago River.)

In 1804 US troops constructed a log fort at the mouth of the river. They named it after Henry Dearborn, the Secretary of War, and a small settlement grew around it. The village didn't last long, though. In 1812 war broke out again between the United States and the British Empire, including Canada. General William Hull, the Governor of Michigan, ordered the evacuation of Fort Dearborn, but Potawatomi Indians ambushed the evacuees, killing eighty-six and capturing sixty-two soldiers, women and children, among them the commandant and his wife, who were ransomed to the British. A posse of five hundred Indians was sent to do the gig, so it was not a small skirmish. Those troops and pioneers got wellied, and their fort was burned to the ground. It was rebuilt in 1816, but it

37

must have been a tough place to live, as various wars with Winnebago and Black Hawk Indians continued to rage. Most of the fort was again destroyed by fire in 1857, and what remained was razed to the ground in the Great Fire of 1871.

I always liked to stand at the crossroads outside Fanny Mae's for a wee while, imagining flaming arrows flying overhead. On one occasion a young woman came up to me, a kind of hippy girl, and asked what I was doing. I told her I was thinking of Indians ambushing the pioneers.

"Oh, you like all that kind of stuff about Chicago?" she said.

"Oh yeah," I said. "Love it."

"Do you like architecture?"

"Oh yeah. You bet."

And it's true — I do. The Michigan — Wacker Historic District in the centre of Chicago, where Fort Dearborn used to stand, is an amazing place for gazing at buildings. There's a remarkable line-up of world-class architecture on both banks of the Chicago River, such as the gleaming white art deco Wrigley Building, chosen by William Wrigley, the chewing gum magnate, to house his company. There are several other stunning granite skyscrapers built in the 1920s and 1930s. But smack in the middle of all that fabulous beauty is a glass monstrosity, erected where another lovely white stone building used to stand. The modern eyesore was built by Donald Trump and, in my opinion, it's a piece of shit, so I always just pretend it's not there. It looks totally out of place, and it makes me quite angry that

Trump was allowed to build it. He wants to be President, but I can't help thinking that the whole country would end up looking like a public toilet if he was ever elected.

Gazing at all of the surrounding buildings with the hippy lass, I pointed at what looked like a big, skinny cathedral. "That's my favourite," I said.

"Oh, mine too," she said.

So we started to walk towards the *Chicago Tribune* Building, and on the way over she asked, "Do you have old buildings in Scotland?"

I'm still laughing about that question now, but at the time I just said, "Yeah."

"We've got buildings here a hundred years old," she said.

"Ooh."

"Oh yeah."

"Do you know," I said, "in Scotland, there's a place called New Bridge. It's called New Bridge because they built a new bridge there . . . in the seventeenth century. Mind you, they're still driving over the old bridge."

The girl looked kind of bewildered, then wandered off. I'm sure she didn't believe a word of it.

It was a short walk from the site of Fort Dearborn to the *Chicago Tribune* Building and I crossed the river on one of the many bridges that could be raised to allow tall shipping to pass into Lake Michigan. On St Patrick's Day, they dye the river green in recognition of Chicago's large Irish community. But the dye wasn't really necessary, as the river had a weird green tint to it all year round. Walking over the bridge, I again had reason to doubt the origins of Chicago's nickname. The city might have more than its fair share of gasbag politicians and boastful locals, but that morning it didn't seem that way. My hair was the clue: a horizontal haircut. Try telling me that Chicago wasn't windswept.

Approaching the *Chicago Tribune* Building, the first thing you notice is the vertical stripes, which makes it seem much taller than its 462 feet. But move closer and it looks more like a Gothic King Arthur's Castle. This combination might sound incongruous, but it works brilliantly. It's a most attractive building, built as a result of a competition held in 1922 to design the most beautiful office building in the world. The architects won a $100,000 prize and the commission to build the tower. If they held the same competition today, I think the same architects would win again. They would certainly get my vote. I love it. I know some breathtaking buildings are being constructed, especially in Spain, but I don't think any of them compare with the *Chicago Tribune* Building. To me, it's a thing of absolute beauty. But there's more to the building than just the original design, as brilliant as that is.

The original owner and publisher of the *Chicago Tribune*, Robert "Colonel" McCormick, had been a war correspondent and he went to Europe early in the First World War to interview Tsar Nicholas II, Prime Minister Herbert Asquith and First Lord of the Admiralty Winston Churchill. While travelling around Europe, he collected chunks of historic buildings, including a lump of stone that had been blown off Ypres Cathedral by the German artillery. Initially, he just kept these as souvenirs, but then he instructed the *Tribune's* correspondents, wherever they were in the world, to start collecting pieces of other famous buildings "by well-mannered means". When the correspondents arrived back in Chicago with their booty, the pieces of masonry were implanted in the outer walls of the lower storeys of the *Chicago Tribune* Building.

Now, walking around the tower, I kept spotting them, and it was difficult not to exclaim whenever I saw a chunk: "Ooh, look, a wee bit of Edinburgh Castle!" or "Wow, a chunk of the Parthenon!" Quite how the correspondents managed to collect all of this stuff "by well-mannered means" was a mystery to me. Did they sneak up Edinburgh's High Street in the middle of the night with a sledgehammer and smash a chunk off the castle walls? I didn't know, so I suppose it was better not to question their methods and just enjoy the result.

There were lumps of masonry from Tibet, the Great Wall of China, the Taj Mahal, the Palace of Westminster, the Great Pyramid, the Alamo, Notre-Dame Cathedral, Abraham Lincoln's Tomb, the Berlin Wall, Angkor Wat — the list went on and on. In all, there are 136 fragments of other buildings implanted into the walls of the *Chicago Tribune* Building. As I walked around the perimeter, I took a wee look at each piece of Colonel McCormick's grand haul: the Royal Castle, Stockholm; the Ancient Temple, Hunan Province; Fort Santiago; St David's Tower, Jerusalem; a piece from the Holy Door of St Peter's Basilica in the Vatican; a wee bit of Pompeii; the Badlands, South

Dakota — that was a nice one; the Monastery of St Michael of Ukraine; the Old Post Office in O'Connell Street, Dublin, where the Irish rebellion started; the Temple of the Forbidden City, Beijing; a roof tile from some Roman ruins; a tiny shard of stone from the Cave of the Nativity in Bethlehem; a rock from Flodden Field in Northumberland, where the English gave the Scots one hell of a doing; then, next to it, a piece from the Tower of Tears in Amsterdam.

But my favourite is a fragment of Injun Joe's Cave, a show cave in Missouri on which Mark Twain based the cave he described in *The Adventures of Tom Sawyer*. I'm a Twain fanatic, so I was really disappointed when it wasn't where I thought it would be. But then, at the very last second, I came around a corner and there it was, my old pal sticking straight out of the wall. Just seeing it made my day. The smallest things can make me happy. I gave it a little rub, just to check I hadn't imagined it. Phew. I wasn't senile like I thought I might be.

From my favourite building I walked a few blocks south down Michigan Avenue, one of my favourite streets, past more magnificent architecture to Millennium Park, which adjoins Grant Park, where Barack Obama held his victory speech after winning the 2008 presidential election. Still marvelling at the fabulous buildings, I reflected that Chicago was a very beautiful place — a stunningly good-looking city — and Chicagoans generally seemed intent on keeping it that way, making it more gorgeous as they went along. It wasn't like Edinburgh, where the city authorities were in the process of plonking a big bloody tram system down the middle of Princes Street, the jewel in the city's crown.

It seemed to me that most of the world's beautiful cities — Venice, Rome, Paris, even Glasgow, which was a gorgeous Victorian city — were constantly under pressure from cretins who wanted to build awful eyesores, or demolish the beauty and replace it with car parks. I could only assume that the people who found themselves in positions of authority, which they achieved because they were desperate for power, seldom had any aesthetic taste. Meanwhile, the people who did have taste didn't seek power. So cities were constantly under threat because the tasteless people were always in charge. It saddened me. But walking down the streets of Chicago really cheered me up, because it was a living example of how a city could improve and get better looking all the time.

Then I arrived at Millennium Park, which was the cherry on Chicago's icing. Close to the shore of Lake Michigan, right in the middle of the city, this was a stunning park, but there was a huge row about it when it was built. Although it covered only twenty-four acres, it cost $475 million, more than three times its original budget, which the people of Chicago funded through a combination of taxes and donations. To make matters worse, it opened four years late, in 2004, long after the New Year's Eve it was meant to celebrate.

However, in spite of its shaky beginnings and huge cost, I thought it was a triumph, and incredible value for money. It will last a long time and Chicagoans will keep reaping its rewards. I only wished we had something similar in Glasgow.

It reminded me of a story I once heard about a city that bought some Jackson Pollock paintings. The authorities were harangued and mercilessly ridiculed by everyone who thought the paintings were worthless junk. Then, ten or twenty years later, the ridicule stopped as those people who'd complained and grouched discovered what a wonderful investment the city had made on their behalf. I hoped the same thing happened with Millennium Park. It was already Chicago's second most popular tourist attraction, and the area around it had the fastest-appreciating real estate in America. But what really mattered was that it was such a life-affirming place, thanks in part to its designer, Frank Gehry — probably the most important architect of our age.

Built over rail yards and parking lots, the centrepiece of the park was an ultra-modern, vast open-air concert venue that accommodated 4,000 in seats and another 7,000 on a huge lawn. A field of thick grass sloped down towards the Jay Pritzker Pavilion, a stage surrounded by 120-foot-high slices of brushed stainless steel that looked like ribbons fluttering in the wind. Above it all, a spider's web of criss-crossing pipes housed hundreds of loudspeakers, suspended above the audience to distribute the sound as effectively as inside a concert hall. It was unbelievable.

Nearby, there was a great sculpture by the Indian-born British artist Anish Kapoor. Although called "Cloud Gate", everybody knew it as "The

44

Bean". If you saw it, you'd know why: it looked just like a 66-foot-long, 33-foot-high, shiny, metallic jelly bean. Created using a huge number of stainless-steel plates weighing more than 110 tons, "The Bean" had been polished to such a fine degree that I couldn't see a single seam. Jesus only knows how Anish Kapoor managed to do it. But what everyone loved about The Bean was the way it stretched and distorted views of the Chicago skyline behind you when you stood in front of it. And when I walked underneath it, I saw myself multiplied, repeated and stretched. It was like looking into a psychedelic kaleidoscope.

The area around "The Bean" is extremely beautiful, and when we filmed there it was full of people, even though it was a very cold day. A mass of really happy visitors were taking photographs, wandering around, and smiling and laughing when they saw their reflections in the sculpture — surely that was proof of its value. Young and old alike were tickled by it. People even did little dances to see how their reflections would move. It struck me that "The Bean" had a quality like the *International Camera Dance Movie* that for years I've been threatening to make. My plan would be to take a movie camera out of its case, put it on a tripod in an urban area, and just leave it running. Children would jump up and down in front of it. Adults would stop and stare. And whatever country they came from, people's reactions would be the same. "Ooh," they'd say in their native tongue, "look — a camera." Then they'd shimmy around in front of it, moving in for a closer look. You might think I'm indulging in my habit of digressing, but there's a point here. Just like "The Bean", and in the nicest possible way, my movie would have no point whatsoever. They're both just fun and interesting and they make us smile. And a lot of good things have no point at all.

So, if you ever get the chance, have a look at the views of Chicago that are reflected in "The Bean". There's no point to it, but just go and see if it has the same effect on you as it has on everyone else. I bet it does.

A short walk from "The Bean" is something else that would blow anyone away. Called the "Crown Fountain" and designed by the Spanish artist Jaume Plensa, it's a pair of 50-foot-tall glass towers that display video images of a thousand Chicago residents in what looks like a big picture frame. I won't even pretend to know how they superimposed the images on to the 50-foot-high glass towers, but it's fascinating to watch as the giant faces smile for a few minutes, then pucker their lips all kissy-kissy while pipes send out large streams of water, giving the illusion that the water is spouting from their mouths. Kids absolutely love it, me included.

Of course, there's always uproar when a government or a council spends public money on something like this, as if art wasn't worth the effort of spending money. But then a government will go and spend billions on nuclear missiles and hardly anybody lets out a squeak. What's wrong with the world? You get an atomic submarine that's good for nothing but maiming and killing, and people almost applaud the thing when it comes into harbour. But spend a few dollars on a beautiful work of art and people are outraged. "The Bean", the "Crown Fountain" and the other parts of Millennium Park are a joy, yet people always moan about how much it all costs. The park is a lovely place to be, dynamic and relaxing at the same time. It's great. And you know what? I think it's a snip at $475 million.

From the park, it's a very short hop, skip and jump across Michigan Avenue to the original start of Route 66 at the corner of Jackson Boulevard. It's traditional for Route 66 travellers to have their final meal in Chicago and their first on Route 66 at Lou Mitchell's, which has been at 555 West Jackson Boulevard since 1923. It's a nice enough place that does an all-day breakfast and very good Danish pastries, but I had an appointment to keep around the corner.

Although the junction of Jackson and Michigan was the original starting point in 1926, it's no longer the place where most people begin their journey. There are two reasons for this. First, in 1933, after the World Fair freed up some land to create Grant Park, the start was moved a few blocks to the east — to Lakeside Drive on the edge of Lake Michigan. Then, in 1955, the City of Chicago turned Jackson Boulevard into an eastbound one-way street, making it impossible to head west on the original Route 66. As a result, the start was moved a block north to Adams Street, another one-way street, but going in the opposite direction.

If all of that sounds complicated, it's nothing in comparison to what happened to the rest of Route 66. Throughout its history, the Mother Road was more akin to a meandering river than a fixed road: its source and destination remained constant, but its route frequently changed to suit local circumstances. So shifting the start from Jackson to Adams is a very apt harbinger of what will follow in the miles ahead.

I arrived on Adams Street without my trike, as I still wasn't quite ready to begin. First, we had to shoot some publicity stills beneath a sign that marked the start of Route 66. I've never been a big fan of having my picture taken. To me, it's as bad as going to the dentist, a kind of root-canal vibe. The photographers are usually really nice guys, but I can't help feeling — when I'm doing something with my face, my eyes, or the angle of my head — that the snapper is thinking, Is this how this prick sees himself? I know it's probably just paranoia, but I can never get shot of it, so I always find the whole process kind of awkward, and I'm usually very glad when it's over.

That evening, I was especially glad when we finished because it was bloody freezing, so much so that I went out and bought some thermals afterwards. Something weird was happening to the weather in the Midwest of America in late April 2011. To the east, west and north of us there were typhoons, hurricanes and probably fucking tsunamis by the dozen. I had no idea what was going on, but it did occur to me that it might be the end of the world.

The next day I was back at the corner of Adams and Michigan, now dressed in my leather jacket and leather chaps, with a nice big crutch cut out of them — just what I needed to let in the freezing-cold air. I pulled on my helmet and threw a double-six to start.

Leaving early in the morning, I didn't need to be told it was a Sunday — it's a strange day all over the world. I've got a theory that if you were unconscious in a coma for twenty years and you suddenly woke up, you might not know where you were, but you would know if it was a Sunday. It's got a particular vibe to it, just like Friday night — my personal favourite. I think that Friday night feeling comes from the days when I had my welder's wages in my back pocket, all aftershave and shoeshine, going dancing at the end of the week at the Barrowland or the Dennistoun Palais in Palermo shoes with inch-vents on the jacket and sixteen-inch drainpipe trousers. Happy days.

Riding off on the magic trike to the sound of a busker playing a saxophone — of all things, it sounded like "Careless Whisper" by George Michael — we soon left Millennium Park and the Art Institute of Chicago behind us. I'd wanted to pop into the Institute to see a specific painting, Grant Wood's "American Gothic" — the one with the guy in his overalls holding a pitchfork, standing next to his daughter. But we never made it, mainly because of all that weird weather. And it was still weird now — we were heading straight towards tornadoes. I dearly hoped we wouldn't run into one. I'd seen a tornado once before, and it was more than enough to last me the rest of my life.

# CHAPTER
# THREE

## A Royal Route

I was travelling light. My golden rule for any trip is to clear out my mind before I leave home. Empty it so that it's wide open to every experience during the journey. It's like travelling with an empty suitcase that I can fill with things I find along the way. I don't understand why anyone would want to gather up all the things that surround them at home — pictures and mementoes and life's little luxuries — and take them on the road with them. The only things from home that are essential to me are my banjo and an iPod packed with banjo music that I listen to when I'm on my trike.

Riding through the centre of Chicago, almost every time I stopped someone called out to me, like the taxi driver who wanted to know what I was riding. "It's a trike," I said. Then a young lad on a skinny bike remarked on the quietness of my engine. "It's got four cylinders," I replied. This makes it a lot quieter than the single- and twin-cylinder Harley-Davidsons that usually cruise the streets.

A woman crossing the road yelled, "Hey, Billy!" I nodded and smiled at her. "What are you doing here?"

she asked as she whipped out a camera and took my picture.

"We're making a film about Route 66. That's why I'm in Chicago."

It was nice to be recognised by fans and passers-by. It made me feel all famous and warm and cuddly.

At the end of the block I passed under one of the most iconic sights in Chicago — the cast-iron legs of the elevated train system. Or the "El", as Chicagoans call it. Nelson Algren, the novelist who wrote *The Man with the Golden Arm*, called it Chicago's rusty iron heart. It works like a subway system, transporting people far away from the traffic of cars, buses and trucks on the roads, but it's above the ground rather than below. I think it's absolutely beautiful. It's like the Forth Bridge to me — all rivets and girders and proof of how clever men can be. And it has the same impact as a red London bus or a yellow New York taxi. As soon as you see any of those things in a movie, you know exactly where you are. Usually there's a car chase going on under the El. Or people running along with guns, with one guy on the road and another way up above him on the El, trying to hide, legging it up and down stairs, or sprinting along the tracks and past queues of commuters, shoving them out of the way.

I wish we had an El in Glasgow. We almost did once. In the 1930s a guy called George Bennie built a prototype rail system called the "railplane" at Milngavie, just outside the city. It was on legs and rails, just like the El, but the cars hung from an overhead monorail and had propellers powered by on-board motors at each end of the carriage. They looked like cigar tubes. Bennie reckoned his trains could travel at up to 120mph., but he couldn't find someone to finance his great idea and build it in Glasgow. That was a shame, because we Glaswegians could have had something like the El, but even more swanky. Sydney's got something similar now — the overhead railway — and it's hugely popular. It makes the traffic flow better and people like it because they can get to work easily. It's comfortable, it's funky and it looks great.

Because I like the El so much, I'd persuaded the director that we ought to film something about it before we set off on Route 66. But when we went to do it I was a wee bit disillusioned because the director took us far down the line, where the El runs along rails at ground level, not suspended above the street. What I didn't realise was that it's difficult to get permission to film on the inner-city section that I like. But then the director told me he had a wee trick in mind. We boarded a train a long way out of town and I interviewed a supervisor called Jackie, who is some kind of expert on the system and its history. While I asked her all about her job and the El, the train started to rise above the streets, and before I knew it we were back in the centre of Chicago. I got off the train and walked down the stairs, with the crew filming me all the way. Result.

It made me very happy, not because we'd found a cunning way to bypass the restrictions, but because I like to celebrate the achievements of the human race. I like to show people at their best. And I think you often see people at their absolute best in engineering. Of course, the El is a staggering feat of engineering, especially the riveting. There must be a zillion rivets in Chicago, and most of them are on the El. Whenever I see something like the El, or a big ship or an impressive bridge, I get so proud of my species. Which makes a change. It's our fault that the jungle is on fire, although I never set fire to a jungle in my life. It's our fault that the spotted lemur has got nowhere to live, even though I couldn't pick out a spotted lemur in a police line-up. I'm a nice guy. I want the world to be beautiful. So I like to point out the beauty of human creations, like the El, to give the human race a nudge, as if to say, "Just look what we can achieve if we put our minds to it."

Thinking about celebrating the beauty of mankind's creativity got me thinking about another of my pet theories, which is that newspaper obituaries should be closer to the front because they are often stories about the great unsung heroes of the world. I realised this when a pal of mine died some years ago. I read his obituary; then I read all the others in the paper that day. And I thought: My God, these are extraordinary people. How come I've never heard of them? They had found cures for diseases or helped children and innocent people escape from dictators all over the world. But we rarely took any notice of them because they were old. If we saw them in a supermarket, we'd never give them a second thought.

So I'm on a little one-man crusade to bring the obituary closer to the front of the paper. Let's sing a bit louder about the unsung. Rather than spending all our time watching stupid people doing stupid things and being filmed by other stupid people on reality TV shows, why don't we spend a few minutes each day reading about good people doing good things? I'm not being a hippy. It's just that we've got to improve ourselves as a species or we are absolutely doomed.

I was thinking about all of this as I passed under the El. As I slipped between its massive iron legs, a train hurtled overhead, as if to say: "Look what you're capable of. Look at *this*." It really is a magic noise — the sound of trains right in the middle of town. I bet the wee boys in Chicago just love it. I reckon they're crazy about it. But not everyone's as jolly and happy about the El as I am. Way back in 1892, the New York Academy of Medicine claimed that "the elevated trains prevented the normal development of children, threw convalescing patients into relapses and caused insomnia, exhaustion, hysteria, paralysis, meningitis, deafness and death. And pimples on the willy."

I'm sure you can guess which of those ailments I added to the list.

Continuing on down Adams Street on the trike, I was enjoying every yard of it. The concrete canyons, where you have to look straight up to see the sky, are really amazing to ride along. But I was soon twisting and turning to follow Route 66 out of the Windy City, passing down streets and avenues with names like Ogden, Cicero, Nerwyn, Harlem and Lyons. I think a lot of people are a bit disappointed when they discover that Route 66 isn't just one long, straight road but all broken up into various chunks and sections.

Not so long ago, in the days of prohibition, these outer parts of Chicago were once undershot with a spider's web of tunnels used by gangsters and bootleggers to distribute their wares to the speakeasies. Chicago is such a beautiful town these days — good and interesting and clean and lovely — and the city authorities now seem very embarrassed by all that Al Capone stuff from the 1920s and 1930s. When you ask them about it, they say, "Well, it was a long time ago. It was a period we'd rather just put behind us . . . blah-di-blah-di-blah." But the truth is that the prohibition era was one of the most interesting periods in Chicago's history, which is why we stopped to investigate it. I reckon you have to go to a speakeasy if you're in Chicago, so we did.

The American government made a criminal mistake in the late 1910s, when it bowed to pressure from the Anti-Saloon League and the Women's Christian Temperance Union and enacted legislation to shut down boozers everywhere. Can you believe it: every bar in America was shut. For thirteen long years, until 1933, it was illegal to make, sell or transport alcohol. As a result — you know everybody needs a wee drinkypoo — speakeasies sprang up everywhere.

Everyone imagines every speakeasy had a wee hole in the door. You know, knock twice, wait for the wee hole to open just a whisker, whisper, "Joe sent me," and sneak inside. But there were thirty thousand of them in New York alone — twice the number of bars there had been before the ban on booze came into effect in January 1920 — so there was no such thing as a standard speakeasy.

The one we visited in Chicago was on Wabash Street, not far south of Adams Street and the start of Route 66. It's now a very good restaurant called Gioco, but you can still see remnants from its prohibition days, when the front was a restaurant but the rear was a boozer that became more and more secretive, and much more interesting, the further back you ventured.

Something many people don't realise about that period in America is that, in the midst of all that prohibition, you were allowed to brew a hundred gallons of beer and fifty gallons of wine in your own house, but you couldn't sell it. No one was allowed to distil hard liquor, but that didn't stop the bootleggers. They called it bathtub gin in northern cities like Chicago. In the rural southern states it was known as moonshine.

Even though people were allowed to make all the beer and wine they could possibly drink at home, they still wanted to go out for a bevvy. Just like now, they enjoyed mixing and doing the how-do-you-do when they were drinking. Seeing a good business opportunity, a guy in his twenties called Al Capone, with a big scar on his face and a white hat, convinced the authorities to let him sell non-alcoholic beer.

I mean, what a lame story.

Capone made thousands of barrels of non-alcoholic beer and delivered them to the speakeasy on Wabash Street, among others. As soon as the police had inspected the non-alcoholic hooch, Al's mates would show up with big veterinarian syringes — the type that you usually shove into a cow's bum — full of ethanol. Pure alcohol, in other words. The ethanol was sourced from all over America, but the bulk of production took place in the countryside. Capone used Route 66 to transport the moonshine from rural areas to Chicago in false petrol tanks. The ethanol would be injected into the barrels and — Ta da! Off we go! — happy days were back again. If the cops turned up when the speakeasy was in full swing, there were escape routes through which the VIPs could make a swift exit. The rest of the clientele would have to face the music. And probably stop dancing.

Prohibition was hugely counter-productive. It actually *increased* alcohol consumption and promoted crime by igniting the bootlegging moonshine and beer wars fought by the Chicago gangs. Capone became the biggest and most notorious gangster in America when he took over the running of the Outfit — the syndicate of Chicago organised crime gangs. He was a major villain — in addition to bootlegging, he was involved in prostitution and bribery of government figures — yet he didn't lurk in the shadows. On the contrary, he became a highly visible public figure. Many Chicagoans even admired him, seeing him as a self-made success story. And Capone responded by giving some of the money he made from his illicit activities to charity, creating the image of a modern-day Robin Hood.

He kept plenty of the cash for himself, though, and lived ostentatiously. He held meetings in the Jeweler's

Building, a forty-storey neo-classical office tower in the heart of Chicago with an automated car lift that jewellery merchants used to make safe transfers of their merchandise. Capone would drive his car into the lift, rise to the top floor, and enjoy a few drinks in Stratosphere, the speakeasy with the best views in town.

But on St Valentine's Day 1929 Al Capone made a big mistake. He sent his boys down the road to wipe out seven Irishmen. Disguised as policemen, Capone's gang showed up with machine-guns and mowed down their Irish rivals. (Curiously, one of the Irish gangsters wasn't a gangster at all, but a doctor. He was a kind of hoodlum groupie — he liked to follow the gangsters around town and act tough.) When the press published pictures of the massacre, the people of Chicago thought Big Al had gone too far and started to turn against him. Eliot Ness and his "Untouchables" in the Bureau of Prohibition took a look at Capone's activities, but they found it impossible to link him to any serious crime, let alone the massacre. He'd covered himself pretty well and had the police in his pocket. Then they had the bright idea of taking a look at Capone's tax records.

Here's a thing. In 1927 Capone had made $106 million, but he hadn't filed a tax return. So they hauled him in for that. He was fined fifty thousand dollars and sent away for eleven years, most of which he served in Alcatraz. While in prison, he contracted syphilis, which affected his physical and mental health to such an extent that he was no longer able to run the Outfit. By 1946, he had the mental capacity of a twelve-year-old.

Eventually, at the age of forty-seven, he died following a stroke and a heart attack brought on by the syphilis.

Amazingly, Al Capone left us with a legacy that has nothing to do with booze. One of his charitable donations was a million dollars to provide milk for schoolchildren. But he insisted that a use-by date must be put on each bottle because he'd always hated the sour milk he'd been forced to drink as a child. It was the first time that anyone had had this idea, and it set a standard that's endured to this day. Isn't that the strangest thing?

The side-effects of prohibition weren't all bad, particularly its influence on the music industry and specifically jazz. Because it was the music of the speakeasies, jazz became very popular very fast, and it helped integration by uniting mostly black musicians with mostly white crowds. Chicago played its part in the development of jazz, but it played an even bigger role in rock'n'roll, which you could say was invented by black men (and women) in a little room in South Chicago, where Muddy Waters and all the other greats — including Chuck Berry, Bo Diddley and Etta James — made their first records.

That room was the recording studio of Chess Records, a legend in the blues and rhythm'n'blues world. In 1928 two Jewish brothers, Leonard and Phil Chess, arrived in Chicago as Polish immigrants. They started a few bars and by the 1940s had a nightclub called the Macomba Lounge. One of the singers who performed there was a certain McKinley Morganfield, who boosted his earnings by busking around South

Chicago during daylight hours. He was better known to everybody by his nickname — Muddy Waters.

The Chess brothers already had an interest in a record label called Aristocrat, so they used it to record Muddy's raw singing style, which perfectly reflected the spirit of the Chicago blues bars. The recordings were a great success, and soon Leonard and Phil were able to buy out their partners in Aristocrat and change the company's name to Chess Records.

Muddy's increasing fame drew other young Mississippi bluesmen to Chicago, such as Little Walter Jacobs and a twenty-stone farm worker named Chester Burnette, who soon became known as Howlin' Wolf. In their footsteps followed Sonny Boy Williamson, Memphis Slim, John Lee Hooker and Willie Mabon. All legends.

In 1955 Muddy introduced the Chess brothers to a twenty-eight-year-old singer and guitarist who was on holiday from St Louis. He sang "Ida Red", a song he'd written himself. Leonard and Phil liked the song but suggested a new title. Renamed "Maybellene", it was the first of many Top Forty hits for the guy from St Louis — Chuck Berry — who went on to write and record a string of hits that became signature songs of rock'n'roll: "Roll Over Beethoven", "Johnny B. Goode" and "Sweet Little Sixteen".

The studios and offices of Chess Records were based at several locations in South Chicago, but the most famous was immortalised by the Rolling Stones in their song "2120 South Michigan Avenue". Nowadays, it's home to Willie Dixon's Blues Heaven Foundation. It's in a rundown neighbourhood that probably has never seen better days. It has that air of always having been a bit on the skids, but it's a real place with a proper sense of identity and a community that holds together when times are tough.

Walking up to the old Chess Records building produced a strange sensation in me. In a nondescript street with a wee garden on one side, initially it felt like a non-event. But then I noticed some iron figures set into the garden railings — like a guy playing guitar, who just happened to be Chuck Berry. Wandering along a wee bit further, I spotted another, recognised the guitar, and realised it was Bo Diddley. Before I knew it, I was standing outside the birthplace of rock'n'roll.

As soon as I stepped through the door, I knew I'd arrived somewhere special. It's holy ground — the Taj Mahal for anyone who likes rock'n'roll. Hallelujah central. And they let me in even though I'm about as black as snow. Then the funniest thing happened. Me and several of the crew all went very quiet and treated the place like a church. Nobody said "Ssshhh!" or anything like that. A silence just fell upon us when we realised we were standing in the actual building where they recorded all those fantastic songs.

There's a wee museum with some posters on the wall from the old Blues Caravan tours. I remember those posters from when the tours came to Scotland in the sixties. They always looked great and the line-ups were terrific. I mean, can you imagine a show like the one I spotted on one of the posters: Jimmy Reid, John Lee

Hooker, T-Bone Walker, Big Joe Williams, Curtis Jones and the Taylor Blues Band, all on the same bill? Even wee Mississippi John Hurt was there. And Memphis Slim. My God — what a night out. We used to love it whenever they came to town.

From the museum, I moved on into a large whitewashed room at the centre of the building. It was the room where all those hits — "Johnny B. Goode" and the rest — were recorded. I touched a key on a piano, just to be sure I'd definitely touched something that one or more of the greats had once touched. Then I imagined Etta James and Bo Diddley singing, and Chuck Berry duck-walking across the floor, and all the others creating magic in that little room. Some of Ronnie Wood's drawings were hanging on one of the walls, but it was still quite hard to believe that the Rolling Stones had made an album in there. Can you imagine how that little room must have rocked over the years? I felt precious and churchy and I'm sure you would too if you visited Chess Records. It's a very special place.

I'd made my pilgrimage to Chess Records earlier in the week, before leaving Chicago on Route 66. But on the Sunday of my departure, a couple of hours before I left Adams Street, I returned to the neighbourhood for a unique experience. It had been a long time since I'd been to church on a Sunday morning, but now I was heading to Quinn Chapel, two blocks south of the old Chess Records building and an equally famous place in music and social history.

Quinn Chapel is the oldest black congregation in America. Services have been held there since the 1850s, when its congregation consisted mostly of freed slaves and abolitionists. When slavery was still a fact of life in the southern states, the chapel was a safe house on the Underground Railroad, a secret network of travel routes that were used to guide slaves to free states and territories in the northern United States and Canada. In the years since then, a succession of black leaders and luminaries such as Martin Luther King, Booker T. Washington and Frederick Douglass, a former slave who became a leader of the abolitionist movement, have spoken from the pulpit at Quinn Chapel.

On its own that would be hugely significant, but Quinn Chapel is also where gospel music really began in America. I've always loved gospel singers, especially Ray Charles and Etta James. So I'd been looking forward to experiencing a service of the African Methodist Episcopal Church, but I was very nervous before entering the chapel because I'm as close to an atheist as you can get. I think I am, anyway. It's probably better to say I don't believe in religion. So I was nervous in case I offended the congregation by being a disbelieving voyeur sitting among them. Even though they didn't know it, *I* knew it. I'm not religious, but I'm not against people who are, and I don't believe in telling people that they're wrong. It's not the right thing to do. All of this was bothering me terribly, but as soon as I got into the church, a big whitewashed hall, I was so overwhelmingly and pleasantly surprised that I forgot all about my qualms.

First of all, there was a choir to one side of the altar and a girl standing front and centre, where the priest or pastor would normally stand. She was half singing and half talking, in that Aretha Franklin soul way. I nearly cried. My lip went all wobbly. I'm not joking, I had to tell myself to get a grip because there were a lot of people around me, singing, "Hallelujah, hallelujah", and I didn't want to draw their attention.

I found a few empty seats and sat down to listen. Beside me was a chair with a Bible on it. After a while, a man in a light fawn suit picked it up, sat down beside me and started reading the Bible and mumbling. The service continued with more singing, more gesticulating and waving and praying, and I must say it pleased me greatly. A wonderful woman sitting behind the pastor was going, "All right, all right" — agreeing with everyone — "Yes, sir . . . yes, sir. All right. Yeah." Then the man in the fawn suit turned to me. "Would you like a Bible?"

I didn't like to say no.

He went off to get me one, returned, then pointed to his own so that I could find the appropriate page. I'm not a Christian now, and when I was a Catholic I didn't know the Bible — we used a missal to guide us through the mass (Catholics and the Bible have a funny relationship, but that's another story for another time). But I could follow the pastor's preaching. I was enjoying it and having fun with a little girl and her young brother who were sitting beside me, faffing around and getting them to laugh and joke and jest with me.

It was delightful. And what amazed me — even though it shouldn't have, because it's happened so many times when I've been among black communities — was the kindness and generosity of spirit shown to me.

The previous day I'd been to the oldest cigar store in America. It's in the centre of Chicago, next to the El. The crowd inside was mostly black and they were all watching the Chicago Bulls playing basketball. I had a shoeshine, bought my cigar and sat down. I'm not much of a basketball fan, but it was a very good game. One of the crowd of black guys recognised me while another thought I'd been in *Monty Python*. (It's a recurring disappointment for me in America. Maybe the association is because I did *The Secret Policeman's Ball* with some of the Pythons and that was a big hit in the States.) The guys were cracking jokes and having fun, then one asked if I'd like a drink.

"No, I don't drink," I said. "But I'd like to smell it, if you don't mind." It was Maker's Mark, a Kentucky bourbon whiskey, and I had a sniff. "Oh . . . memories. Memories."

The guys all laughed and smiled. Then one of them stood up, came over and handed me a ten-inch-long Bolivar cigar. *A Havana.* "Welcome to Chicago, Billy," he said.

I nearly fell off my seat. Such friendliness, such overwhelming *bonhomie* and *joie de vivre.* And for *nothing.* All I had done was walk into the shop. And they had shown me such outstanding hospitality and kindness.

So I should have known better than to be surprised at the homeliness that was shown to me in Quinn Chapel as everyone who came near me shook my hand, wished me a good day and said they were glad I was there.

As I said, I'm not a believer any more and I don't think I ever will be again. I used to be quite a sincere Catholic when I was a boy, but it hasn't stood the test of time for me, especially when a child dies and some fool says, "Jesus wanted him for an angel." I just want to lash out when I hear something like that; I want to get violent. I think religion's time has come and gone. They're having a lot of fun just now throwing bombs at each other, aren't they, all the peace and love merchants. That said, the spirit and the sheer enthusiasm in that room persuaded me that if I was going to be religious again, that might be the religion I'd go for. I certainly came out feeling much, much better than when I went in.

It was just a joy watching that congregation of people at their best, worshipping as they saw fit. And what they saw fit, I saw fit. I wasn't jealous of their faith, but I admired it. I thought a wee bit of it would do me some good. It took me back to when I was a boy, when I had faith. And although that's gone now, visiting Quinn Chapel and being among a congregation of good people doing good was a happy experience, a wholesome thing to do. I'm glad I did it.

Chess Records and Quinn Chapel border on to a neighbourhood of Chicago called Bronzeville, which in the early twentieth century became known as the Black Metropolis after half a million African-Americans fled the oppression of the South and migrated to the city in search of industrial jobs. The city authorities confined the new arrivals to this borough, which extended over a very small area between 29th and 31st streets. The conditions were extreme at times. For instance, twenty thousand people were housed in four twenty-two-storey buildings within very close proximity to one another. However, this mass migration brought music into the area. Bronzeville was a haven for jazz, blues and gospel. The great Louis Armstrong's trumpet ignited the borough's many jazz clubs. Muddy Waters and Buddy Guy created electric blues here, while Quinn Chapel and the Pilgrim Baptist Church gave birth to gospel music.

Ever since then, Bronzeville has continued to bustle with celebrities, intellectuals, musicians and artists. The Regal Theater, located in the heart of the area, was demolished in the 1970s, but in its heyday it played host to the cream of twentieth-century American music. Nat King Cole, Ella Fitzgerald, Sarah Vaughan, Lena Horne, Dinah Washington, Miles Davis and Duke Ellington performed there frequently. The Supremes, the Temptations, the Four Tops, the Jackson 5, Gladys Knight and the Pips, Count Basie, Dizzy Gillespie, Louis Jordan, Solomon Burke, Dionne Warwick, James Brown, the Isley Brothers, John Coltrane — the list of performers at the Regal is like a *Who's Who* of soul, rhythm'n'blues and jazz. What would anyone have given to be present at the Motown Revue in June 1962, when "Little" Stevie Wonder, Smokey Robinson and the Miracles, Mary Wells and the Marvelettes and Marvin Gaye were on the bill? What a line-up.

But until the mid-1960s, when the Civil Rights Act was passed, travelling through America was frequently fraught for African-Americans. Restricted to segregated zones in the South and often discriminated against in other areas too, their journeys along America's highways — including Route 66 — were far from simple. Some motel and restaurant owners welcomed black Americans; others blatantly discriminated against them.

In 1936 a postal employee from Harlem, New York, came up with the idea of producing a guide to integrated or black-friendly establishments. Although initially it focused on businesses in New York State, Victor Green's guide was such a success that within a year its coverage had spread nationwide. Under a banner of "Now we can travel without embarrassment", *The Green Book* was particularly helpful to African-Americans who travelled through what were called "sunset towns", which publicly stated that "Negroes" had to leave by sundown or face arrest. Known unofficially as "The Grapevine", the book became the inspiration for that fantastic song, "I Heard it through the Grapevine", recorded by Smokey Robinson and the Miracles, Gladys Knight and the Pips, and of course, in its definitive version, Marvin Gaye.

I went to meet Preston Jackson, an artist and activist who lives and works in Bronzeville, whose family made it across America using *The Green Book*. I'd intended to ask him about his family's experiences, but we ended up talking more about the effects of growing old — like those single hairs that grow out of your ears or eyebrows — and the absurdity of Pat Boone singing "Tutti Frutti". This lovely, intelligent, committed, talented man had come to the same conclusion as me and thousands of others: when Boone recorded "Tutti Frutti", that paragon of clean living didn't have a clue that the song was about prostitution and gay sex. (The original opening lyrics were: "A wop bop a loo mop, a good goddamn!/Tutti frutti, loose booty/If it don't fit, don't force it/You can grease it, make it easy"!)

Preston has remained militant in the most gentlemanly, pure way. He's a good man with a very good heart who cares deeply about the culture of his people and he tries to portray it through his art. He showed me his sculptures, many of which portrayed Harlem in its heyday and the years of its decline. We chatted about all sorts of things. Then, at the end of the meeting, my nemesis caught up with me again.

As I mentioned earlier, in America I am often mistaken for one of the Pythons. Don't ask me why, as I don't look anything like John Cleese, especially when my long, grey hair is down, as it was that day. Nevertheless, it often happens. People will come up to me and say, "Excuse me. Are you John Cleese?"

Or they'll say, "I love your work."

"Oh, thanks very much," I'll respond.

"So how are the other guys?"

"Who?"

"The rest of the *Monty Python* crew. Eric? Michael?"

And my heart sinks.

Sometimes I tell them I'm not John Cleese. "No, I'm a Scottish comedian," I say. "My name's Billy Connolly."

"Oh? Incognito?" And then they do the nudge, nudge, wink, wink thing.

As it happened, earlier that day I'd told the crew about being mistaken for John. I could see that some of them only half-believed me. After all, no Brit would confuse my Glaswegian brogue for John's clipped English vowels. But then, as I came downstairs from Preston's gallery, a big black guy tapped me on the shoulder.

"Are you John Cleese?"

"No, I'm Billy Connolly."

"Oh . . . incognito?"

Nicky, the producer, just exploded. The truth was revealed before her very eyes.

Now I was back on my trike, heading southeast on Route 66, gradually coming to the edge of Chicago. It's always weird when you leave a city. No matter how much you like the place, the outskirts always suck. You go from these gigantic palaces in the sky, like the *Chicago Tribune* Building and the Sears Tower (which I could see in my mirrors for ages) and then the surroundings get more and more shabby and rundown.

The Windy City is a brawny kind of place, and here at its fringes are the factories, slaughterhouses and foundries on which it built its industrial might and reputation. The road darts between warehouses and over railroad tracks and makes a few turns. Then, suddenly, we were out in the countryside, joining Interstate 55 for about eight miles (it was built directly over Route 66 here, so you can't avoid it) before leaving it to rejoin old 66. Even here, out of town and in the proper outdoors, it was a bit shabby, largely because it was reclaimed mining land and there was still a kind of messiness to it. And the weather didn't help. It was another grey and windy day. Although I like rain and what it does, I was starting to feel we really hadn't been blessed with good weather since arriving in Chicago. A bit of sun would have been welcome, especially now that we were on Route 66. Everybody's image of the Mother Road involves bright colours — red and yellow, white and blue — rock'n'roll, hamburgers and hot dogs, Jerry Lee Lewis and Chuck Berry. But I was getting rained on all the time and somehow it didn't fit.

A few minutes later, I entered Romeoville, a town about thirty miles southwest of Chicago. Nestling between urban areas, this part of Illinois was mostly agricultural country, and Route 66 was flanked by wide-open plains that looked like potato fields, only occasionally broken up by sparse lines of trees or telegraph poles. Much of the produce from these fields used to be shipped from Romeoville along the Des Plaines River, which passes through the town, and the

71

Illinois & Michigan canal system. Nowadays, nearly all of it goes by road.

Romeoville used to be called Romeo when it was part of a twinned community with Juliet, a few miles further down Route 66. That romantic association ended in 1845, when someone realised that Juliet was most likely a misspelling of the name of the French pioneer Louis Jolliet, who first explored the area in the 1670s. The town decided to change its name in honour of him, but it still didn't get the spelling quite right. It's now known as Joliet. Meanwhile, jilted by its twin, Romeo acknowledged the busted romance and became Romeoville. Nowadays, it plays very much second fiddle to Joliet, which is the first significant city beyond the sprawl of Chicago.

You might have heard Joliet mentioned in television crime programmes. It used to be a quarry town, nicknamed "Stone City". Much of that lovely white stone seen on skyscrapers like the Wrigley Building in the heart of Chicago came from Joliet's quarries. But these days the town is most famous for its prisons. They are the biggest industry in town. Imagine prison being your biggest industry — holy moly! — but that's one of the strangest things about America. The Land of the Free incarcerates more of its people than any other country on earth.

Joliet's most famous prison, the Joliet Correctional Center, is known to millions of *Blues Brothers* fans as the lock-up from which Jake Blues is released at the beginning of the movie. It is also name-checked in Bob Dylan's "Percy's Song". But it closed in 2002 and all the prisoners were moved to a much larger maximum-security facility, the Stateville Correctional Center, a vast compound on the edge of town that used to have a death row and conduct executions by lethal injection. It's the kind of isolated place in which the US government is hoping to house some of the terrorist suspects who are currently stuck down in Guantanamo Bay. There's another clink, the Will County Adult Detention Facility, on the other side of town, so you could say Joliet is book-ended by slammers.

Driving through the outskirts of town, I passed an ice-cream parlour with a couple of *Blues Brothers* figures on its roof. Gimmicks like those two figures have been features of Route 66 ever since its heyday, when restaurants and motels would go to extraordinary lengths to attract the attention of passing drivers.

There's not much more to say about Joliet. It's a pretty wee town with a river flowing through the middle, but, based on my experience, no people in it — except for one guy running along a pavement. I hope he hadn't escaped from prison.

# CHAPTER
# FOUR

## It Starts in Illinois,
## Let Me Tell You Boy

A few more miles through the tall-grass prairies of Illinois, I arrived in Wilmington, turned a corner and came face to face with a wonderful sight — a twenty-eight-foot-high green spaceman in a silver helmet who advertised a drive-in restaurant called the Launching Pad.

Big guys like him are still common sights on Route 66. Some travellers make a thing out of trying to spot as many of them as possible. Originally, these giants were designed to catch the eye of potential customers who were driving past so that people would say, "Gee look, a giant. Let's go and eat there." Later, when the interstates bypassed a lot of the communities on Route 66, even bigger giants were built, to catch the attention and wallets of people cruising past.

The owner of the Launching Pad bought his spaceman at a restaurateurs' convention in 1965 for three thousand dollars. Which begs the question: what kind of person lugs a twenty-eight-foot spaceman to a convention? I always thought conventions were held in hotel suites, and I can't imagine anyone dragging a twenty-eight-foot astronaut into the Glasgow Hilton, no matter how much I stretch my imagination. But this fella had bought his giant spaceman for three thousand bucks and good on him, the entrepreneur that he was. I just wonder what he said to his wife when he brought it home. "Darling, I've got you a present . . ."

When that fella bought the big guy, it was just a big semi-naked model. Someone used to make a standard roadside giant — they all had the same trousers and always held their hands out in front of them. So the owner of the Launching Pad held a competition to give his giant a name and decide how he should be dressed. A ten-year-old girl won the contest with her suggestion of Gemini — after the Gemini space programme, which was all the rage at the time. They made a big space helmet and a rocket, which they put in his hands. The helmet made him look a bit like a giant welder, but maybe that's just me. Strangely, two rockets have been nicked from his hands so far, although I can't imagine what the dirty swines do when they steal a six-foot polystyrene rocket. It's rather tragic. Did they take them home and play with them?

As far as luring people off the interstate, the Gemini Giant would certainly work for me. I can just imagine my kids when they were younger — "Dad, take us there. I wanna go to where the rocket man is. Take us there, Dad. Come on, Dad, *come on*." I'd cave in. And anyway, I've always loved that kind of thing myself — that part of America that's always viewed as big and vulgar, but which really appeals to me. Things like the biggest chair in the world, the biggest frying pan and the tallest thermometer. I love all that. There's something of the sideshow about it, something Coney Island, that tickles me. It's fun and Americans know what fun is. After all, they've got the only constitution in the world with the word "happiness" written into it.

American adults believe in having fun. They've got more toys than us Europeans. If you go into an American's garage, you'll find a four-wheeled vehicle and a three-wheeled vehicle and bicycles and boats and dirt bikes and a motor home. I'm in total agreement with them. Life is supposed to be fun. It's not a job or an occupation. We're here only once and we should have a bit of a laugh. So these big men by the side of the road totally appeal to me.

Wilmington itself is a nice enough place. There's a dinosaur model on top of a tyre garage and a few other remnants of Route 66's heyday in the main street, such as a boarded-up drive-through restaurant.

Pushing on, heading for Pontiac, I was cruising happily when my eyes darted from the road and right there, in a diner's car park in Bramlington, I spotted Elvis, James Dean and Betty Boop. Yelling at the crew, who were driving ahead of me in the truck, I pulled over. The Route 66-themed, 1950s-style joint — the Polk-a-Dot Drive-In — was a charming place, but this was Easter Sunday and it was closed. In Britain it would have been open, but they take the Christian thing more seriously in these parts. Outside the diner, lined up along a wall, stood those three fibreglass, slightly larger-than-life-size effigies. There was space for one more, which I later discovered had been occupied by Marilyn Monroe, with her white dress billowing in the classic pose from *The Seven-Year Itch*. I had some fun with Elvis and Betty. I cleaned up her skirt and posed and jived around in front of them, making a fool of myself, before moving on down the road.

After just two miles I came to Godley, a tiny place with a population of less than six hundred but a racy history. Not so much a town as a single street with a collection of buildings on either side, Godley has a geographic quirk that shaped its destiny. The left side of the main street, which crosses Route 66, is in one county and the right side is in another. You might think that's nothing special, but in the 1930s, when the Illinois coal mines and stone quarries were in full swing, it made Godley the hottest destination for miles around on a Friday night. Loaded up with their end-of-week pay, the miners and quarrymen would head for Godley, knowing there was a brothel there that had a unique way of evading the law. Some enterprising resident had turned a railway carriage into the brothel and parked it on the line. The lads would turn up and get down to drinking and shagging their earnings away. If word came down that there was going to be a raid, a shout would go up and all the lads would interrupt their activities to push the carriage into the neighbouring county. Once across the county line, neither police force could do anything about it. The crime had been perpetrated in one county, but they were now in the neighbouring county, so unless they got down to business again, they were back to being law-abiding citizens.

Driving through Godley, I could barely concentrate on the road, I was laughing so much at the mental image of all those bare-arsed men diving out of bed to push the carriage into the next county while the hookers looked on and the two counties' police forces scratched their heads, unable to do anything about it. The thought of a bunch of mad-shagging train-pushers made my heart sing. There's something wonderful — and very pragmatic, in that typically American, no-nonsense way — about a brothel on wheels. And to think the little village was called Godley. It should have been called Godless.

At first glance, Pontiac is just an ordinary town, like hundreds, maybe even thousands, of others in the Midwest of America. Located smack bang on Route 66 and built around a town square with a county courthouse on one side, it's like so many small towns portrayed in so many Hollywood movies. It was even used as the setting for *Grandview, USA*, a 1980s romantic comedy starring Jamie Lee Curtis, Patrick Swayze and John Cusack. *Time* magazine called it one of the best small towns in America. You can imagine the kind of place — there are shops and restaurants around the square, and the courthouse has a clock tower, just like the one in *Back to the Future*.

It's the kind of place where you can picture that whole American Dream thing happening — people setting up in Pontiac and making successes of their lives in a modest, wholesome way. Those sitcoms of the fifties and sixties suddenly come alive when you're in Pontiac; you realise they were based on real life. Then, in June 2009, the town's local government did an amazing thing. It invited 160 artists to paint nineteen murals in the town in just four days. The council put up the artists, fed them and gave them booze, and the whole thing turned into a huge party. And, if you ask me, it was a huge success.

The murals were painted by a group of artists called Walldogs, which is what the commercial painters of old were often nicknamed. The group's members came from all over the world, and their paintings aren't anything like those ghastly murals that look half like graffiti and always give me the pip. These murals are handsome replicas of the advertisements that used to be painted on the sides of businesses at the turn of the twentieth century. They are very detailed figurative paintings, beautifully executed, and they make the town look smashing.

Residents of Pontiac stumbled on the idea of having their lovely town bedecked in murals after they had commissioned a Route 66 mural for the centre of the town. It was a simple image — the Route 66 highway shield — but it immediately drew visitors to the town. The nineteen murals painted in 2009 have been even more successful, doubling tourist numbers. I'm not surprised.

I went for a walk round Pontiac to have a good look at the murals. They were all a delight, but I was most tickled by the one for the Allen Candy Company. It appeared to have been painted by several artists (the signatures read: "Roy, Noah, Brad, Teddy and Jackie"), and apparently one of them had owned a dog that died the week before the mural was painted. So the artist had the dog cremated and mixed its ashes in with the paint. Now the dog is part of the mural. I loved that.

There's more to Pontiac than the murals. They've also had funky wee cars inspired by Route 66 — each about the size of a kiddie's pedal car — placed around the town. With the cars dotted all over the place and bolted to the ground, I had to watch my step, particularly on street corners. On the steps of the courthouse there's a particularly weird car with a windswept Abraham Lincoln sitting in the back seat. Long before he became President, Lincoln had tried his first case as a lawyer in Pontiac. It was a strange thing to imagine as I strode around the town, dodging the wee cars and other artworks and admiring the murals.

Some of the cars were painted in rainbow colours. One, a wee beauty called "Pussy Footin' around Downtown", had a leopard-skin pattern. Another, with big sunglasses and a cheesy smile, was called "InCARgnito". Then there was a brightly coloured van called "Vincent 'I'm not a Van' Gogh" that had a reproduction of one of Van Gogh's paintings on it.

There are also pyramids and all sorts of nonsense, such as a pair of man-sized footprints in the concrete pavement next to a set of doggie paw-prints, so that it looks like some guy was just there, walking his dog. It's terrific that a town will go to such lengths to cheer itself up. When you see so many towns falling into the abyss with pound shops and charity stores everywhere, it's lovely to see one making the effort to tart itself up a bit.

Before I give the impression that Pontiac is a wee bit of heaven on earth, I ought to get something off my chest that bothered me right from the start of the trip. It's not something unique to Pontiac, but by the time I reached the town it had become really hard to ignore. If this book inspires you to travel along Route 66 and you're hoping to eat well, think again. There's not much decent or wholesome — or even particularly healthy — food to be found along the Mother Road. There are plenty of pancakes and burgers and shakes and fries, but after a while it becomes a very monotonous diet.

The night before I toured Pontiac, I visited a restaurant and ordered the broasted chicken. I only had it to see what *broasted* was. I soon discovered it meant broiled and roasted, or what most people would call burned. Maybe I should have known better when I saw the menu. It had pictures of the food, which is always a dead giveaway (unless you're in Japan, where the food is invariably fantastic, even though the restaurants often have wax replicas of their dishes in the window). If you're on Route 66 and you stop at a place where the menu has pictures of the grub, you'd be well advised to carry on until you find somewhere better. Unfortunately, along Route 66, there aren't too many better places. I know it sounds deeply snobbish, and I probably shouldn't say it, but the amount of fat and sugar and junk eaten in Middle America is scary. That's why everyone's getting obese.

However, there's a silver lining to every cloud. In this case, we have the inventor of one of the staples of unhealthy fast-food cuisine — the Cozy Dog — to thank for also creating one of the greatest artists associated with Route 66 — Robert Waldmire. Route 66 attracted a lot of poets, writers, painters, wanderers and all sorts of scallywags who were just in love with the road and made it their whole life. Bob was one of them. He was due to paint a mural in Pontiac in 2009, but he died before he could carry out the commission. Now a bunch of artists are going to get together and paint one in his memory.

Bob grew up watching the Route 66 traffic pass by his parents' restaurant in Springfield, Illinois (which was where his father, Ed, came up with the Cozy Dog, of which more later). In 1962 Ed took the whole family on a road trip along the 66 to California. Bob, who was already an accomplished artist at school, was hugely inspired by what he saw and fell in love with everything to do with the Mother Road — the motels, diners and truck stops, and particularly the Arizona and New Mexico deserts. He decided he wanted to spend his time travelling the route, but first he went off to university, where he spotted a fellow student's illustration of the local town. Wishing to do something similar for his hometown, Bob had a brainwave: he would get local merchants to pay him to include their businesses in his poster.

Bob appears to have been completely different from his father. He was a hippy type, a big, bearded vegetarian who ate "not dogs" rather than hot dogs. His illustrations are very like those of Robert Crumb, very intricate and detailed, with little buildings in the plan of a town, all seen from above. He'd include all the details, like telegraph poles and street signs. They're very, very good.

His first poster was a great success, both critically and commercially. Bob made even more money from selling it to local residents than he'd made from getting the businesses to pay up front to be included in it, so he set off to visit college towns, repeating the formula as he travelled. This one idea changed his life for ever. Provided he lived relatively cheaply, he could travel back and forth across America supported entirely by his illustrations. Best of all, it meant that Bob, who hated the cold, could spend winters in his beloved desert, drawing the buildings, towns and landmarks of Route 66. These drawings became famous icons of the road themselves, as did the orange 1972 VW campervan in which he travelled. When Pixar made *Cars*, they based Fillmore, the VW bus character, loosely on Bob Waldmire.

Some of Bob's best work was his set of four large and highly intricate state posters of Route 66 winding through California, Illinois, New Mexico and Arizona. Filled with hundreds of drawings of scenic vistas, sketches of the wildlife and historical attractions, they also contained short philosophical comments, quotes from literature and pleas for peace, non-violence and sound ecological practices, many of them quietly rebellious. "It is estimated that Lake Mead and Lake Powell [two massive reservoirs created by the damming of the Colorado River] evaporate more water per year than the multi-billion-dollar central Arizona project will provide annually," it said on the Arizona poster. And on his New Mexico poster: "The state has a cradle to grave affair with nuclear technology — the atom bomb was born here, nuclear wastes are buried here."

But, personally, I think Bob did his best work when he turned his pen on hunters and really went to town. "The campaign to 'control' the coyote is more like a war of extermination," he wrote in small print on his poster of Silver City, Arizona. "The Steel Jaw-Leghold Trap . . . Scourge of the Earth." However, a hunting shop spotted the comments and threatened to sue Waldmire. Fortunately, he managed to get the law on his side and avoid court.

While I was in Pontiac, they were displaying Bob's old converted bus in which he used to spend the winter travelling through the southwestern states. It's one of those yellow American school buses with corrugated sides, but Bob added solar panels, rainwater collectors, a solar oven, a sauna and solar shower, and all sorts of gizmos so that he could live off-grid when he was in the desert. From the outside, it looks a bit ramshackle, but it's an absolute dream machine. It's even got a veranda and an observation deck on the back. I was so jealous.

It was a bit of a squeeze to get in the bus, but well worth the effort. With his old shoes still lying near the steering wheel by the front door, and all his bits and pieces dotted about on shelves and tables and walls, it's the cosiest place. All of Waldmire's wee favourite things are still in there — ornaments, pictures, photographs of

Mahatma Gandhi and Martin Luther King, key rings and things that other people would consider junk — so it's like stepping into Bob's dream world. I don't know what would have happened in an emergency stop in this bus. Everything would have ended up beside him on the floor, I imagine.

All in all, the bus is an amazing thing. A great way for an artist to live, going away for four or five months every winter, a real free man. Before visiting it, I was kind of reluctant to go and see it. I wondered what the hell I'd have to say about a school bus in which a guy buggered off to New Mexico every winter. It seemed a limited subject. But when I got there I was delighted. It made me wish I'd known Bob Waldmire personally. He seemed like an amazing fella. And Pontiac is all the better for having his bus parked there.

Outside the town, there's another Route 66 landmark that's worth a look if you're passing. In 1926 Joe and Victor "Babe" Seloti built a diner and petrol station on the road that would become Route 66 in a couple of months' time. They named it the Log Cabin Inn. Close to the railway line and built of cedar telephone poles, it seated forty-five customers. The interior still has the original knotty pine walls. After the war, Route 66 was widened to four lanes and moved to the west side of the Log Cabin, which left the back of the restaurant facing the road, so Joe and Victor took a wonderfully pragmatic approach to their problem. First they jacked up the building. Then, using a team of horses, they turned it round to face the new road and dropped it back on to the ground. Business continued as usual.

Pushing on from Pontiac, past Normal, through Shirley and McLean (neatly separated by Funks Grove, famous for its maple "sirup", made since the 1820s by successive generations of Funks), I arrived in Atlanta. This is another lovely town, the highlight of which is a slightly strange story that makes the Seloti brothers' ingenuity seem like child's play.

It reminded me of an old joke from Scotland about a railway station in the Highlands where people got off the train with their suitcases only to discover there's nothing there. The village was away down the road, so they walked and walked with their cases until they finally reached it, exhausted.

One of them asked a local, "How come the station isn't closer to the village?"

And the local said, "Well, we thought it would be much handier if the station was closer to the railway line."

That's an old music-hall joke, but — believe it or not — life imitated comedy in Atlanta. The town began its existence as Newcastle in 1854 and was happily minding its own business until a year later, when the railway came to town. Or rather the railway *didn't* come to town — for some reason, they laid the tracks more than a mile away from Newcastle. That worried the residents, who thought they'd miss out on all the passing trade, so they uprooted the whole town, lock, stock and barrel, and hoiked it up to the railway line. When they'd finished, they renamed it Atlanta. I find this an absolutely wonderful, inspiring story. It's a very American, let's-get-up-and-do-it kind of thing.

A lot of old Atlanta is no longer standing, but it still has its outstanding 36-foot-tall clock tower, which dates back to 1908 and is one of the few in America that continues to be wound by hand. I met a guy called Bill Thomas, the owner of a café called the Palm Grove. Like a lot of places on Route 66, the Palm Grove had crumbled after the interstate bypassed Atlanta, but Bill had brought it back to life, partly through his championship-winning pie-making skills. He'd promised me a piece of his award-winning pie, but first I had to wind up his wee clock. I'm not belittling the Atlanta clock when I call it wee. It's just that I've wound up Big Ben, and when you've done that, every other clock in the world is wee.

Bill fixed a crank to the mechanism and let me at it. "How many cranks will it take?" I asked.

"About fifty-three total. And Billy, see what you're doing? Right up here." He pointed to a weight on a wire. "*That*'s what you're actually lifting."

"It's exactly the same method as Big Ben, although it's smaller scale."

"And see this? You want to stop." A white mark on the apparatus had reached a bar. "Stop. You've done it."

"Oh, glory be."

Then, because I'd wound the mechanism correctly, he declared me an honorary "Keeper of the Clock". I even got a certificate.

"Lucky me!" I said.

"It might help with the police or in a bar or something."

"And you've spelled my name right and everything. Thank you very much. Now, to the pies."

I'd really enjoyed it. And my new status as an official clock-winder of Atlanta has improved my CV no end. I'm sure I'll pick up loads of work in that field as I wind my way through life from now on.

Bill's café was a delight. He had worked very hard to make it look like it might have done in the 1930s. I had the last piece of peach pie. I nearly went for the apple, but I thought: Oh come on, be original. My super-duper favourite is key lime pie, especially from diners on the road. I also like coconut cream and banana cream, but Bill recommended the peach. As soon as I took a bite, I could appreciate why he'd won awards. It was delicious. The crew wolfed down blackberry, strawberry, apple and all sorts of other pies. A wonderful time was had by all.

Over the road from Bill's café stood another Route 66 giant — exactly the same size as the Launching Pad's spaceman, but this time holding a big hot dog in place of the rocket. In the time since I'd seen the Gemini Giant, I'd found out a bit more about these massive figurines. Most of them were made in the 1960s by International Fiberglass, a company based in Venice, California. The first, designed to hold an axe, was made for the Paul Bunyan Café on Route 66. Most similar statues along the road came from exactly the same mould, albeit without the axe, which explained why they all had their hands held out in front of them.

The one with the huge hot dog had spent thirty-eight years outside a restaurant in Cicero, Illinois. Then, in 2003, someone from Atlanta spotted it for sale on eBay and cheekily asked the seller if he could have it for nothing.

"Fine," said the seller. "Come and get him."

So the giant with the big hot dog arrived on permanent loan in Atlanta, Illinois. And the seller, whoever he is, booked his place in heaven.

I'd already had a great time in Atlanta, then things got even better. Having broken the banjo badge I usually wear on my lapel, I went into a shop to buy a new one. It was a funky wee shop, full of esoterica and built with Route 66 travellers in mind. The owner, Gene, who was a really friendly guy, had heard I was on a bike and asked me about it.

"Actually, I'm on a trike," I said.

"Can I see it?"

I let Gene sit on the trike — because he asked me nicely — then he invited me to his home. He said I could visit any time I liked and that he'd take me up in his aeroplane. I'm very tempted to return to Atlanta just for that. We returned to his store and I bumped into a woman from York. She'd been following me around because her sister was a huge fan, and she asked for an autograph. When I'd finished writing a wee note and signing it, she thanked me, then dug something out of her bag.

"Here's some decent tea," she said, holding out four Yorkshire teabags. "You'll have trouble getting a decent cup of tea as you go along Route 66."

I don't recall ever meeting so many nice people in such a short space of time. Atlanta was an absolute joy.

My next stop was Springfield, where Abraham Lincoln lived before going to Washington, DC as the sixteenth President of the United States. For the first time since leaving Chicago, I was back on an interstate. Riding in torrential rain, it was quite heart-stopping at times, especially when passing trucks. With the spray and the shit flying everywhere, it was tough going. And as I've said, I'm a poser, so I don't believe in riding in the rain. I don't want to be wringing out my underwear every time I stop. I've seen some guys who are even prepared to ride in the snow, but that's a different trip. That's pure sado-masochism. I like the fun of bikes. And this was no fun.

But I made it to Springfield. It was a totally crap night by the time I reached the hotel, but I told myself that something good would come of it. I'm a great believer in carrying on and not stopping just because it's raining.

Ahead of me, less than a hundred miles down Route 66, a tornado had struck Missouri. Watching the television news in my hotel room that night, I saw a bus sitting on top of the airport building in St Louis. Outside the room, thick branches were flying past the window. I couldn't foresee any kind of lush day hanging out in the sun, covered in suntan oil, coming up any time soon. Ever since we'd arrived in Chicago, the weather had taken a turn for the weird, but I was determined to make a go of my Route 66 trip. It *will* be good, I kept telling myself. It *will* be fun.

90

# CHAPTER
# FIVE

## Travel My Way,
## Take the Highway

I'd stopped in Springfield to see Lincoln's home and tomb, but to be honest I wasn't looking forward to visiting either of them. In America, Lincoln is often portrayed as a leading opponent of slavery, but having recently read about him, I'd started to doubt how much liberty he was really willing to grant the slaves. Everyone assumes he wanted total freedom, but I wasn't so sure. Although he was anti-slavery, I suspected he wasn't too keen on former slaves and other black Americans having the vote. So I was in two minds about one of America's most revered statesmen, frequently referred to as the greatest President in American history.

Going to Lincoln's house, a charming and handsome — but still quite modest — painted-frame building in a shady residential neighbourhood with wood-plank pavements, started to change my mind. It might sound ridiculous to describe it this way, but Lincoln's house was a really human home. He came over as a father, a man who had been a good dad to his children and a good husband to his wife, quite apart from being the President of America and leading his country through one of the bloodiest civil wars in history.

Lincoln was born in poverty to a Kentucky farming family. With illiterate parents and only a year's formal education, he had few prospects, but while working as a storekeeper and postmaster he developed a love of reading and a keen interest in politics. In 1834 he was elected to the Illinois State Legislature, and two years later he passed his bar exams to become a lawyer. Seeking work in his new profession, in 1837 he arrived in Springfield, the state capital of Illinois. A wee while later, he met Mary Todd, and they married in 1842. The next year, the couple's first son, Robert, was born, and in 1844 they bought a little house, painted white with green shutters, from the Reverend Charles Dresser, who had performed their marriage ceremony. Over the years, the Lincolns enlarged the house to a full two-storey Greek Revival-style home for their growing family. By 1853, the couple had four sons, although only Robert reached adulthood, married and had children of his own. The others died of pneumonia, tuberculosis or yellow fever, spread by flies from the Washington swamps.

The Lincoln home has been declared a national historic site and forms part of a small national park dedicated to the President. Four blocks of a section of Springfield that used to be quite rundown and occasionally dangerous have been restored to something approaching their mid-nineteenth-century prime. Lincoln's house is the centrepiece, and you can walk right through it. You can even inspect his outside loo. Around the house, several other buildings have been equally well restored. Most of them were once occupied by friends of the Lincoln family.

It's always very strange to visit a place where a great person used to live. When they're dead and gone, it's hard to imagine them inhabiting the space. And yet you can touch things that they've touched. Lincoln's house is particularly peculiar in that way because it's such a historically important place. In 1860 the Republican Committee arrived in his front room and offered him their nomination for President. I stood on the exact spot where Lincoln stood, all six feet four of him, when they made the offer. He pondered what to do, saying, "Well, I don't know." At the time, he was on the court circuit and still a member of the State Legislature, so I suppose he was quite comfortable with that. I like the fact that he clearly wasn't one of those hell-driven careerists. That's probably what made him such an outstanding leader of his country. He knew that accepting the presidential nomination would launch him from the relative anonymity of Illinois to national fame. Of course, we all know what happened to him in the end, though.

Walking around the house, I started to feel great warmth for the man. There were little bits of paper on the desk where he worked. And the dining room where the family used to have their meals still had the stand on which Mary, who did most of the cooking, placed the cakes she made for them. I'd imagined a huge dining room to entertain great dignitaries, but, like

**93**

everything about the man, it was very modest and homely. Upstairs, the bedrooms were just as interesting. I especially loved the wallpaper, an intricately patterned design that was possibly made by a French company. It said so much about Lincoln and his wife. I bet they were a really modern couple for their time.

But the kitchen was my favourite room in the house. With a wood-burning stove — a bit like an Aga — it must have been like hell in there, with smoke and flames everywhere. When they moved to Washington, Mary wanted to take the stove with her, but someone put their foot down and said, "No, come on, behave yourself." But I could see why she wanted to take it with her: it's absolutely beautiful.

The more I learned about Abraham Lincoln, the more I liked him. In the parlour, where the family spent a lot of their time, the kids would roll around and play on the floor, and Abe would either read or roll around on the floor with them, while Mary would do a bit of sewing and stitching. Apparently Lincoln was very fond of his children and liked to spoil them. One of his kids once had a birthday party and Lincoln invited sixty children, so the place must have been in uproar. He was often seen pulling his kids along the street in a cart, something that was considered very unmanly and feminine in those days. I liked the sound of that because I remembered pushing my own son around in a pushchair in Glasgow. It was the delight of my life at the time, but even then people responded to me strangely and often looked at me as if I was a bit of an odd hippy. They'd say, "Aren't you embarrassed? That's a woman's thing to do." So I could only imagine how the residents of Springfield must have reacted to Lincoln in the nineteenth century.

Another thing I like about him is that he lived in a sort of suburbia, a modest neighbourhood. He was born in a log cabin, so the Springfield house must have been a huge move up for him, and it was the only house he ever owned. He moved straight from Springfield to the White House in February 1861. Four years later, it was *boom*, goodnight Vienna, when John Wilkes Booth, a Confederate sympathiser, shot him in the back of the head.

Lincoln was a giant and I came away from his old home in great admiration of the man. And I'll retain that admiration, I think.

Clearly, I'm not the only one to hold Lincoln in such high regard. For evidence, you only need to look at his tomb, built in Springfield after that stumer shot him. ("Stumer" is a Scottish word that really appeals to me. I don't know where it comes from, but I like to think of it as a cross between "stupid" and "tumour". It means you're no good for anything.) The centrepiece of Oak Ridge Cemetery, Lincoln's final resting place is surrounded by towering oak trees in a gently rolling landscape. His 117-foot-tall granite tomb also contains the bodies of Mary and three of their four sons — Edward, William and Thomas.

Although relatively modest by the standards of presidential tombs, this is one of the most revered places in America — and rightly so. It's worth a visit just to see the sculptures of Lincoln, both inside and outside the tomb, the most impressive of which is a large bronze bust of the President at the entrance. A facsimile of a marble bust that stands in the US Capitol in Washington, DC, the bronze was created by Gutzon Borglum, who also sculpted the vast Lincoln figurehead at Mount Rushmore. Many visitors rub the nose of the Springfield bust for good luck. It's not encouraged, but I've never done what's encouraged, so I gave it a rub.

Inside the building, other bronze statues portray Lincoln in various stages of his life. Some include excerpts from his most famous speeches. Walking down a circular hallway to a marble burial chamber, I was confronted by the sombre words that Edwin Stanton, Lincoln's Secretary of War, uttered at his death: "Now he belongs to the ages." Stanton's next words after the assassination — "There lies the most perfect ruler of men the world has ever seen" — aren't displayed in the tomb, but I think they would have been quite appropriate. Standing in the chamber, there's a very real sense of the terrible human cost of the American Civil War, almost as if Lincoln died yesterday.

A red marble marker stands above the underground vault where Lincoln's coffin lies. People have twice tried to steal the body, so the vault has now been reinforced with concrete and steel to foil grave robbers. God only knows why anyone might want to steal it. What would they do with it? Put it on eBay?

One of the things that sums up Lincoln for me is that he spoke for less than three minutes at the dedication of the Soldiers' National Cemetery in Gettysburg, Pennsylvania, where four and a half months earlier, the

Union armies had decisively defeated those of the Confederacy. Before the President's concise, powerful and deeply moving speech, Edward Everett, a former Secretary of State, had talked for two solid hours. Everett's seldom-read, 13,607-word oration was slated to be the main event of the day, but Lincoln's "few appropriate remarks", which summarised the war in just ten sentences, is now recognised by everyone in America as *the* Gettysburg Address.

He began the speech with a reference to the American Revolution of 1776: "Four score and seven years ago our fathers brought forth on this continent a new nation, conceived in liberty, and dedicated to the proposition that all men are created equal." Then he invoked the principles laid out in the Declaration of Independence and redefined the Civil War not merely as a struggle for the Union but as "a new birth of freedom", which would bring true equality to all of America's citizens, ensure that democracy remained a viable form of government, and create a unified nation.

Now one of the best-known speeches in American history, Lincoln's Gettysburg Address was greeted first by a stunned silence and then by wild, prolonged applause for the man who was guiding the nation through the Civil War and preserving the Union. He was a fantastic guy and a true lover of freedom. His assassination did nobody any good. John Wilkes Booth simply killed a very good man.

As I mentioned at the start of this chapter, I had arrived in Springfield swithering, as we say in Scotland, between whether Lincoln was a truly great guy or just an ordinary guy made to look great by history. By the time I left, I was in no doubt. To abolish slavery and to keep the Union of America intact were two extraordinary achievements. I ended the day wishing I'd had the chance to meet Lincoln. I think he would have been a friend of mine. I reckon I would have liked him and I hope he would have liked me.

In a few hours I'd completely changed my opinion of the man. And I kinda like that. I'm not locked closed on everything.

Moving from the sublime to the ridiculous, I climbed on to my trike, headed out of the cemetery, passed the Illinois State Capitol Building (built from Romeoville limestone) and arrived at the home of the Cozy Dog, one of the birthplaces of fast food.

This was the place where Bob Waldmire, that fabulous artist who lived on a bus, grew up watching the traffic on Route 66. His father, Ed, invented the Cozy Dog after visiting Oklahoma and eating a speciality of the state — a corn dog — which is a sausage baked in cornbread. Ed liked it, but thought it took far too long to prepare. He mentioned it to a pal, but then the Second World War intervened and he thought no more of it.

A few years later, when Ed was stationed in Amarillo, Texas, with the US Air Force, his pal wrote to say that he had developed a batter that would stick to frankfurter sausages, allowing them to be deep-fried. He sent some of the batter to Ed, who tested it in the air force kitchens, creating a thickly battered hot dog on a stick. Ed called them "crusty curs".

These meat lollipops became hugely popular on the air force base and around town, so when Ed was discharged in 1946, he decided to set up a restaurant to sell his creation. But his wife thought "crusty cur" was a terrible name and suggested Cozy Dog instead, possibly because it was like a hot dog in a blanket. Their Cozy Dog restaurant in Springfield was the first fast-food joint on Route 66. For the first time in history, big groups of people were driving long distances and they needed places to grab a quick bite to eat. Cozy Dogs could be prepared in advance, so the customers could grab one and then just keep driving.

Incidentally, did you know that it took a wee while for anyone to come up with the idea of putting a frankfurter in a bun to make a hot dog? The story goes that a Bavarian sausage seller called Anton Ludwig Feuchtwanger had been selling frankfurters with a pair of white gloves so that his customers could eat the hot sausages in comfort. But when the customers started keeping the gloves as souvenirs, Feuchtwanger responded by serving his sausages in rolls. Nobody seems to know for sure whether he first tried this at the 1893 World's Fair: Columbian Exposition in Chicago or the 1904 Louisiana Purchase Exposition in St Louis. Whichever it was, Feuchtwanger is credited with inventing the hot dog, although I can't believe that nobody thought to put a frankfurter in a bread roll between the thirteenth century — when the sausages were invented in Germany — and 1893. By the way, if you've ever wondered why a hot dog tastes the way it does — with that unique flavour that no other sausage or meat has — well, the answer is coriander. That's the secret ingredient. Tell your friends. And tell them who told you.

The people at Cozy Dogs were terrific and the souvenirs were great, but something was not sitting well with me. Then I realised what was bothering me. In 1996 they'd moved from their original location. I knew the building didn't look like the kind of restaurant that would have been built in the 1940s or 1950s, the kind of roadside eatery that a young Bob Waldmire would have sat outside, watching the world drive past. It fed into my irritation about parts of America rejecting Americana. They used to build roadside diners and restaurants that were very funky, but now they've stopped doing that. Instead, they build plain little brick sheds that all look like public toilets. The Cozy Dogs had a plainness about it that I found kind of sad. What a shame.

As for the Cozy Dog itself? Well, I guess it's an acquired taste. But the chips are to die for, and the decor inside the restaurant is brilliant, so it's still well worth a wee look. I just wish they sold vegetarian "not dogs". Considering the restaurant's association with Bob Waldmire, they really ought to have them on the menu. They've got his artwork up on the walls, so they should sell his favourite snack.

Leaving Springfield, the weather immediately improved. The sun came out for a wee while for the first time since I started my journey. The rain had been belting down non-stop and I was getting a bit bored with it. I don't mind weather if it changes all the time, but constant rain and greyness really get to me. And I'm speaking as someone who comes from Scotland. So I know of what I speak.

I was making my first detour off Route 66 since leaving Chicago, and rode for what seemed like thousands of miles across vast empty plains of wheat, corn, soya bean and potato fields. Known as the Prairie State, Illinois has some of the most fertile soil in the world. The cold winters allow it to replenish itself, while the long, warm summers and reliable rainfall produce ideal growing conditions. The state produces enough soya beans each year to fill the Empire State Building more than fifteen times.

My destination was the largest Amish community in Illinois. As I approached Arthur, about ninety miles due east of Springfield, it soon became obvious that I was entering a religious community where the way of life had changed little since the current residents' ancestors had settled there some 150 years ago. About ten miles from town, there was a road sign I'd never seen before: a black silhouette of a horse and buggy on a yellow background. The sign warned that the local people lived and farmed in a unique way, one firmly based on centuries-old traditions and practices. Then I rode past a field in which the soil was being ploughed by horse.

About four thousand Amish people live in Arthur, where they humbly follow their community's strict but simple rules. Each family traditionally owns around eighty acres of farmland, which is used to feed the family and the wider community. They use only horse-drawn machines with metal wheels, and their main crops are wheat, oats, clover and corn. However, this pastoral way of life is changing for the Amish, who are struggling with ever-increasing land prices and decreased demand for home-grown, non-mass-produced food. In response, some members of this resourceful community are turning their hands to other skills, such as furniture- and machine-making, in order to supplement their agricultural income. Tourism is also becoming an important part of the Amish existence, as the cottage industries and country shops continue to thrive.

That's why I found myself pulling up outside a large, plain wooden shed and offices that served as the workshop of Mervin, the Amish furniture-maker I mentioned at the start of the book. I liked Mervin from the first moment I met him. He has an easy smile and a gentle manner, as well as that fantastic pudding-bowl haircut. Dressed in a plain shirt, dark trousers and button braces, Mervin was very welcoming and offered to show me around his workshop. He answered every question honestly, such as when I asked how he took orders from customers, given that the Amish weren't meant to use modern appliances like telephones.

"We've got a phone that we use to take orders," he said. "We're not allowed to have phones for ourselves, but they're all on the outside of the building." He indicated something that looked like a payphone, bolted to the side of his office. As an Amish businessman, he can receive calls from people who have no other way to contact him, but he can't phone out, except in an emergency. "More and more of them have their own phones," said Mervin, referring to the other Amish residents of Arthur, "since more of them run businesses in the area."

In my ignorance, I'd always thought that Amish communities didn't extend any further than Pennsylvania, but Mervin explained that they had spread across large parts of the United States. Originating in Switzerland, the Amish are a Christian group who migrated to America in the early eighteenth century in search of freedom to practise their religion as they pleased. Although I was right in thinking that they initially settled in Pennsylvania, which is still home to one of the largest Amish communities in the world, some families eventually travelled further west in search of more land.

For years, the Amish lived very enclosed lives, almost entirely self-sufficient and spurning contact with the outside world. But times have changed, and Amish furniture-makers, renowned for their old-fashioned, high-quality woodworking skills, now sell their goods outside the community in order to survive. Mervin showed me how his team of cabinetmakers made every piece by hand in a large joinery workshop that he'd set up in 1996 after working for another Amish carpenter. Surprised to see some power tools in the workshop, I asked Mervin whether the Amish way of life allowed him to use electrical machinery.

"No, all the tools in the shop are run off hydraulics and air," he said. For instance, Mervin's saws and sanders were hydraulic, rather than electric. "We've got some electric lights and appliances. We're allowed to have some electrical power, but we run it off diesel generators. We're not allowed to have it come off the line, so we produce it ourselves."

"Why's that?" I asked. "Because it would connect you to the outside world?"

"Not just that," he said. "Mostly it's to stay away from as much modern stuff as we can."

"It seems to be working well for you. You seem to be managing pretty well without it."

"Yeah."

Mervin asked if I would like to have a go at putting a cabinet together, but I turned down his kind offer. "I'm too clumsy," I said. "I don't want to waste one."

The wood is mostly imported from Canada, although a small amount comes from the northeastern US states and the South. Mervin said the most important member of the team was the man who cut the wood. "If he doesn't get it right," he said, "then it's real difficult for the guys who put it all together." Clearly, the man who cut the wood was doing his job extremely well, because the finished products were all beautiful, with an astonishingly smooth finish. Such well-made pieces of furniture are surely destined to become the antiques of tomorrow.

In his showroom, Mervin showed me an entire kitchen that had been constructed in his workshop. With excellent craftsmanship and fantastic attention to detail, it was splendid, top-of-the-line stuff — the kind of furniture you buy only once, because it lasts a lifetime. I'd dearly love to have something like it in my house.

Mervin had a charming, very practical, down-to-earth attitude to making furniture. "Who designed this?" I asked, pointing at one of the kitchen cabinets.

"We see it," he said, "and then we just make it."

It was at this point that Mervin suggested we should go for a ride in his horse-drawn buggy, something I'd always wanted to do. He showed me out to the yard, then directed me into the stable so that I could bring out the horse. As I explained earlier, I'm a wee bit wary of horses, but Mervin helped me lead out a lovely chestnut. Very gently, Mervin attached some tackle to the horse while I continued to pepper him with curious questions.

"As we were driving here I noticed that many Amish were waving at us from their buggies. Is that normal?"

"Oh yes," said Mervin. "We think that if you don't wave, you're stuck up."

"Really?"

Mervin laughed. "That's the way a lot of people feel. It's like: try to be friendly to everybody."

"That's wonderful."

Mervin then attached the horse to a black buggy, which, like Mervin's furniture, was a beautiful example of skilled craftsmanship. It had two sliding panels on each side, so the passengers could travel either entirely enclosed and protected or with the sides open.

"She's a little worked up today," Mervin warned as he adjusted the horse's reins.

"Why's that?" I asked, even though the horse seemed perfectly calm to me.

"A few strangers about. She's not so used to them."

As he fixed the horse, he told me that most Amish families owned a buggy or two, all of them made by local craftsmen. A larger model typically costs around seven thousand dollars. We set off and Mervin explained that he learned how to control a buggy as a kid. Then he showed me the ropes.

"It's not hard at all," he said, as I took the reins.

"Not with you here, it isn't," I replied.

We pootled along for a little while, chatting idly.

"You know what I find very impressive, Mervin? You keep talking about the rules for this, the rules for that, and the rules for the other. You seem very comfortable with it."

"It's something you get used to, you know."

"From the outside, people think it's kind of fanatical. But up close you seem very happy with what you're doing."

"It's nice to keep your family together and just kind of do your own thing." We plodded on a bit further in silence, then he said: "I guess, as far as the rules and stuff go, it's . . ."

"Do you find comfort in it?"

"Oh yeah, oh yeah."

"You certainly seem to," I said. "You seem to be a very happy man."

"Yes."

**106**

"Another thing. On the way here we stopped at an Amish restaurant, and when we were among Amish people there, I thought they would keep themselves separate, but they made a point of saying 'hello' and 'good morning'."

"Oh yeah." Mervin nodded, then turned to me. "So, you got any children, Billy?"

"Four girls and a boy."

"How old are they?"

"The youngest one's twenty-two and the oldest is forty-one."

"All still living with you?"

"Well, two of them still live with me."

"I see."

"The rest are out working in different places."

Mervin interrupted our conversation to explain that if I wanted the horse to go a little faster, I should give her a gentle tap and click my tongue. "There you go," he said, showing me how.

"How many children have you got?" I asked.

"Five. We had six but the youngest one passed on," said Mervin. He hesitated before continuing. "We had an accident when he was fourteen months old."

"Oh, fourteen months. That must have broken your heart."

"It was kind of a sad situation. I was out in the barn and I was using the skip-loader to move a hay-bale and I backed over him."

"*Oh no.*"

"Yeah, and . . . so it was kind of sad."

107

I looked at Mervin. He was telling me about this tragedy in such a quiet, calm, matter-of-fact way that it broke *my* heart. He'd simply accepted that it had been God's way. Whether I agreed with that was a different story, but he accepted it and that was the whole cheese.

"It's been twenty . . . The second of April. It was twenty years ago, so it was kinda . . ."

The anniversary had just passed, a couple of weeks before. "Oh, my goodness me," I said.

"You know, it's still tough."

I nodded. "That must have taken a bit of getting over."

"Yeah. We still think about it a lot."

"I bet you do."

"But, you know, life goes on and . . . you've just got to make the best of it sometimes."

"Of course you do."

"It's one of those things."

"Yeah."

We sat in silence for a few moments, watching the countryside slowly slide past and listening to the clip-clop of the horse's hooves.

"We had a lot of rain lately," said Mervin, "and we got water across the road here." He explained how you get the horse to cross a deep puddle. "If she runs, that's fine; but if she wants to walk, let her walk." It seemed like a good approach and the horse took us through the water.

Next we took a spin around the fields, a vast, flat landscape with little protection from the elements. Winters here are long and hard, but Mervin said they were bearable and I could understand why. Sitting behind a horse clip-clopping down the road was a lovely way to travel, and I seemed to have got the hang of it.

"It's not hard at all," repeated Mervin.

"It's very nice. I would love to go into town like this." We both cackled.

"And when you're young and single," I said, "is this how you go out with your young lady?"

"Yeah, we can. They get those gatherings and then they'll sometimes end up taking the lady home and getting acquainted and so forth."

"Is that allowed? Are you allowed to be alone with your girlfriend? Or do you need a chaperone?"

"It's allowed."

"And do you do that thing here where you . . . Is it called *rumspringa*?"

"Yeah, they call it *rumspringa*."

*Rumspringa* literally means "running around", which is an apt description. It's the period between the ages of sixteen and eighteen when adolescent Amish kids decide between being baptised and officially joining the Amish Church or leaving the community. It's also when they look for a spouse. It's a rite of passage, and maybe a time for sowing a few wild oats. Some Amish communities allow their young men to purchase small "courting buggies", while some families paint their yard gate blue to indicate that a daughter of marriageable age lives there.

It seems a very sensible system to me. By recognising that adolescents need to rebel and defy their parents, it allows a degree of misbehaviour to be tolerated. Some of the kids turn their backs on Amish practices, wearing non-traditional clothing and styling their hair differently (they call it "dressing English"), driving vehicles, drinking or taking drugs and engaging in pre-marital sex. Up to half of them may temporarily leave the community or eschew the traditional practices, but almost all eventually return and choose to join the Church.

I told Mervin I thought the *rumspringa* was a very sane thing to do.

"Yeah, but there's some things that go on that I don't really like or . . ."

"That you don't approve of?"

"Some of the kids get carried away."

"Of course."

"And people's people, you know? People's people."

"Do people get disappointed if the youngsters don't come back?"

"Some do. That varies from family to family. It might be more disappointing to one person than it is to another."

"It all seems very basic and understandable to me."

"Well, we just try to be simple, you know? A lot of them get it out of their system and then . . ."

"Settle down?"

"Yeah. We're all humans, just like the rest of them."

I like that attitude. There's something very accepting — and very Scottish — about it.

I was intrigued how Mervin met his own wife, so asked: "How would an Amish guy find an Amish wife?"

"Well, a lot of them have activities going on. Or, like what I did, I met her, my wife, at a certain place and got acquainted. Then we started dating each other. I'd take her places."

"Did you meet in a sort of community thing, a dance or a get-together or something like that?"

"I was probably where I shouldn't have been."

That made me laugh.

Mervin told me that the various Amish communities across America all have the same basic rules, but with some variations, according to geography. "You know, because you live in a certain circumstance, a certain rule doesn't work." A few are allowed to have mobile phones or to fly on aeroplanes because they are considered necessities. Occasionally, Mervin will take a train into Chicago for business purposes, but in his community aeroplanes are still forbidden. I'd love to have seen him with his hat and beard striding through the Windy City.

"In this area we don't fly," he said. "But it's one of those things — maybe one community needs something where another one doesn't. When I was younger, I asked one of the bishops how we should decide what's appropriate and he said it's important that everybody agrees to whatever we're doing."

"That seems to bind everything you do. With the Amish, everybody has to agree."

Mervin nodded. "You know, it varies. It's not all one hundred per cent. Just everybody tries to do their part. It makes it easier for everybody."

"I like the way you combine resources. If someone's got cancer and the treatment is expensive, you all take part in paying for it. I think that's a wonderful thing."

"I really appreciate that, too. Helping each other binds people together. It's kind of the key thing."

"Visitation" is another big thing among the Amish. It's all about maintaining their community. They'll gather at each other's homes to drink coffee and eat popcorn. Alcohol is not permitted, but Mervin said the youngsters often have a drink anyway. "They go through that age when it's an attractive thing, even though it's not allowed." Weekends and holidays are spent dropping in on friends and relatives. "If someone needs visiting, maybe they're sick or they need company, we go see them."

In their spare time, many of the Amish folk fish for bass or sing in choirs, particularly on Sunday evenings, when all the generations congregate together. They go to church at least every fortnight, often visiting other churches in the district, although communion is only ever taken in their local church.

Mervin and I kept talking until, about half an hour later, we arrived at the family farm and he invited me into his parents' house. Mervin himself lived next door.

"Your stomach getting empty?" he asked. "Are you ready for lunch?"

"Absolutely."

After several days of eating rubbish on the road, it was a delight to sit down to some proper home-cooked food, prepared by Mervin's wife and mother. They were both dressed in long, plain dresses, pinafores and bonnets. Near by, a small girl, no more than two years old, wandered around, also dressed in traditional Amish dress and bonnet, a dummy in her mouth. I listened as the family chatted in what sounded like a combination of English and High German.

Mervin invited the director, the producer and the rest of the crew to join us as we sat down to a huge spread, including chicken, ham, pie, salad, vegetables, potatoes, noodles, corn and bread. It all tasted wonderful.

After dinner, Mervin showed me how the gas lighting in his parents' house worked. It gave out a lovely glow. Then he asked where I was going next.

"St Louis. It'll take about two and a half hours." I told Mervin that the throttle on the bike was a bit tight and made my thumb sore. "So it'll be a little painful by the time we get to St Louis, but all in all it will be good fun . . . if the rain stays away."

As we prepared to leave, I told Mervin that this had been one of the nicest days of my life.

He just laughed.

"Going around with you in the buggy was delightful. I'd like to thank you very, very much. It's been such a pleasure meeting you."

"You're welcome. Appreciate you stopping in."

"I'm very happy. You've made me very happy."

I rode away from Arthur thinking it had been the best day's filming I'd done in a long, long time. Mervin is a lovely man. A complete man. He knows exactly who and what he is, and what he does. He makes beautiful things, and he makes them extremely well.

It's lovely to know that there are still people in the world who are making wonderful things. I'd thought that when it came to furniture-making, maybe the best days were over. But they're not. There are still guys like Mervin making fantastic things that will be handed down in families from generation to generation. It fills my heart with joy.

And Mervin is not just a master craftsman — he laughs easily and can take a joke. At one point I'd asked him to put on his Amish hat. I'm sure plenty of guys would have refused, not wanting to conform to some outsider's stereotype. But Mervin immediately agreed and plonked his hat on his head with a big smile.

I still know very little about the Amish way of life, but it seems very humane to me. I don't know of any other religion that has that. The fact that most of them choose to come back and live that way after the *rumspringa* says a lot. And there's a wonderful social side to it. For instance, I really liked the way that Mervin and many of the other Amish guys grew beards but not moustaches, just because they all wanted to look the same as each other. Like, for instance, when I asked Mervin, "Why no moustache, why just the beard?"

"Nobody else has moustaches," he said, "and we like to all be the same." That's a lovely sharing concept which really appeals to me, and it's not phony.

Being Amish is not for me, because I'm too long in the tooth and set in my ways, but if I could have my time again, I'd be proud to be Amish. I think I would have made a pretty cool Amish guy, with my hat and bib and brace overalls, making beautiful furniture. I would have settled for that.

My day in Arthur left me with a similar feeling to when I'd visited Quinn Chapel. It's nice to see people happy in the knowledge of who and what they are.

The weather was still crap — there were even reports of more tornadoes in St Louis — but I was content now. It was what it was, and as much a part of the journey as the road and the people I'd meet along it. Everything doesn't always have to be in primary colours. But I must admit, I could have done without the permanently wet crotch.

# CHAPTER
# SIX

## Go through St Louis;
## Joplin, Missouri

I arrived in St Louis to find I was staying in the Moonrise Hotel's Buddy Ebsen Suite, which was strangely appropriate, as Buddy was the reason why I was on the journey. A movie star in 1930s Hollywood, Buddy later played the dad in *The Beverly Hillbillies*, one of the most successful sitcoms of all time. I used to watch it at home in Glasgow in the 1960s and delight in its bluegrass banjo theme song. It made me rush out and buy a banjo, thereby kick-starting the whole long story that took me out of the shipyards, into playing in folk bands and from there to comedy, movies and ultimately a television series about riding a trike along good old Route 66.

If it hadn't been for Buddy Ebsen and the other guys in *The Beverly Hillbillies* — and Earl Scruggs, who played that theme song — I would never have written this book. So it was kind of nice to be in Buddy's suite. It put a big smile on my face when I went into the room and saw pictures of him all over the place.

The journey to St Louis had been longer and harder than I'd anticipated when I left Mervin's place in Arthur. The rain battered down, drenching me until I was freezing wet and shivering. Then, mercifully, Mike, the director, offered to take over on the bike. He rode twice the distance that I did and was nearly drowned by the spray of passing trucks. It was terrifying. Driving along on a three-wheeler with your arse eighteen inches off the floor as forty-ton trucks come whooshing past is not fun. It's not a game for children at all. But Mike did it, and we all arrived in St Louis to tell the tale, so I was a happy boy. It felt like a good day's hard work.

We had arrived in St Louis by crossing the Mississippi on Poplar Street Bridge, the route since 1966. In the 1920s Route 66 took the McKinley Bridge, a three-arch structure, across the river, but in the 1930s, Route 66 was diverted on to the Chain of Rocks Bridge, allowing travellers to bypass St Louis. It soon became a well-known landmark on the road west, so I decided to take a look at it. But good intentions can result in tricky outcomes, and when I arrived at the bridge with the film crew my first thought was: What am I going to say about *this*? It was just a wee bridge over a wee river. How would I entertain the great British public with that? Some of them would have bigger bridges in their back gardens.

Then the crew took a run up the road to investigate and discovered we were at the wrong bridge. A big, proper bridge was just around the corner. Relief all round.

Straddling the border between Illinois and Missouri, the Chain of Rocks Bridge follows a line of large rocks, which at one time could be seen stretching across the Mississippi like a giant's stepping stones. But the rocks created rapids, making that particular stretch of the Mississippi extremely dangerous to navigate, so in the 1960s a low-water dam was built across the river to raise the water level. Now you can see all the rocks only during extreme low-water conditions. On the day I visited the river was very high, so we couldn't see any of them — not that it detracted from the fabulous bridge.

Standing in front of the bridge, you can see why it has become an icon of Route 66. It has eleven truss sections that look like they're made out of giant Meccano pieces, and it bends by twenty-four degrees about halfway across the river. The construction company had purchased land on each side of the river, but the parcels were not directly opposite each other. Initially they planned to build the whole bridge on a diagonal, but the US Army Corps of Engineers objected to that plan on safety grounds. So they built the first section, which crosses the major navigation channel, straight across the river from the Illinois shore. Then the remaining part was built at an angle to meet up with the Missouri shore.

Now decommissioned and out of use for motor vehicles, the Chain of Rocks Bridge takes only bicycles and pedestrians these days, but we had secured special permission to drive my trike across it. Built in 1929 as a toll bridge, at first it wasn't very successful, mainly because it didn't connect easily to downtown St Louis.

Soon after opening the bridge, the company that built and operated it went bankrupt, so it was handed over to Madison, Illinois, the city at its eastern end. In 1936 it was included in Route 66, and traffic numbers soared. By the time it was closed in 1970, the city had made seven million dollars profit from it. Not bad, eh?

For years a wee mystery surrounded the bridge. Every year a huge bouquet of flowers would appear on it. Nobody knew what these signified until 1959, when someone noticed an envelope attached to the flowers. Inside, they found a tragic wee note dedicated to Todd Costin, who had worked on the bridge and had fallen off in 1929, just before it was completed. Engineers had predicted that there would be ten fatalities during construction, but only Todd was killed. He was dragged to the bottom of the Mississippi by the weight of his tools.

In the mid-1970s Madison City wanted to demolish the bridge, but a recession put paid to that when the market price for scrap iron collapsed. At the time, the cost of demolishing the bridge would have been several million dollars more than its scrap value. So the bridge was left to rust, largely forgotten until a local bicycle group rediscovered and renovated it to create what might well be the longest pedestrian and bicycle bridge in the world.

The bridge is still in a pretty rusty state, but I like it. It has a rural, funky, southern feel to it. And it was lovely rumping along it on my bike, with the metal rattling and the noise of the engine echoing all around me. At the far end of the bridge, I arrived in *Missoura*.

Did you notice how I went all local there? We know it as Missouri, but all the locals say *Missoura*. And it's St *Lewis*, not St *Louie* — you have to pronounce it that way if you don't want them thinking you're a square.

From the bridge, I had a good run of a few miles down the road with a helicopter following me, which is always a gas. I feel like such a star whenever I do that, like Ray Liotta in *Goodfellas*. I was scared to look around for the helicopter, so I just leaned back on my trike and posed. I was being moody and bikey and overtaken by trucks, and it was a jolly day — the kind of day when I feel like I'm being successful at what I do. Usually I don't actually know what I'm doing. It's the same on stage — I do what feels good, but I don't know how it looks. I don't practise in front of mirrors and I don't look at rushes. Instead, I rely totally on how it feels . . . and as long as it feels good, that's fine by me.

It can be weird, because people tell me that my movement on stage is getting funnier and better, but I've still got no idea what I'm doing. All I know is that they're laughing while I'm poncing around. And I don't go and look at other people, in case I inadvertently steal their moves, so I've not even got anything to compare it to. I also avoid watching other comedians, because I know I'll just absorb their material and then think it's mine later.

A lot of comedians who are accused of stealing stuff don't intentionally nick it. They just become a sort of comedy black hole, sucking in material. They see and

120

hear so many funny things when they go to clubs, performing with other guys, and everything they hear goes straight into their mental filing system. Months or even years later, it'll pop out and they'll swear it's their own idea. But actually they heard it ages ago in some obscure club in Chicago or wherever. Then the guy who actually did come up with it gets mad — and quite rightly so. But we all pick things up by mental osmosis, and comedians are no different to anyone else.

To avoid this problem, I go completely by feel — a bit like reading Braille — whenever I'm on stage or making a television show. It's a weird and frightening process because I never know how I'm doing. And making the series about Route 66 was no different. I was sure the director and half of the crew thought I was fishing for compliments because I kept asking them how it was going, but I genuinely didn't know.

So it was a gamble, but quite an exciting one. I knew it could backfire. I could have spent these seven weeks doing a live tour, where thousands of people would have paid good money to see me and would have given me a warm welcome. But one night of television would reach *millions* of people. Which meant I had to be good, even though I hadn't scripted a single word beforehand. So, before arriving at each location, I immersed myself in my research notes and just hoped it would all come out in the correct order. As on stage, whenever I remembered something interesting, it would just plop out. There was no preconceived plan. But it seemed to work, and it always gave me a boost when I saw the crew laughing. That was my quality-assurance test.

St Louis is a rather beautiful city, with lovely people. In fact, every town I'd passed through up to this point had been beautiful, clean and tidy. America really is a country of small towns, most of which are handsome and well kept, although some are stultifying in their dullness. Driving through them, the streets are often empty, with nobody walking along, something I've never encountered in Britain. Whenever I stopped to eat or have a pee, I'd meet charming people in the shops and restaurants, but on the street the towns and villages were invariably completely dead. It lent a sadness to these places — like the locals had all given up their streets to the car.

Before riding back into the centre of St Louis, I visited an area that one of those tornadoes I'd seen on the news had torn apart only a few days earlier. Riding towards it, there was no sign of anything out of the ordinary, but then we turned a corner and arrived in the district of Bridgeton. *God Almighty*. With wind speeds up to 200mph., the tornado had cut a swath half a mile wide and twenty-one miles long through several counties in and around the city. Within that zone — total devastation. Three feet outside the zone — everything perfect and orderly. From a distance, it looked like a big machine had cut a valley clean through the town. Houses had been decimated, leaving only the foundations and enormous mounds of crap. Huge trees had been uprooted, just pulled right out of

122

the ground, showing the awesome power that the tornado must have possessed. Officially, it had been designated an EF4, the second-worst type of tornado. I couldn't imagine what the worst type must be like. We sometimes get wind speeds of about 100mph. in Scotland, but when you're talking double that, well, that's just fantasy land for me. It must be so terrifying to have your house turned to scrap around you.

The first thing I noticed in Bridgeton was the amazing silence. There was an awe and drama about the place. Churches were missing their roofs. At the Ferguson Christian Church, they'd been watching Mel Gibson's *The Passion of the Christ* when the storm showed up. As the congregation watched Jesus being whipped, the roof was ripped off, frightening the bejesus out of them. They must have thought they'd been sent for. Meanwhile, the house next door and a big Buddhist temple further down the road were left untouched. I didn't think for a moment that it meant anything significant, but it still amused me a lot.

The second thing that struck me was the cheeriness of everyone. The police, the fire service, the victims — they were all in a good mood. I visited a house in which only the concrete basement, where the family had hidden from the worst of the storm, was intact. A friend was helping them sort through the detritus, looking for valuables and anything of sentimental value. I introduced myself and asked a few questions about the house, or what was left of it.

The friend pointed at a pile of wood and rubbish. "This was the deck and the pool."

"*This* was the deck and the pool?" It was a complete mess.

"Yes," she said. "They were down in the basement."

I looked. "This was their basement?"

"Yes. Where the refrigerator is lying."

"They were down there? And they came up to see *this*?" I pointed at the devastation.

"Actually, I think he stuck his head out of that stairwell right there and just kind of looked around and said, 'Our house has gone.'"

As we were chatting, Bridget, the daughter of the house, turned up. She was in great shape, just pleased that she and her family had survived unhurt.

"Were you here when it happened?" I said.

"No. I had just recently moved out of the house, about three weeks ago."

"Good timing!"

"Well, I left about half my stuff here. I hadn't completely made it out of the house, so . . . good timing for me, but bad timing for my stuff!"

She was incredibly jolly. And yet, all around us, it was total chaos, as if vast garbage dumpsters had been turned upside down either on the houses or beside them.

"I can't imagine how it must have felt," I said. "What was the noise like?"

"My dad said it sounded like a freight train was going right through the house. He said that the instant his ears popped, he knew it was coming. It was the pressure of the tornado."

124

"Is that when he was still up here?" I pointed to where the deck had been.

"As he was going down the steps. He made it down just before it hit."

"Oh my God!"

"My dad was standing at the top of the steps, watching the news, looking out the window. My mum was already in the basement. My uncle called and said, 'There's a tornado that landed in Bridgeton. You guys need to be downstairs!' No sooner had he gotten down the steps than it hit."

Her father sounded just like me — the type who ignores advice until the last possible moment. As soon as he locked the basement door behind him, it started to shake. Looking up the stairs, he could see debris flying everywhere.

Then Bridget told me that her father had recently been diagnosed with colon cancer, and he was recovering from surgery. On the day that the tornado hit, he was on a portable chemotherapy pump.

"Oh my God!" I said again.

"It makes him feel pretty sick, but he's been out here digging and doing his thing."

Bridget explained that they had a couple of days to sift through the wreckage before everything would be bulldozed away and the clean-up operation would start.

"So you're just going through all this rubble, hoping to find precious things?" I said.

"Yes. We've found a couple of very, very valuable things, like my engagement ring. It was at my parents' house, sitting on my night stand, and she found it in the rubble." Bridget pointed towards her friend. "When she found it, we all cried. Everybody did."

"Oh my God!" Of course I hadn't known she was engaged. What an amazing story. "I'm going to touch it for luck."

"It had travelled about seventy-five feet, so it's definitely one of the luckiest pieces of jewellery I know. And my wedding dress survived, too. It has a little bit of mud on it, and a small hole in one of the seams on the side, but all that can be fixed before I get married."

I told Bridget that I thought her community's optimism was extraordinary.

"In the first few days my parents were very upset. But now my mum's talking about wanting a new big front porch. She's already designing the new place. This was just a one-storey home and they're discussing whether to make it taller instead of having it so long. They might go for a two-storey home." Apparently, she was also planning a whole new deck area and a veranda.

"You're all insured, aren't you?" I asked.

"We had full coverage on the house."

"I love thinking about your mother redesigning." It made me laugh.

"The first thing she said was 'I want that big front porch.' She likes the big country style."

"I know what she means. I'm married to a woman like that."

It's such an American thing to be so pragmatic and optimistic, always looking at what the future might bring, rather than reflecting on what has been lost in the past.

"This was our party place for all our friends," said Bridget. "There was a pool and a hot tub in the yard, and a trampoline. So they're planning somewhere to continue having parties."

Remarkably, no one was killed by the tornado. In fact, not so much as a pet had been reported missing. But I wondered what it must be like to live in a place where tornadoes are a permanent threat.

"Have you had tornadoes here before?" I said.

"Not anything like this," said Bridget.

"About 1967 was the last one that was equal to this," added Bridget's friend. "And it was two miles down the road. I was a kid and I remember that one; it was on my fifth birthday. I spent it in the basement waiting for a tornado to pass."

"You wouldn't need to blow your own candles out that time!" I said.

"No, I didn't even have a cake that day. And people died in that one. It was really severe."

She told me that they got lots of tornadoes, but their routes were unpredictable, so the outcome was always a bit of a lottery. In fact, St Louis is one of the most active urban areas for tornadoes in the United States. Every April, on average, 163 tornadoes will strike America, most of them in Tornado Alley. In this zone cold, dry air from Canada and the Rocky Mountains meets warm, moist air from the Gulf of Mexico and hot, dry air from the Sonoran Desert. When they collide, the air streams create rotations, like the swirl of

127

cream being stirred into coffee. In storms, when the air streams are fast and powerful, the rotations can turn into tornados. Tornado alley stretches from the Eastern Plain of Colorado and the Texas Panhandle, through Oklahoma, Kansas and Missouri, and up to Nebraska and South Dakota. But this year, by 25 April, they had already experienced 292 tornadoes. And everyone was nervous, because May usually has twice as many as April.

They were right to be worried. A fortnight after I'd visited Bridgeton, one of the worst tornadoes in American history, a mile-wide whirlwind, struck Joplin, Missouri, killing 138 people. At the same time, Arizonans were fighting some of the largest wildfires they had ever known; and the greatest flood in US history was spreading down the Missouri River. Meanwhile, Texas was suffering its eighth year of "exceptional" drought in the past twelve years. Something very weird was happening to the weather.

The next day, we took the trike to a garage to get the throttle fixed. It was now so stiff that it made my thumb and forefinger ache. It was all I could think about when I was riding along, and that was dangerous. My mind ought to have been on the road, not my throbbing thumb, when I was flying up an interstate or bumping along Route 66. With the bike out of action for the day, I took a taxi down to the Gateway Arch.

The world's tallest man-made monument (they really like superlatives in America), the arch is America's symbolic gateway to the West. Four million people visit it each year. They just want to touch it or gawp at it or be near it.

According to those who know about these things, it's an inverted catenary curve — the kind of organic shape that forms naturally when you hang a piece of string between two points. The designer, Eero Saarinen, also designed the Tulip chair and the TWA Terminal at JFK Airport in New York (that's the funky, space-age one). He came up with the design of the Gateway Arch by dangling a twenty-one-inch length of string between his fingers, held seven inches apart, and scaling it up from there. Saarinen said he chose the shape of a dangling necklace in tribute to the great explorers, hunters and trappers of the West. As most people know, those pioneers always wore a wee single-strand pearl necklace and a twinset underneath all their rawhide gear, just in case they were ever invited to a tea dance in the outback. (Okay, I made that up. But they did always make sure they had a wee black dress in their saddlebag in case of emergencies.)

A lot of people rave about Saarinen's Tulip chair, but the Gateway Arch is surely his finest piece. I'd seen it maybe half a dozen times before, but always from a distance, between buildings. It's a bit like Paris and the Eiffel Tower — you keep seeing it from unexpected angles. But when you get to see it properly, it's a thing of amazing beauty. My only slight disappointment was that I'd always thought that it straddles the Missouri River, but in fact it stands alone, on the west bank of the Missouri. But that doesn't detract from how magnificent it looks.

The 630-foot arch was gleaming in the sun when I arrived. There were nine hundred tons of stainless steel standing in front of me, the most used in any single project in history. It fascinated me that they did the surveying during construction overnight, when it was cooler, so that expansion of the metal would be minimised. They built the arch as two separate legs, and then joined them together at the top. And do you know what the margin of error was for the base of each leg at ground level? One sixty-fourth of an inch. *One sixty-fourth of a bloody inch*. Any more than that, and the two legs would not have met at the top. It made me imagine the builders finishing the two legs to find that they'd built them perfectly, but a foot apart. Can you picture it? "Excuse me, mate, you wouldn't happen to have a twelve-inch piece of stainless steel on you? We're a bit short up here."

I descended into the basement to take a lift all the way to the top. When I say lift, I mean a strange little pillbox that goes sideways as well as up and down, which of course it has to do as the top of the Gateway Arch is not directly above the base. Designing it presented a unique challenge for some of civil engineering's finest minds, who knew that no conventional lift would be able to carry passengers all the way to the planned observation deck at the pinnacle of the arch. They suggested that two or more lifts would be needed, with passengers hopping from one to the next on their journey to the top. Nobody wanted that — it had to be a single-lift design. But after a lot of scratching of heads, the Harvard- and Yale-educated engineers drew a blank. No one could work out how to put a single lift into a structure that didn't rise in a pin-straight line.

Then a young man came forward. A lift repairman by trade, his only qualification was a high school diploma, but he reckoned he had designed a lift that could ascend the whole parabolic structure. When he'd finished explaining his idea to a room of architects and engineers, he asked if there were any questions.

"Yes," said one of the audience. "Who are you?"

"I'm thirty-four," he said. And left it at that.

A few years later, the mysterious lift repairman's design was adopted and installed in each leg of the arch.

It's a very curious lift. Officially, it's called a cantilever railway. I climbed into a tiny cabin, almost bending double to get through the door. Four adults can just about fit into one cabin, which at first goes up diagonally in one direction. Then there is a lot of clanking and grinding of gears and the little wagon rises in the opposite diagonal direction. It was kind of weird, a bit like being on an underground train, except moving in a different direction. I couldn't see much, aside for some rivets and girders, but I quite enjoyed that. As I've said before, I like engineering. I like things that are built to be beautiful and to show off the skill of the human race.

The trip took about four minutes, near the end of which the little pod appeared to go straight up for a short time before resuming its strange zigzag movement and arriving at the top.

I'd been in a few other monuments in my time, like the Atomium in Brussels and the Walter Scott Memorial in Edinburgh. And I'd always wanted to go inside the Statue of Liberty, but never managed it, although I can tell you a story that will make you jealous. Once, on Elton John's birthday, he took me on a trip around Manhattan in a helicopter and we flew around the statue. Then we hovered right in front of her face and had a good look. Are you jealous yet?

Anyway, back to the arch. At the top, there's a small observation capsule with a great view. I've always loved being up high, so it was fantastic to gaze down at the State Capitol Building and the riverboats far below on the Mississippi. I was a bit disappointed that no one asked me how to spell Mississippi, because it was one of those words that they tested us on again and again at school. Back in those days, I'd never have dreamed that one day I would be at the top of a huge monument looking down on it. Isn't life the strangest thing?

Just as I'd done from the top of the Sears Tower in Chicago, I gazed west, contemplating where Route 66 would take me next. Whereas Chicago had been the central distribution point for goods coming from and going to the West, St Louis was often the starting point for people moving westwards. This was made possible when President Thomas Jefferson bought fifteen US states and two Canadian provinces from the French in 1803. Doubling the size of the United States, the Louisiana Purchase included all of present-day Arkansas, Missouri, Iowa, Oklahoma, Kansas and Nebraska, as well as parts of Minnesota that were west of the Mississippi River, most of North Dakota, nearly all of South Dakota, northeastern New Mexico, northern Texas, the portions of Montana, Wyoming and Colorado that lie east of the Continental Divide, and Louisiana west of the Mississippi, including the city of New Orleans. In addition, it contained small portions of land that would eventually become part of the Canadian provinces of Alberta and Saskatchewan.

Jefferson commissioned two Virginia-born veterans of the Indian wars in the Ohio valley, Meriwether Lewis and William Clark, to survey all the rivers and land west of St Louis. Accompanied by a fifteen-year-old Shoshone Indian girl called Sacagawea, they crossed the Rocky Mountains and reached the Pacific Ocean in present-day Oregon, claiming all the territory that lay beyond the nation's new boundaries for the United States. This led to the biggest migration in history, as people from all over the world first arrived on America's East Coast, then moved west.

While up in the observation deck, I met a nice family from Newfoundland. I've never met a Newfie I didn't like — they are fabulous people from a breathtakingly beautiful part of the world — and these Newfies didn't disappoint. They even knew who I was, which made a pleasant change from being mistaken for John Cleese.

From the Gateway Arch, I headed to St Louis station, to see its own famous arch. I took a taxi again, but a huge parade was blocking off several streets, so I was forced to continue on foot. On the way, I passed a park known as the Citygarden, which was chock-a-block with some fabulous sculptures. I was fascinated and went to have a closer look. Some girls were trying to squeeze inside one of the sculptures, a giant man's head lying sideways on the ground. It would have been great to film them as they messed around, but by the time we'd set up the camera, they'd moved on. Not to worry — before long, some other children were climbing all over it.

This art was so alive. Most towns have statues of dowdy characters with big moustaches, dressed in frock coats and covered in pigeon shit. They're the great and the good of the town, but nobody gives a toss about them. People swan straight past, even if they're Robbie Burns or Robert Tannahill, rather than some general or lord mayor. Abstract and modern sculptures are so much more accessible. People are drawn to them and like to touch them. I love the fact that abstract art can do that for people, entitle them to go up and touch it. To me, it gives the art a life of its own. If I was the artist, I would be absolutely over the moon if I saw those kids reacting to my work in that way.

As I walked through the park, I saw another bunch of kids treating a big red abstract sculpture like a slide, whizzing down it on their bellies. Another statue had water squirting out of the ground and the kids were running through it, getting soaked. It made me so happy. It was such a joy to see these inert statues brought vividly to life.

I spotted a sign as I was leaving. It warned that playing in or near the water and sculptures was inherently dangerous, but it didn't say, "Keep Off!" It just asked visitors to exercise some caution and common sense when they let children loose on them: "Treat it and one another with respect, thereby maintaining an atmosphere which provides enjoyment for all." It was that easy to get people to behave responsibly. Much better than the usual threats of "Clear off or we'll call the police, you scoundrel." What a wonderful place. A public garden with spectacular landscaping and internationally renowned sculpture in a completely open, accessible setting — what more could anyone want?

After that delightful, unplanned detour to the Citygarden, I must admit I was dreading my planned trip to the railway station. I was on my way to see its "whispering archway", but I was wondering what on earth I could say about a station, no matter how beautiful. Even Grand Central Station in New York is difficult. You say it's stunning. Then what?

However, I was very moved by some of the details of this station, such as that two million soldiers passed through it every month in 1943. I wondered how many of them returned home after being shipped over to Europe and Asia. All those goodbyes and cheerios and tidings of "good luck" and "look after yourself". And the arch turned out to be quite interesting, too. Most whispering galleries work on the horizontal inside a dome. For instance, at St Paul's Cathedral in London, you whisper against the wall and the sound goes round horizontally. But this one goes up the wall, across the ceiling and down the opposite wall in a channel. Apparently no one realised it carried whispers until a workman hit himself with a hammer and swore. One of the other workmen on the other side of the arch heard the expletive distinctly. Now some guys say to their girlfriends, "Stand there. There's something I want to tell you. I want you to hear this." Then they shoot over to the other side of the arch and whisper: "Will you marry me?" Lovely.

I tried it out and it works perfectly. But I had nothing more to say about it, so we packed up the camera and went for lunch.

Entering a Japanese restaurant, I looked up at the television to see *The Last Samurai*. It stars Tom Cruise, Timothy Spall . . . and me. We asked the manager to rewind to the beginning and then we all watched it, something I've never done before. Usually I don't even go to the premiere of a film in which I've appeared. If can get away with it, I'll sneak away. But enough time had passed since I'd filmed this one, so it was fun to watch. All in all a rather jolly time was had in St Louis.

The next day, we collected the repaired bike and I was itching to get back on the road. But first I wanted to stop off at a soul food restaurant run by a remarkable woman.

Robbie Montgomery used to be one of the backing singers for Ike and Tina Turner — an Ikette — shaking her tail feathers and singing fabulous soul songs such as "River Deep, Mountain High". That meant she'd got to know everybody. She'd sung with Mick Jagger and lots of other sixties and seventies stars like Dr John, Stevie Wonder, Barbra Streisand, Elton John, Pink Floyd, Rod Stewart and Joe Cocker. When she'd been starting out, restaurants on the road would often refuse to serve black performers, so Robbie and others in the band would cook dinner in an electric skillet in their motel rooms. Eventually forced to quit singing because of a lung disorder, Robbie turned to her second love, cooking soul food. She opened a restaurant, and after many years and a lot of hard work, she now owns two fantastic restaurants called Sweetie Pie's, one of which is in South St Louis.

It was a real privilege to meet a woman I'd previously admired in a soul revue. Now seventy years old, she is still very beautiful, with a shock of white hair tied back under a chef's hat.

"I never thought I'd stand this close to you," I said. "The only time I ever saw you before, you were . . ."

"Shaking my tail feathers?"

We both laughed.

"That was my favourite," I said. "Shaking the tail feathers!"

"Really? Well, the tail feathers broke. I can't shake it any more. I've gotten too old for that now."

It was very easy to laugh with Robbie.

"Well, welcome. Are you going to come on in?" she said.

"I hear I have to stand in line like everybody else. That's democratic. I don't need special treatment. I don't seek it, I don't need it."

"Oh, good."

Robbie's dishes, learned at her mother's hip, are best described as from-scratch cooking. The menu features recipes like baked chicken, ox tails, candied yams, macaroni cheese and peach cobbler made in the traditional way.

"White people call it home cooking," she said. "Black people call it soul. We call it comfort food. Or we call it Mississippi-style cooking, because these are all my mom's recipes and she was born in Mississippi, like me, and she taught me to cook."

I was really looking forward to my first taste of soul food, but I was nervous about sitting there — the only white guy in the restaurant. It was nothing to do with race. I just didn't like being the only guy who didn't understand what was on the menu. But Robbie guided me, and it was just darling.

"It's Sunday," she said, "so most people have collard greens and candied yams; and if you like meatloaf, that's your choice."

"I like meatloaf," I said. "And I haven't had it in such a long time." I'd never had candied yams or collard greens. I'd only read about them in William Faulkner books. They were fantastically good, but the experience was made so much better by being able to sit and talk to the woman who had sung such sensational songs. We talked a lot about music, food and life in general, and Robbie was the best company. It was a great start to the day.

So far on Route 66, my meetings with black people — from Preston Jackson in Bronzeville and the Quinn Chapel congregation to Robbie here in St Louis — had been a joy and a constant surprise to me. If I was black in America, I think I'd be angry at the way black people have been treated over the years. And I'm not just talking about slavery. From the Civil War through to Vietnam and Iraq, black people have fought for America, then returned home to bloody shoddy treatment. Yet they seem unfazed by it. Their experiences haven't broken their niceness. On this trip I was constantly amazed and pleased by their attitude. I know that sounds hellish — like I was a fucking explorer — but I'd expected them to be angry, and they just weren't. There was a quality to black people in America that I found unbelievably impressive, especially when I was talking to Robbie. I was glad to meet her, and I was even gladder that I ate her food. It was unbelievable.

All that said, though, my macaroni cheese would smash Robbie's out of the park. But my macaroni cheese would smash *anybody*'s out of the park. I'll take on anyone. And I do a mean fishy pie, too.

# CHAPTER
# SEVEN

## You Haven't Seen the Country 'til You've Seen the Country by Car

Leaving St Louis, I stopped off at Jefferson Barracks, the oldest operational military base west of the Mississippi River. Established in 1826 on land obtained as part of the Louisiana Purchase, these barracks assisted and supported the westward expansion of white settlers by keeping hostile Indian groups at bay.

Exactly 150 years before I visited, Missouri was torn apart by the Civil War, an appalling event that left 625,000 Americans dead, more than perished in the two world wars combined. Missouri endured more than a thousand battles and engagements between 1861 and 1865. On the day that I passed through, a Civil War re-enactment group was recreating the Camp Jackson Affair, which set Missouri on the violent, turbulent path to war between the opposing Confederate and Union armies. On 10 May 1861, Union forces clashed with civilians on the streets of St Louis — at least twenty-eight people were killed and another hundred injured. The incident polarised the border state of Missouri, leading some citizens to advocate secession with the Confederacy and others to support the Union, thereby setting the stage for sustained violence between the opposing factions.

Eleven southern Confederate states fought twenty-five northern Union states, but even today nobody can be certain *why* they went to war. This very complex issue sells millions of books in America every year, and thousands of academics dedicate their lives to studying it. To Abraham Lincoln, the President at the time, the conflict was entirely about slavery; but a recent poll in America found that two-thirds of people think it was actually about issues to do with how much power the federal government had over individual states and that it had nothing to do with slavery at all.

Whatever the true cause, I was enjoying the smell of cordite at the re-enactment. Held over two days in a green, rolling Missouri field, it involved several hundred participants in grey and blue coats watched by several thousand spectators. Like some other scheduled stops on the trip, I must admit that I hadn't been looking forward to this one. I didn't expect to have a good time with people who re-enacted battles during their weekends. But I was proved wrong yet again. The re-enactment was beautifully executed, although it was hampered by one fatal flaw: none of the re-enactors wanted to die, because that meant lying on the battlefield for hours on end until the entire shooting match was over. I spotted only one dead guy. He was lying face up and was so still that I wondered if he might actually be asleep. There were far more wounded guys, limping off the field. The bastard that I am, I watched them closely to make sure they kept playing their part right to the end, but I didn't spot any who gave up hobbling when they thought no one was looking.

It was all very impressive, but I still didn't have a clue what to say to the camera crew about it. I made a few comments, and an American guy standing next to me started to laugh, so I felt reassured that I'd not overstepped the mark by making fun of the Civil War. He seemed like a good guy, so I asked him to explain exactly what was going on.

"This battle kept St Louis in the Union," he said. "So the Unionists are supposed to win, I guess."

"Well, they have to in the end, don't they?"

"The bit about America losing 625,000 Americans, that's the tragedy. I heard you talking about it."

"That's right. And we keep doing it. We keep sending people to war. Young, healthy, bright people."

"In England you send them on honeymoons, right?"

This guy had a sense of humour. A couple of days earlier, Prince William had married Kate Middleton and now everyone was talking about where they might be going on honeymoon. You couldn't escape it — even in the middle of America. "I don't know why you're so interested in it all," I said. "Didn't you have a war to get rid of them?"

He laughed, then nodded at the re-enactment. "This is the first time I've ever done this."

"Me too." One of the re-enactors suddenly put his hands in the air. "Oh look, he's surrendering and he's a bluecoat!"

The bluecoats were Unionists, whereas the Confederates traditionally wore grey. Not the easiest of colours to tell apart at the best of times, but what made it even worse was that the Confederate Army struggled to find grey material, so some of their soldiers wore dark blue. Unsurprisingly, this led to considerable confusion. For instance, during the Battle of Shiloh, some of the Confederate forces fired at their own soldiers. As if that wasn't crazy enough, the Union then ran out dark blue cloth, some of their old uniforms faded to grey as the dye washed out, and many Unionist troops were given grey jackets to wear over their blue shirts. No wonder so many soldiers died.

After a few hours, the re-enactment ended with no sign of who had won. Several of the participants recognised me and wandered over for a chat. They told me they'd all made their uniforms themselves and had been very accurate about the details, to the point where one of them had a period pipe that he kept smoking, staying in character throughout. They were great fun. I couldn't have asked for better company.

From the re-enactment, I drove directly to Jefferson Barracks National Cemetery, a military graveyard on the banks of the Mississippi. More than 220 generals from the Civil War spent time at Jefferson Barracks and many of them were laid to rest in the cemetery, which covers more than 330 acres. Established after the Civil

War, it contained nearly 160,000 graves by 2005. Since then, several thousand more have been added.

There wasn't much I could say about this place. The sight of all the graves said it all, really. Every grave was identical — each one a uniform size in an indistinguishable serried rank. Tombstones in civilian graveyards are often engraved with poems and little one-liners, but there's none of that in military graveyards. Just the bare details: name, regiment, date of birth and date of death. Occasionally, the tombstone would have a few additional words, such as "Loving Father" or "Dear Brother", but more often it was just the basic facts in row upon row of tombstones, rolling over hill and dale.

To me, it seemed a wee bit obscene to make something so horrible look so neat and tidy. I know that's a very cruel thing to say, because I'm sure the people who designed the cemetery did it with the very best intentions, but it reminded me of the National Memorial Arboretum in Staffordshire — a monument to all the British forces killed on duty or as a result of terrorism since the end of the Second World War. When it was opened, a commentator on television explained that some of the walls listing the dead had been left blank. Apparently, there was space for about ten thousand more names to be added. When I heard that, I thought: Does this bastard know something I don't?

What horrifies me most about war memorials is that no antiwar sentiments are ever displayed. It's as if war is fun or noble, when actually it's all about shit and snot and blood and guts and soldiers' stomachs hanging out and people with their faces blown off. But they never showed that side of it. Perhaps, if they did, there'd be less of it. I remember seeing a picture of a soldier in Vietnam who was sitting, waiting to die, with his jaw missing. His head now started at his top row of teeth; everything beneath that was gone. They didn't put that on the recruitment posters, did they? But that's what war is to me. And I don't care who we're fighting, I don't hate them enough to do something like that to them.

Maybe all of this hit me particularly hard at the Jefferson Barracks National Cemetery because I visited it shortly after Osama bin Laden was nailed and America was rejoicing in a huge wave of triumphalism. I found all of that rather horrifying — that delight in death and that attitude of "Why don't we just kill the bastard?" We have to move beyond that kind of thinking or we're doomed as a species.

Fortunately, my mood, which had got more than a bit dark at the cemetery, immediately lightened as I rode west from St Louis and Route 66 entered some of the most pleasant, verdant country along its entire length. Scenic wooded drives through hills and valleys, far from the superslab of Interstate 44, gave a tantalising impression of what riding the road must have been like in its heyday. But the weather was still remarkably turgid and *dreich* (a Scottish word for dreary) as I pulled up at my next stop, a wolf sanctuary in Eureka, Missouri.

I've always had great respect for wolves. Many years ago, when I was a boy, I read that the wolf's fierce reputation was the creation of writers who had never even seen one. Sitting in London, Birmingham or Manchester, they wrote about the call of the wild with little or no experience of it. If they'd seen these magnificent creatures, they would have realised immediately that they're terrified of humans. Absolutely terrified. There's no chance at all of that cartoon image of them sneaking up behind you and tearing out your throat with their vicious teeth. The wolves I saw at the sanctuary couldn't get far enough away from us.

Tucked away in a wooded area, the Endangered Wolf Center is home to forty animals from five different species, including the two most endangered species of wolf — the Mexican grey and the red, which used to be native to Missouri. Only around a hundred red wolves exist in the wild and they're all in North Carolina. As for the Mexican grey, there are only about fifty left anywhere outside captivity.

A lovely young lady called Regina showed me around, explaining that their mission was to breed wolves in captivity and then release them into the wild. "We're unique in that aspect," she said. "We don't pat the animals, we don't talk to 'em, we don't play with 'em. We want them to keep that fear of humans, so when they go into the wild, they stay away from people."

They had already released some Mexican grey wolves in the New Mexico — Arizona border area — the only spot where they can still be found in the wild.

Some red wolves had been released in the Alligator River National Wildlife Refuge in North Carolina.

"Sarah Palin likes to shoot wolves from helicopters," I said.

"Yeah. In Alaska and a few other areas, that's their practice."

"It's ridiculous, isn't it?"

"It's different management styles. These guys, you definitely don't do that with them" — she pointed at one of the red wolves — "because there are so few left. They're the most endangered mammal in North America, so they're very protected." We both watched the wolf, which was bright red with big ears and exceptionally long legs that made it walk funny, like it was wearing high heels.

In addition to the wolves, the sanctuary houses some brilliantly coloured African wild dogs — all yellow, white, grey and brown. Fucking great, they are. Superb hunters and killers with massive strength in their jaws, second only to the hyena, they're also hugely social animals. When they wake up in the morning, they all greet each other like they've never seen each other before. Then, in the afternoon, they have a wee kip, wake up, and do it all over again. They really seem to love each other.

The final two species in the sanctuary are maned wolves from South America, which have manes of black hair, like horses, and swift foxes from North America. All of them are kept for education, research and breeding purposes.

"Swift foxes?" I said. I'd not heard of them before.

"They are," she said. "Their name kind of gives away what they do."

I laughed.

"They are the fastest animal we have here. About forty miles per hour."

"Really?"

"They're pretty fast. So whenever we have to give them their vaccines and catch 'em, it's a challenge."

I told her that I'd always liked wolves.

"Yes. They're a creature that really touches your heart. One of my favourite things about working here is that I get to work with species that are going to be released into the wild."

"They've been lied about for so long, you know. Fiction writers have written such nonsense about them for years."

"That's true. Kids grow up listening to *Little Red Riding Hood* and *The Three Little Pigs* and stories about werewolves and they become scared of wolves. But the old cliché — that they're more scared of you than you are of them — is true."

Then she asked if I'd like to help feed a deer to one of the wolf packs. I could see several wolves lurking among the trees in the distance, looking very nervous. The dead deer had been donated by the Missouri Department of Transportation after it was hit by a car. Instead of going to waste, it would give the wolves a welcome taste of their natural prey.

The warden handed me a long stick. "It's your protection stick," she said. "The wolves won't come up to you, but if you feel threatened, you can wave it. But

148

like I said, they're gonna be at the back of the enclosure."

A protection stick. I liked that. "I'm sure wolves are terrified of white sticks," I said.

"You'd be surprised."

There were six animals in the pack — an alpha male, a female and their cubs. As well as an occasional deer, the wolves were fed a dry mix made specifically for them and they could hunt raccoons, possums and even any turkeys that wandered into their enclosure.

"Do those animals just stray in not knowing?" I asked.

"Yep, they don't know there are wolves in there, so it's quite a shock. And these guys get to practise their hunting skills."

The deer was frozen stiff. "Will they be able to eat this?" I said.

"Oh, yes. Think of the wolves in Yellowstone. They come across deer that have been killed by the winter cold. They're still able to get in there and break apart the carcass and get the healthy, nutritious stuff."

After dropping the deer in the enclosure, I watched from a distance as the wolves approached it very warily. The alpha male took the first bites, eating the best meat; then the female tucked in. Finally, they let the cubs come in and eat, too.

"In the wild," said the warden, "the entire pack helps take down a deer or an elk, and they all have their roles. One of the cubs distracts the deer or the elk and then the alphas come in and take down the deer from the rear, by the neck. Then the rest of the pack helps bring

**149**

'em down. You'll actually see 'em kind of take roles when they're chasing. One will chase for a little bit and then take a break, then the next one'll chase until they get 'em down. And they all help. So when they say it's a family pack, they really mean that every animal works to get the dinner."

When wolves hunt, they're successful only about 10 per cent of the time. A well-placed kick from an elk can break a wolf's leg or jaw. And there are no vets in the wild. It would be like us going to the supermarket and being chased out with a baseball bat nine times before we were able to buy any food. And the one time that we managed to buy anything, the food would be kicking and fighting us the whole time.

I looked up to where one of the wolves was watching me, the warden and the camera crew. "Look at that one — on top of the shed."

"He's checking you out. We think we're being quiet, but these guys have amazing hearing. They can hear from several miles away. One of the ways they communicate is by howling, which they can hear up to ten miles away, depending on the wind speed. So even though we're quiet, they can hear us. They can smell us, too. When you're out there hiking, they can hear you coming before you even know and they'll take off running."

"They're really wishing we weren't here, aren't they?"

"They are. They're ready to go for dinner and we're making 'em nervous."

"You can see them coming round and saying, 'Oh God, they're still there.'"

"They're very shy. And that makes them tough to study out in the wild. You want to observe their behaviour and learn about them, but they know you're there before you even know you're there, so they run away. But being shy helps them survive."

We watched the female wolf circle the deer cautiously. Tall and weighing about forty-five pounds, she was very light on her feet. All legs, like a supermodel, she backed off the deer when she sensed that the alpha male was returning for another wee snack. Then he peed on the deer, marking it as his own.

Wolves have the most awful reputation for crowding and circling hikers, pulling them down, tearing out their throats and killing them in a fevered bloodbath. Well, it's all a load of bollocks. There's no recorded instance of wolves attacking humans in history. They're the most delightful, tender creatures, and the people working with them at the sanctuary are lovely. They've dedicated their lives to looking after these beautiful animals and I'm full of admiration for them.

I also think we could learn a little about social interaction from those African wild dogs. The French have learned it already: they all shake hands in the morning, as if they are being introduced for the first time. I really like that, and was inspired to try it myself. So, at breakfast the next morning, I shook hands with one of the crew. Maybe he was surprised, but I can be quite human when I try.

★　★　★

My journey continued through green farmland, across little bridges over creeks and past red-brick and wood farmsteads, for about thirty-five miles to Stanton, site of one of the best-known and most hyped attractions on Route 66: the Meramec Caverns. So far, I'd travelled nearly four hundred miles along Route 66, and most of that distance had been regularly punctuated by large billboards advertising these limestone caverns, often accompanied by a painting of the outlaw Jesse James. The billboards draw over 150,000 visitors each year to the caves, so they're clearly doing something right.

The Meramec Caverns are a weird combination of phenomenally beautiful and utterly awful. They're a wee bit showbiz, with neon signs, souvenir shops and a moonshiner's cabin outside, all of which I thought was pretty unnecessary. They were first opened up in 1722, when a French miner met an Indian who told him the caverns contained seams of gold. The miner found no gold, but he discovered lots of saltpetre, an essential component of gunpowder. During the Civil War, the Union Army used the caves as a saltpetre plant, but it was discovered and destroyed by Confederate guerrillas, among them Jesse James. Years later, Jesse and his brother and partner in crime, Frank, reportedly used the caves as their hideout. One legend claims that a sheriff staked out the caves, waiting for Jesse and his gang to emerge, but they found another exit and sneaked out that way.

By the early twentieth century, hundreds of tons of saltpetre had been extracted, creating vast underground

152

chambers. In the 1920s the locals started to hold dances down there. One of the largest caves was named "the ballroom" and it still has a tiled floor and a stage. Bands and their audiences would drive their cars right into the caves and dance the night away. Later, the likes of Dolly Parton played concerts there. The sheer size of the place is quite breathtaking. It's so high that I didn't even feel like I was underground. There's no sense of claustrophobia at all, and it has a kind of magnificence.

In the 1930s a guy with big ideas called Lester B. Dill set about tarnishing that magnificence. He bought the caves, explored the full extent of the underground system, and claimed to have found artefacts belonging to the James boys. It's entirely possible that Dill added more than a wee bit to local legends about the caves being the James Gang's hideout, and he certainly knew a good marketing opportunity when he stumbled across one. But in my opinion he didn't need to push the James angle, because the caves would be much more remarkable without all the hype. For instance, in one of the caves there's something that looks like an art student's attempt to sculpt a vast Scottish clootie dumpling. In fact, it's the world's largest stalagmite, and it's very impressive and beautiful.

But Dill just couldn't stop himself when it came to promoting his investment. While sightseers were in the caves, looking at the stalagmites, stalactites and supposed Jesse James relics — as well as genuine Pre-Columbian Native American artefacts that were found later — Dill hired wee boys to tie adverts on to the visitors' car bumpers. In one fell swoop, he had invented the bumper sticker, so you know who to blame the next time you're stuck behind a particularly offensive one on the motorway.

I loved the stalagmites and stalactites, and I particularly liked the huge pendulum in the main cave. It was supposed to rotate in concert with the spinning of the earth, but the ball at its end was the wrong weight — it should have been a thousand pounds heavier — so it didn't work. To compensate, someone would just give it a shove every now and then to get it going. Fantastic — the idea of a wee guy whose job it is to slink along when nobody's looking and give it a big push.

However, the climax of any visit to the caves is a light show that has to be seen to be believed. To the accompaniment of a musical soundtrack that culminates in "The Star Spangled Banner", a fella flicks switches on a board to light up various stalagmite and stalactite sections in garish colours, ending with the American flag superimposed on one section of rock. I couldn't understand why people thought something as staggeringly beautiful as a cave needed a light show to improve it.

Sometimes there's a tackiness about Route 66 that out-tacks any tackiness I've ever seen anywhere else. And the Meramec Caverns are the pinnacle of that tack.

Relieved to be moving on, I rode through the village of Bourbon, where the huge water tower, built in 1853 and labelled with the small village's name, has delighted countless tourists and passers-by over the years. (Bourbon called itself a city, but with just over 1,300 residents and occupying little more than one square mile, and no cathedral or university, it's a village in my book.) A few miles further, I arrived in Cuba, Missouri, where I spent the night.

I woke the next morning feeling depressed and fed up. I didn't think I could take another shitty, grey, rainy day, freezing my bollocks off on the bike. Route 66 wasn't meant to be like this.

Then I opened the blinds and let out a big "Oh yes!" The sun belted into the room. It was a glorious, warm, bright day. My mood immediately changed. I was even upbeat about the itinerary for the morning: a visit to the world's biggest rocking chair. Another bit of tack, I thought. But it might be a laugh.

The rocking chair is in the town of Fanning, right alongside Route 66. And would you believe it, it's the most beautifully made, smashing piece of (giant) furniture. It was the brainchild of a funny, big man called Danny Sanazaro, and it really is vast: forty-two feet tall with thirty-one-foot rockers, each of which weighs a ton. Standing beside it would make anyone feel like they'd woken up in one of those 1950s B-movies like *The Incredible Shrinking Man*. In the grand Route 66 tradition, Danny commissioned it to persuade drivers and riders to stop at his store. It was designed by a local acquaintance with no formal engineering training, and built by the owner of a local welding company. The designer's plans were off by only a fraction of an inch, Danny told me. The chair was formally unveiled on April Fool's Day, 2008 — a particularly nice touch.

Unfortunately for Danny, apparently there's a sixty-foot chair somewhere in Italy. But when I visited, the back of his rocker still boasted "World's Largest", not "America's Largest", so I guess that news of the Italian titan hasn't reached Fanning yet.

Danny let me climb up on a ladder to sit on the seat so that the camera crew could film me saying that I was going to stay up there until someone made the biggest coffee table in the world and brought me a cup of tea. It had been a long time since a piece of furniture had made me so happy. I spotted one great failing, though: it didn't actually rock.

After climbing down, I had a pootle around Danny's store, which also included a taxidermy place and an archery range. He invited me to have a wee arch and showed me how to fire an arrow. I scored rather well, although that worried me a bit. You start off shooting at targets, like the ones they use in the army with a soldier running towards you with his gun blazing. Then, after about a hundred shots, you think: I wonder how it would be with a real guy who shoots back? I've never done it, but it crossed my mind.

When I'd finished firing arrows, Danny and his wife, Carolyn, invited the whole crew back to their house and gave us the best barbecue I've ever had. Standing on their raised deck in golden evening sunlight, looking out over the treetops in the valley below, they cooked the most tasty, juicy fish from the river, which they called suckers. We'd been joined by their son Laine, who did all the cooking, and Carolyn's twin sister, Cheri. The twins were identical blondes and really stunning.

"Did you have fun growing up identical?" I said.

They both nodded.

"I used to be in a band with a guy who had an identical twin," I said. "It was almost spooky."

"We had a lot of fun with it," said Carolyn.

"Oh, I bet you did. Did you have fun with guys?"

"Yeah," she said. "We still mess with Danny. He'll grab her ass" — Carolyn gestured at Cheri — "and she'll go along with it."

She said that they often catch suckers, which look similar to trout, by spearing them in the river at night. The boat is fitted with a big light on the front to attract the fish. "It's fun," she continued. "It's just a big party. You light a big fire down there and you kill 'em and then you clean and you eat 'em right there on the river."

"That sounds amazing," I said. "God, what a lovely place."

Below us, the woods seemed to be teeming with wildlife.

"I was just watching a deer over here." Cheri pointed into the woods. "It's gone now, but we see turkeys and deer and coyotes, all kinds of stuff out here."

"Most people don't know the turkey's an American animal," I said. "They nearly chose it to be the national bird. Somebody insisted on the bald eagle and they went for it, but it could have been a turkey. Of course, you never think of a turkey as being a beautiful thing because it's got that kind of Christmassy, overfed look about it, but the wild one is a thing of beauty, isn't it?"

"Oh, it is," said Carolyn. "It's nothing like the white, tame turkey. No, the wild ones, they're pretty."

"And all the Christmas ones, they never have sex. They can't; they're the wrong shape. Fancy living without sex and then you die at Christmas. What a party."

Carolyn and Cheri offered to take me out on a hunting trip the next morning. They pointed at a ridge where they said there were many wild turkeys. They'd been hunting since they were little girls, when their father had made them a turkey call — a piece of wood that they would strike to attract the birds.

"I was with a woman, away up in the Arctic," I said, "and she was hunting for moose with a bow. The guy with her had a sort of megaphone and he would go *whoaaa*. And you could hear the moose answering, *whoaaa*. It was the most thrilling thing. It got nearer and the *whoaaa* got louder. But I won't tell you how the story ends. It was a disaster. You would hate it."

"Did she get it?" asked Cheri.

"No, she didn't. One of the crew did a terrible thing."

"Oh?"

"The director farted . . ."

"What did you say when he did that?"

"Well . . . there was no more *whoaaa*, you know."

Danny, the twins, his son and all the crew cracked up with laughter.

**158**

"But the hunter made a living from manipulating people's bodies. She was a naturopath or something. And she cured the director. He had been sick for days, making these terrible noises and running to the bathroom every five minutes with that funny run. You know the one, with the knees together."

"Squeezing it in, yeah." Carolyn was giggling again.

"She did all sorts of things with him. She knew things about the body I'd never seen in my life, you know? Asian opposition muscle stuff. And she messed around with him and made him better. She told him what not to eat, what definitely to eat, and what to eat less of . . ."

"Lay off the beans, huh?"

"Yeah."

"God, I hope that don't happen in the morning," said Cheri.

"I'm in show business, so I've never farted. When you're in show business, you have a de-farting operation. Some people get a new nose at the same time. You can have the wrinkles taken away and be de-farted all on the same day."

There was little danger that the barbecue would cause any problems. As well as the sensational fish, Laine cooked the best mushrooms I've ever tasted in my damn life. Actually, they were the only barbecued mushrooms I've ever tasted, but that didn't make them any less stunning. The previous night, I'd eaten in a barbecue restaurant — oh fuck, what a disappointment that had been. Again I'd seen just how dodgy the food could be in the middle of America. On the whole, it was edible, but eating fast food almost every day was really taking its toll. I'd begun to think there was something wrong with me, like I'd left a bit of my body behind . . . or added a bit. Fast food is okay once or twice a week; but it's a fucking disaster for your digestion if you eat it every day. So it was doubly delightful to share a proper barbecue with Danny and his family.

Up before dawn the next morning, I found myself crashing through woods before I'd even had breakfast. In semi-darkness — with lights, cameras and a non-farting director in tow — I was following Carolyn and Cheri on a turkey hunt. I reckoned I could hear the turkeys running away. There was a turkey noise — *buck-buck-buck-buck-buck-buck* — that I think translated roughly as: "Let's get the fuck out of here, boys. There's a crowd of people with cameras and sound equipment coming."

After stumbling through the woods for a while, we reached a turkey blind. A camouflaged canvas tent, it was large enough for three of us to fit inside. We peered through a netted slit, watching for wild birds. It was freezing and we sat there for an hour or two while one or other of the twins wandered around with the turkey call. Whenever she stopped, all I could hear was the sound of real turkeys getting further and further away, which delighted me, as I don't know how I would have reacted if we'd killed one. I like eating them, but I'm not in the killing business. Even when I go fishing, I don't use barbs on my hooks, so I know that the fish will be unharmed when I release it. I'm fine about people who go fishing and eat whatever they catch, but to catch something, kill it and not eat it is a very bad thing. I'm not a fishmonger, I'm an angler, and I don't like to kill things. And I think that hunting with guns fitted with telescopic sights gives the human a deeply unfair advantage over the animal. When you're hunting with a bow and arrow or a crossbow, at least you're really at the sharp end. You have to be very good to hit anything, and you have to get in close, which demands a bit of cleverness.

Going turkey hunting reminds me of a joke that my daughter Kara claims I told her years ago, although I can't remember doing so.

"How do you keep a turkey in suspense?"

"I don't know."

"I'll tell you tomorrow."

I wish it was my joke — it's quite a good one — but I think Kara must have confused me with someone else.

Incidentally, do you know what the Scots call turkeys? Bubbly jocks — because that's the noise they make when they're chatting away. *Bubbly jock, bubbly jock.* We've got some great names for other animals, too. Frogs are puddocks, sparrows are speugs, owls are hoolits and a linnet is a lintie, which is lovely, I think.

"Oh, have you heard Margaret's big lassie?"

"Aye, she's a lovely big lassie."

"Have you heard her singing? Sings like a lintie."

That always pleased me: sings like a lintie.

★  ★  ★

After the turkey hunt had thankfully ended in abject failure, I left Fanning and the gorgeous twins and had a lovely run on the proper Route 66, away from the interstate. As I've said, much of the original route has now disappeared. Some stretches of it hit dead ends while others simply run out of tarmac. And, of course, many miles have been widened, paved over and turned into interstates, leaving no choice but to travel on the freeway.

So, with the sun shining properly at last, it was terrific to bump along the real Mother Road, with railway tracks to my right and the interstate on my left. Rolling agricultural country stretched far into the distance as I entered the foothills of the Ozark Mountains. Above me, jet planes were playing noughts and crosses with their vapour trails in the sky. I passed a field dotted with bunches of flowers. It was a graveyard, but all the gravestones had been laid flat on the ground, so, from a distance, the commemorative flowers looked like a really peculiar crop.

A train passed me, so I waved. I think we all have a duty to wave at trains. This doesn't apply to planes or cars, but trains always get a wee wave from me, partly because I love those huge American locomotives, but mainly because I always hope to see a hobo looking out of one of the carriages. Apparently there are still loads of them around, catching goods trains across America, although I've never seen one.

This was God-fearing country, the buckle of the Bible Belt. At one crossroads, I stopped to wait for the traffic lights to turn green and spotted churches on three of the four corners. I passed a big billboard that featured a single word — "Jesus", it said. This got me wondering why certain areas tend to be more evangelistic than others. I reckon it might be the lack of choice of things to do in small towns and agricultural communities. Churches don't loom quite so large in the sights of people living in Manhattan, Los Angeles or Chicago.

The previous day, I'd lain on my bed and watched a woman on television saying she had ascended into heaven and fought demons. According to her, the demons were red and black dragons, and God had given her a sword to slay them. The icing on the cake came when she told the viewers that she could teach them how to slay demons, too. All they had to do was buy her CD for twenty-five dollars. It sounded fanciful. And what a bunch of ninnies who fork out twenty-five dollars. Do you know what always strikes me as ironic? Jesus was such a pleasant person and he had some intelligent, earth-shaking views. So why are so many of his followers such ninnies? There seemed to be a church every five yards in Missouri, and some of them were monstrously huge. I didn't get it. Everyone I'd met in this state had been bright and likeable, but clearly a lot of them are gullible, too.

I stopped for a lunchtime pizza in an ordinary wee place. A woman was sitting in the restaurant with two boys, and one of them asked, "Are you Billy Connolly?"

"Yeah."

"I saw you in *The Last Samurai*. Could I have a picture taken with you?"

"Sure."

"Is that your trike?" He pointed out of the window.

"Yeah."

"It's a beauty."

"Come on out and have a look at it."

I showed him around the bike, then he said, "That's my pickup over there."

It was a lovely green truck, old and very beautiful, so I complimented him on it.

"Yeah, I love it." Then he pointed across the street. "And that's my church, over there."

It was one of those gigantic Midwestern churches, the type where a TV evangelist fraud might preach. God, you're so nice — and you seemed smarter than that, I thought. That might sound arrogant, but I've watched those preachers for years on American television. Almost to a man, they're frauds. They've got that politician look about them — two haircuts a day, whitened teeth, all that crap — and they talk a load of bloody nonsense. They're very selective about the Bible. None of the bits that hammer slavery ever get mentioned, but they're very keen on quoting the bits that hammer homosexuality. Oh yes.

Riding on, I was confronted by a typical example of why Route 66 was dying. Half a mile to my left, Interstate 44 surged through the landscape, sucking all the businesses towards it, like iron fillings to a magnet. On 66, lying in the shadow of the freeway, every business seemed to be crumbling. I could sense the local communities trying different things to attract any passing trade, but it was no good. The choice for the motorist was between whooshing along, seeing very little and contributing nothing to the local economies, or creeping along, seeing lots and keeping the local communities alive. A lot of people were still trying to keep the Mother Road alive, with murals and other tourist attractions, but almost every driver was in a hurry to get where they were going. You needed a lot of time on your hands to take Route 66. So it was collapsing. It was a shame, but it was a fact. I'd already seen hundreds of closed shops and decrepit businesses, and we were still only in Missouri.

Following what was left of Route 66 wasn't easy. The roads chopped and changed, and eventually I got lost, so I stopped at an old store, the Mule Trading Post, to ask directions. That was a stroke of luck, because it was run by a nice old fella and was full of bits and pieces of junk and memorabilia. It also turned out to be a bona fide Route 66 landmark, so I was closer to the Mother Road than I'd thought. I bought some badges and key rings from the old boy and we chatted about fly fishing. I really liked him, but I couldn't stay for long. Ahead of me were Springfield, Missouri, and Tulsa, Oklahoma, which always made me think of that Eric Clapton song, "Living on Tulsa Time", and, of course, Gene Pitney or Dusty Springfield singing "Twenty-Four Hours from Tulsa".

The relentless road beckoned.

# CHAPTER
# EIGHT

## Springfield, Illinois . . . Springfield, Missouri too

Rolling on, I passed Rolla — which modestly calls itself "The Middle of Everywhere" — and a string of places with evocative names — Doolittle, Hooker Cut, Devils Elbow, Buckhorn and Laquey — until I arrived in Springfield, Missouri, widely regarded in the folklore of Route 66 as the road's birthplace.

The Mother Road didn't get its snappy name by accident. In 1925 highway officials in Washington came up with a plan for assigning names to the 96,000-mile network of interstate highways that was being constructed and linked across America. Those running east to west would be given even numbers, while odd numbers would be assigned to the north — south routes. The longest east — west routes, stretching from coast to coast, would all end in a zero. But they decided to make one exception — Route 60 — which would head diagonally from Chicago to Los Angeles, crossing Routes 20, 30, 40 and 50.

Maps were printed and signs painted for the proposed Route 60, running from Illinois to Missouri,

Oklahoma, Texas, New Mexico, Arizona and California. But then the influential William J. Fields, Governor of Kentucky, kicked up a fuss. Upset that none of the prestigious routes ending in a zero would run through his state, he persuaded the authorities in Washington to assign Route 60 to a road from the Atlantic coast in Virginia, through various states — including Kentucky — to Springfield, Missouri. As a result, the road from Chicago to Los Angeles would now have to be relabelled Route 62.

Meanwhile, the owner of a restaurant and service station outside Tulsa, Oklahoma, was following all of this with a great deal of interest. Cyrus Avery was acutely aware of the impact of a busy road on business. As chairman of the Oklahoma Department of Highways, he had already successfully lobbied to ensure that the Chicago to Los Angeles road would not follow the old Santa Fe Trail, which bypassed Oklahoma. Instead, thanks to Avery, it would follow a lesser-known trail from the California Gold Rush era that ran straight through his hometown of Tulsa. Now, faced with the humiliation of losing the prestigious Route 60 designation, Avery joined forces with a counterpart in Missouri — A. H. Piepmeier. Telegrams flew between Springfield, Tulsa and Washington, but Avery and Piepmeier couldn't manage to convince the federal bureaucrats to reverse their decision to award Route 60 to the road running through Kentucky.

Then, during a meeting with Piepmeier in Springfield, Avery noticed that the catchy number 66 had not yet been assigned to any road. He swiftly fired off another telegram to Washington and this time the bureaucrats were happy to comply with his suggestion. As the first reference to Route 66 was made in that meeting in Springfield, the town has since claimed to be the road's birthplace. A few months later, the US Highway 66 Association was founded. At its inaugural meeting, Avery coined the name "The Main Street of America" for the route, and the mythologising began.

Springfield is an attractive little city, the third largest in Missouri, and for the first time I felt that I was bordering the Deep South of America. Towards Springfield's centre, there are long avenues of large Victorian homes. With wicker porch swings on covered verandas, some of them look like southern plantation houses. It's a relaxed, calm kind of place. But if you're a cowboy at heart, which I am, it's also a hugely significant place.

In 1865 a guy called James Butler Hickok was living in Springfield. Tall, lean and muscular, with long blond hair falling to his shoulders and two pistols shoved into his belt, Hickok looked like a Western hero straight out of central casting, particularly with the lawman's badge pinned to his chest. We know him better as Wild Bill Hickok, although quite how they got that from James Butler, I don't know. Nevertheless, in July 1865, Wild Bill did something that set a trend for decades to come.

The final shot of the Civil War had been fired only a month earlier when Wild Bill, who had fought on the Union side, came face to face with his arch enemy, a Confederate veteran called Davis Tutt. Even though they'd fought on opposite sides in the war, they'd

**168**

originally been gambling buddies, but had fallen out over a woman called Susanna Moore. There were also suggestions that Hickok had dallied with Tutt's sister, possibly fathering her illegitimate child. Whatever the cause, they now hated the sight of each other.

On 20 July, Hickok was playing poker when Tutt walked into Springfield's Lyon House Hotel. Wild Bill was doing well, so Tutt started loaning money to the other gamblers and offering hints on how to beat him. It made no difference — Hickok's winning streak continued and he had soon amassed more than two hundred dollars (several thousand dollars in today's money), much of it straight from Tutt's pocket. Remembering that Hickok owed him forty dollars for a horse trade, Tutt insisted that he repay it there and then. Hickok shrugged and handed over the money. Then Tutt demanded another thirty-five bucks, for a gambling debt. This time Hickok disputed the figure, saying he owed only twenty-five. A furious Tutt grabbed Hickok's watch, which was lying on the table, pocketed it, and announced that he was keeping it as collateral. Faced with a room full of Tutt's allies, Hickok reluctantly agreed, as long as Tutt didn't wear the watch in public. That would have been a public humiliation, and retribution would have to be sought.

"I intend wearing it first thing in the morning," said Tutt, with a sneer.

"If you do, I'll shoot you," Wild Bill replied calmly. "I'm warning you here and now not to come across that town square with it on."

The following day Wild Bill came round the corner into Springfield's town square to find Tutt swanning around, asking people if they wanted to know the time. Flaunt, flaunt, flaunt.

Wild Bill warned Tutt to cut it out, but Tutt ignored him. They attempted to reach an agreement over the outstanding debt, but failed. After a drink, they parted.

Later that day, shortly before 6p.m., Hickok returned to the square, this time with a pistol in his hand. Onlookers scattered, leaving Tutt standing on his own in the far corner of the square.

"Dave, here I am," shouted Hickok from a distance of about seventy-five yards. "Don't you come across here with that watch."

Hickok had cocked his pistol and returned it to his hip holster. Tutt stood his ground with a hand on his own pistol, silent. For a few seconds, the two men faced each other down. Then Tutt pulled his pistol from its holster. Hickok drew his gun too, steadied it on his forearm and fired at exactly the same moment as Tutt. Wild Bill's bullet hit Tutt in the ribs, sending him staggering back on to the steps of the courthouse, where he gasped, "Boys, I'm killed." He was dead right. Meanwhile, Wild Bill escaped without a scratch. He span on his heels, levelled his gun towards a crowd of Tutt's supporters, and, cool as an alligator, warned them not to interfere.

"Aren't yer satisfied, gentlemen? Put up your shootin' irons or there'll be more dead men here," he said.

They took the hint.

This was the first recorded example of one of those face-to-face, in-the-street, Hollywood-style gunfights — the quick-draw duels that are so familiar from the movies. However, they were not as common as the Westerns would have us believe. In fact, this was one of very few occasions when such a gunfight happened. More often, cowboys shot each other in the back. But Wild Bill's story was quickly seized upon and exaggerated by the dime novels of the time. He even went on to act in a Buffalo Bill production — the forerunner of the Western movie.

Nowadays, a couple of brass markers in Springfield's town square show where Hickok and Tutt stood during the face-off. On the day I visited, there was a huge building site in the middle of the square, obscuring the line of sight between the two markers. But they were so far apart that I started to grow suspicious about the whole story. I reckon that Wild Bill must have arranged for a sniper on the roof of one of the buildings, because it's almost impossible to hit anything from seventy-five yards with a handgun, especially the pistols they had in those days. That's why so many people were shot in the back, from point-blank range.

Hickok was arrested for the murder of Tutt, then charged with manslaughter, but he was acquitted at trial. As Tutt had initiated the fight, been the first to display overt aggression and, according to two witness reports, reached for his pistol first, Hickok was absolved of guilt. He was even praised for giving Tutt several chances to avoid the confrontation, rather than simply shooting him the moment he felt disrespected — which was how matters of honour were usually resolved in the Old West.

Hickok went on to become the law in various other Western towns. Often his reputation alone was sufficient to persuade dusty cowboys to think twice about disrupting the peace, but his fame was a double-edged sword. To some reprobates, killing a man of such high repute was a trophy worth pursuing. During the afternoon of 2 August 1876, Wild Bill was playing cards in the No. 10 Saloon in Deadwood, Dakota Territory. For once, he'd abandoned his usual precaution of sitting with his back to the wall, and somebody shot him in the back of the head. Crack — straight through the skull. None of that quick-draw nonsense. *Boof*. Dead. Bill was holding two pairs — aces and eights — a decent poker hand. Ever since that day, it's been known as the "dead man's hand".

Back in Springfield, the square is now radically different from how it was in 1865. When I visited, it appeared to have become a place where people with nothing much to do hang out. I saw one poor guy being moved along by the police. All he was doing was having a little snooze on the pavement. I always find something like that sad, but here it struck me as peculiar, too, because I'd met unparalleled kindness since arriving in the city. The people had been unbelievably friendly and helpful.

Earlier in the day, I'd been standing at a cash machine in a garage. A very pretty black girl, probably only fourteen or fifteen years old, was being served at the next counter.

172

"Excuse me," she said.

"Yes?" I replied.

"Your shoes are beautiful," she said. "Have a nice day." Then she simply left the garage.

Isn't that lovely? My shoes *were* beautiful — black and white with tassels — but how often would somebody take the time to compliment you on something like that? And everyone I met in Springfield was exactly the same. Exceptionally friendly, those Springfielders and Missourians — or Ozarkians, as they call themselves, because of the Ozark Mountains.

I can't tell you precisely where I went next, because it's kind of a secret. I'm not joking. I was off to meet a man called Rob Lurvey, a self-confessed recluse who hasn't received a letter addressed to his house in more than forty years.

Rob has collected things all his life. As a boy, he started with stamps, like everyone else, but then he diversified. He now has one of the largest personal collections of guitars in the world, including more than five thousand historical pieces. And he had an entire room dedicated to the trusty banjo, with some dating back to the 1800s. Rob's collection wasn't for sale or auction, and he didn't want anyone knowing where he kept it. So we weren't allowed to film the approach or the exterior of his warehouse. I thought that was fair enough, and I couldn't wait to see the collection.

Inside a nondescript warehouse, I met Rob, a man in his fifties with a big, beaming smile. "You must be Billy," he said.

"And you must be Rob. Lovely to meet you."

"You look just like yourself."

That immediately broke the ice and we both laughed.

It was soon obvious that the stringed instruments were only a small part of Rob's collection. He also collected all kinds of memorabilia, and especially anything to do with 3D — like stereoscopes and Viewmasters and holograms. But I was primarily interested in the instruments, so he took me to them.

Guitars, ukuleles, banjos, harps, zither banjos and mandolins — he had them all. The first thing I saw was a long row of zithers — those alpine instruments most of us know from the soundtrack of *The Third Man* — hanging on a wall. Most of them were made between 1865 and 1905 by a company called Schwarzer that had been based in Washington, Missouri. The company folded around the time of the First World War because of anti-German sentiment in America. Rob told me he was one of the few zither collectors anywhere in the world. "I don't know anybody else who's crazy enough to buy them," he said.

I love the zither, though. "I've got a friend in Amsterdam who comes to my stand-up shows and he can play one," I said.

Rob's collection was so extensive that he even had consecutively numbered zithers with their shipping records from the manufacturer. He bought one in 2002 and the other in 2003, reuniting them after 113 years apart. Some of them were real beauties, like a Smithsonian zither that had taken more than a year to make. It had more than five thousand inlaid pieces of wood, carved ivory and gold plating.

"Do you have people look for stuff for you or do you do it all yourself?" I asked.

"I have people."

"Spies?"

"Not really spies, but I've been going to shows since 1985, so most everybody knows what I buy, and there's people out there looking for me all the time."

At one time, Rob had twenty guys searching for a Gibson toy guitar that was missing from his collection. He couldn't even know for sure that it existed — having seen it only in rough illustrations in books — yet he'd spent more than two decades looking for it.

"I was on my way to a national sports collectors' convention in Cleveland — I collect baseball cards too . . ." he said.

"Of course you do."

"And we stopped at the Heart of America antique mall in Springfield, Ohio. [Yes, there's yet *another* Springfield.] It's the largest antique mall in America. I was with a friend who doesn't care about collecting and we got there when it opened at nine-thirty in the morning. I started going through the mall and my friend was checking with me every two hours to see if I was done yet, but I wasn't."

Rob's eyes were sparkling with excitement as he continued to tell the story.

"I was getting ready to go down to the last wing and in a showcase was this toy. I knew immediately what it was and so I immediately rang the buzzer to get somebody there. Nobody would come. They were all busy, I guess. But I wouldn't leave. I didn't want to take a chance of missing this toy. They finally got to me about twenty minutes later and I didn't care what it cost. But I saw it was a hundred and ninety-five dollars, so I asked if they'd take a discount. You gotta ask, you know?"

"Oh yes," I said. "Part of the gig, isn't it?"

"So they gave me ten per cent. I got it for one-seven-five. I'd been looking for one of these for twenty-four years and I started to shake. It's like the Holy Grail. I just couldn't stand it. It was one of the real thrills of my life to finally find one. Other guitar people, they'd all known about it, but nobody had ever seen one. They were all just amazed."

The variety in Rob's collection was astounding — the first double-neck electric guitars, dozens of twelve-string guitars, obscure stencil guitars. It was fabulous to see so many fantastically good instruments, rooms and rooms and rooms of them, one after the other. I'd never seen a music shop with that many guitars. It was absolutely amazing.

"I've never met anyone like you before," I said.

"Oh, I'm out there. When people ask who I am, I say: 'Well, I'm an obsessive, compulsive, manic depressive, eccentric eclectic or eclectic eccentric' — it depends on what day it is."

Some parts of his collection were especially astonishing — like dozens of almost identical versions of the same guitar, each with some obscure, minute

**176**

difference that only an obsessive fanatic like Rob would notice.

To my great delight, Rob had something that he hadn't identified yet, but which I knew well. With only one string, it looked a bit like a banjo and a bit like a ukulele, and it had a wee funny bridge. "It's a one-string fiddle," I told him proudly. Rob's example was a toy version. "It's played with a bow vertically. They used to be popular in Victorian times. You held it between your knees, there was a metal board going down and a horn at the bottom, and you played it like a cello, but it just had one string." It was wonderful to tell Rob, a man with such a vast knowledge of stringed instruments, something he didn't know already.

The fiddle produced a pleasant sound that I remembered from childhood, because a busker used to play one in Byres Road in Glasgow. He had fought in the Battle of Hill 60 on the Western Front in the First World War, and I used to like watching him.

As I continued to look around the vast collection, something intrigued me. "What'll happen to all this, Rob, when you disappear?" I said. "When you leave this mortal coil?"

"It's kinda set up right now to where my nephew gets everything I have. I've got it set up to where he can keep it, he can sell it, or he can donate it to one of several museums. One is the National Music Museum in Vermillion, South Dakota. It's a really cool collection. Or the Ralph Foster Museum, which is down in the College of the Ozarks — it's called the Smithsonian of the Ozarks. That collection down there belonged to a guy named Ike Martin. When I first moved to Springfield, I was in the cub scouts and we'd go down to Ike Martin's music store. In the basement he had this museum. And he'd collected everything. He was really a big influence on my life. He collected arrowheads, he collected guns, he collected just anything you can think of. He was kind of the impetus for getting me started. I mean, I always collected stuff. I've been collecting baseball cards all my life and coins and stuff like that."

Rob's collection is truly unique and I really liked the guy. But that's nothing new — I tend to like people who collect things. I once met a woman who collected ice-cream cones, and a guy in Scotland who collected space guns. And I heard about someone who collected matches with something wrong with them — like the Siamese-twin matches with two legs and one head that sometimes pop up in matchboxes. Over the years, he had apparently collected enough to fill a frame. Something like a paperclip might be completely ordinary, but if you meet someone who collects paperclips, and they proudly show you their collection, it takes on a kind of majesty.

When I was a kid, I had a friend who used to collect bus tickets — each one of which had a five-figure number running along the top. But he didn't collect just any old ticket — the five numbers always had to add up to twenty-one. If they didn't, he wasn't interested. He had a load of them in a shoe box. I think that's the oddest hobby I've ever known.

Personally, I used to collect snow globes. I've still got hundreds of them at home. In fact, if anybody has been inspired by this and wants to start collecting something, I'd be happy to give you my snow globes to get you started. Although, now that I think about it, one of my daughters — Scarlet — would probably kill me if I did. I think she's got her eye on them.

Having collected the snow globes for years, I just decided to stop one day. I do that kind of thing sometimes. I kept a diary for eight and a half years and then suddenly stopped. My wife says it's possibly the most boring thing she's ever read in her life. "Oh God, rain again today. Hope it clears up tomorrow." Riveting stuff. I started to ask myself why I was writing it. Was I hoping that somebody would read it when I was dead? Or was I hoping to publish it so that people could see how windswept and interesting I was? Then I decided I would rather have a big book with random writings and collections of theatre tickets and bus tickets and things I had done that day. So, if it was a boring day, I wouldn't write anything. I finished only one page of that before I got bored shitless and didn't do it any more.

After Springfield, I headed towards the Kansas state line, riding on Route 66 out of sight of the interstate through rolling wooded hills and wide-open green prairies. It was perfect country for leaning back, enjoying the road and singing its fantastic signature tune to myself.

Although most of us associate "Route 66" with Chuck Berry, or maybe Nat King Cole, or the Rolling Stones, it was actually written by a former marine called Bobby Troup. He'd made a bit of money writing a few tunes for Frank Sinatra, Tommy Dorsey and Sammy Kaye, so he bought himself a second-hand Buick and set off with his wife for America's entertainment capital, Los Angeles. According to Troup, they stopped for a bite to eat in a restaurant and his wife suggested he should write a song about travelling west by car. At the time, they were on Route 40 east of Chicago, and Troup didn't feel at all inspired, but the idea intrigued him.

A few days later, having joined Route 66, Bobby's wife tapped him on the shoulder and said, "Get your kicks on Route 66."

"God, that's a marvellous idea for a song," replied Bobby.

He wrote half of the lyrics in the car, but then got stuck. A while later, Bobby was working with Nat King Cole and played him the sections he'd written. Nat immediately urged Bobby to finish the song. More in frustration than anything else, Troup simply used the names of some of the towns and cities he'd driven through during his trip: St Louis, Joplin, Oklahoma City, Amarillo, Gallup, Flagstaff, Winona, Kingman, Barstow and San Bernardino. (Winona is the only one out of sequence, as it was included to rhyme with "Flagstaff, Arizona".) Somehow that list of places managed to encompass the allure, sense of freedom and romanticism of the open road.

Nat King Cole recorded the song and it was a big hit, earning Troup, who went on to write many more songs and star in movies and television series, more than four million dollars in royalties. Over the years, dozens of artists have recorded it, although they often change the lyrics. In most cases they use a shortened version of the song that omits a couple of verses and doesn't mention a string of towns that appeared in Nat's original version — Tulsa, Albuquerque, Tucumcari, Needles, Essex, Amboy and Azusa. All of these places still lay ahead of me.

Approaching the Missouri — Kansas state border, my eye was caught by a sign for a place called Precious Moments. Then, outside Carthage, a town near Joplin, huge billboards started to loom up on both sides of the road. They all featured pokey wee characters similar to those "Love Is" cartoons that used to appear in the British press. The wee figures on the billboards would always be saying holy things to one another under a "Precious Moments" banner. My curiosity had been well and truly piqued by the time I came to a sign for the Precious Moments exhibition, so I pulled off Route 66 and went to have a look. What I found, in my opinion, was absolutely horrific.

Riding through double gates, I entered a landscaped park with hedge-lined drives that led me to a car park in front of a pink and peach building. Inside was a gift shop the size of bloody Selfridges, and scenes from the Bible depicted by the same little cartoon characters I'd seen on the billboards. Each one conformed to that gooey, soppy, syrupy idea that some Americans have of something good. I wanted to scream.

Leaving the hideous building, I followed more hedge-lined paths that weaved through the little cartoon characters — this time modelled in stone and blowing trumpets, as if they were welcoming us to heaven. Before long, I was walking towards a pink and orange chapel. Clearly inspired by Michelangelo's Sistine Chapel in Rome, it was highly decorated inside, with the same little dinky-poo characters acting out scenes from the Bible. Moses, for instance, had a wee roundy face and a tear in his eye. It was nightmarish. The climax of the thing was a whole wall, supposedly heaven, featuring hundreds of little boys and girls in togas — all playing basketball or spinning hula hoops. Above, it said: "No more tears".

I was close to vomiting. But some people — usually fat adults in T-shirts — were busy proclaiming how much they loved Jesus, so I kept my mouth shut. The camera crew and Mike, the director, were standing beside me, waiting to shoot something, but I just couldn't bring myself to do it. I'm not in the business of taking the mickey out of people, and I've got no time for television shows that try to entertain by making fools out of people. I've never liked it, and I wasn't going to start indulging in it now. Far be it from me to kick a person's faith away from them, no matter how sick it made me.

The funny thing was that Mike and I had entered the place feeling quite jolly, laughing and smiling. But we exited in silence, like we'd been to a funeral. It was very odd. Seeing the extent to which people will twist religion was very weird and kind of scary. It was a side of the Bible Belt that I just didn't understand. The way they seemed to have removed all of the dignity from religion was really quite creepy.

It would have been all too easy to stick the boot in. But then little grannies and aunties, people who take their religion very seriously and practise it with quiet dignity, would be wounded by someone like me clumsily tearing into their faith. I admit that part of me was desperate to get in there with my big swinging boot, but I was quite proud of myself and the crew for just walking away that day.

After the bizarreness of Precious Moments, I needed something to jerk me into a different mood. A few miles further down Route 66, a sign announced that I was leaving Missouri and entering Kansas. Galena lay ahead, then Tulsa — less than a day away if I rode straight through. But with plenty of places to stop, it was going to take me significantly longer than twenty-four hours.

The Mother Road only clipped the southeastern corner of the Sunflower State. Blink and you'd be in Oklahoma, as the Kansas stretch lasted a mere thirteen miles. However, every mile of it was genuine, historical Route 66 hardtop because Interstate 44 completely bypassed the state of Dorothy and Toto, leaving a perfectly intact section of the old Mother Road.

There isn't much to say about Galena, a perfectly nice but unremarkable former mining town with an air of its best days being long behind it. Like so many

American small towns, nobody was in the street. Not a soul. Riding down Main Street, I spotted the obligatory church and, directly opposite it, a poker house offering Texas hold'em. Apparently Galena had all the bases covered for anyone hoping for redemption from the pressures of the world.

Whereas "Missouri" comes from a Sioux word, *ouemessourita*, meaning "those who have dugout canoes", and "Oklahoma" is Indian for "red people", the origin of "Kansas" is an Indian word that means "people of the wind". It's a sadly appropriate name for this part of the world, as it lies in the heart of Tornado Alley.

As I continued to ride through the Sunflower State, I became slightly despondent. I'd been assured that although Route 66's passage through Kansas was short, it boasted a surprisingly large number of fried chicken shacks — fourteen in just thirteen miles — and all of them teeming with customers buying up to five thousand chicken dinners a day. I'd even been promised a Scottish connection, because fried chicken was allegedly a traditional Scottish dish. This was news to me, so I was determined to investigate. But do you know what? There was nothing but a great big hole where I was expecting hustle, bustle and the sweet smell of chicken fat.

Making a television travelogue can occasionally turn into a crap shoot. And I hate it when that happens. I arrived at Chicken Annie's in Pittsburg, Kansas — a slight detour off Route 66, but I'm prepared to suffer for my art — expecting to find hundreds of people wolfing down their dinner. Instead, there were about four cars in the car park, and inside it looked like the dining room in an old folks' home. I'd schlepped all the way over there only to discover it was the dullest fucking place on earth. I'd been promised a string of chicken businesses, all jostling with each other for trade, but when I stood outside Chicken Annie's, I couldn't see any sign of a single shack. There was one other chicken shop, but it was way behind some trees. There was no fucking competition whatsoever.

I had this weird feeling, like I was spiralling downwards. I couldn't think of anything to say about the place, and I started to doubt everything. Kansas was turning into a big disappointment. I'd not been there before, and I doubted I'd return. As for the suggestion that fried chicken was a traditional Scottish dish . . . that was bullshit, too. I've never known a single Scot who makes a fuss over chicken. And I've never seen a single Scottish cookbook that features recipes for fried chicken. It was a non-story and it left me feeling a bit like the centre of a doughnut. Empty.

The combination of Precious Moments and the chicken shack fiasco meant I finished the day in a foul mood. But sometimes I find a kind of comfort in being grumpy. There's a feeling of righteousness, a sense of being the great misunderstood, which is probably bollocks, but comforting all the same. At least I knew it would pass, and that something else would show up. Something interesting would stick its head up, and I'd be intrigued by it. That's the glory of Route 66 — there's always something new around the corner.

It would have been great to end the day with a feeling of a job well done. If I'd achieved anything, I could have nipped upstairs to my room, lain back on my bed and watched *Ghost Finders* on the telly before falling asleep with a sense of satisfaction. I didn't see that happening tonight. But then I remembered Rob and his crazy collection. It seemed so long ago that I'd met him, but it had only been that morning. I'd had a good chat with him. I'd known my stuff and he'd certainly known his. Maybe the day hadn't been so bad after all. In fact, as long as I thought about Rob surrounded by all his instruments in his anonymous warehouse in the middle of nowhere, I felt pretty good.

# CHAPTER
# NINE

## Oklahoma City Looks Oh So Pretty

A sign by the side of the road, then a slight thud under the wheels as one section of tarmac ended and another began. Those were the only indications that I'd slipped out of Kansas. "You Are Now Entering Oklahoma On Historic Route 66", said the sign.

In many ways, Oklahoma is the heart and soul of Route 66. Although Springfield was the birthplace of the road's moniker, Oklahoma was the home state of Cyrus Avery, the man who chose that name. And it boasts more miles of original Route 66 than any other state. Somewhat ironically, it was also the first state to bypass the Mother Road, dealing an early death blow in 1953 when it opened the Turner Turnpike (later part of the oppressive Interstate 44), which replaced more than a hundred miles of America's Main Street. Oklahoma is also the state from which the characters fled in *The Grapes of Wrath*, in which John Steinbeck coined "The Mother Road" to describe Route 66, immortalising it as "the path of a people in flight" from dust bowl despair and starvation. It was also the first state to recognise Route 66's historical and social significance. Enthusiasts established the Oklahoma Route 66 Association to preserve and promote the road, and they designed the "Historic Route 66" signs that now punctuate the landscape all the way from Chicago to Los Angeles, having been adopted by most other states.

Route 66's first miles in Oklahoma pass through fairly nondescript towns and villages. First there's Quapaw, another former mining town, followed by Commerce, now semi-deserted, then Miami, from which a magnificent section of original 1926–37 Route 66 — bumpy, gravelly and only nine feet wide — stretches for two miles. A little while earlier, having passed through a wee ghost town, I'd spotted a handwritten sign by the side of the road: "Swamp Sale", it said. Let's have a look, I thought. You never know your luck. I'm one of those guys who sees a sign for a car-boot sale and thinks he's bound to find a great guitar for twenty bucks. Maybe watching all those auction shows on television has done it. Whatever the reason, I was curious, so I pulled over and went for a wander.

Near the entrance, dressed in dungarees and lounging on a plastic garden chair, was a character straight out of *The Grapes of Wrath*. Shading himself from the sun under the raised rear door of a people carrier and some low trees, Vernon Willoughby looked kind of poor, but happy. A well-worn blue vest barely held in an impressive belly, and a greying beard framed his ruddy face. Around him, his family lazed in the sun, waiting for someone to take a look at their wares.

"Are you selling those chickens and all?" I pointed at some birds in a cage.

"Yeah." Vernon had a twangy Oklahoma accent.

"How much does a chicken cost?"

"A lot of people sell 'em for fifteen dollars a piece when they're grown, laying eggs."

"Yeah? And you?"

"Anywhere from eight dollars to fifteen dollars."

"Eight to fifteen?"

"Yeah." Vernon spoke very slowly and deliberately.

"And how much is a duck?"

"That's for five. Because they grow quicker than chickens do."

"But the duck eggs are delicious, aren't they?"

"Yeah."

"Where do you come from yourself?"

"A little town called Quapaw over here in Oklahoma."

"Oh yeah?"

"66 runs right through it."

I nodded. "I'm going to Tulsa and then Oklahoma City."

"That's a good ride on that 66."

"Yeah?"

"Long one, though."

"They're all long. It's too big, this country."

As well as fully grown chickens, Vernon was selling some guinea fowl and those wee yellow fluffy chicks. On another table there were various ornaments and bits and pieces, presumably from his house, nice items of Americana, a well-crafted wooden box, a ceramic buffalo with the ubiquitous "Made in China" imprinted on its base, and an elephant-shaped incense holder. It all looked a bit desperate. A duck for five dollars seemed like a bargain — they lay eggs for ever — but of course I couldn't buy one.

Further up the lane, another half-dozen stallholders were displaying their wares. The first I came to shouted, "Whoa, no, no, no! Get the camera away!" He was a nice fella, but he was selling guns and knives and didn't want to be filmed. I was happy to respect his wishes. I'm not one of those people who thinks everything about guns is bad. Not everyone who's interested in them is a potential murderer or a militia man — just some of them. Many of them are simply into hunting and collecting knives. The working knife is a big thing in America.

The next stallholder was similarly reluctant to be filmed. "No problem whatsoever," I said. "I understand."

So I moved on to another stall, where a large man called Olen Robbins, dressed all in black and wearing black shades was standing in front of a large black pick-up truck.

"Yeah, go right ahead," Olen said when I asked if we could film him. "Where are you folks from?"

"I'm from Scotland."

"Really? Well, welcome to the United States."

"Oh, I live in New York, but I'm from Scotland."

"You'll find a variety of interesting stuff along old Route 66 and quite a bit of history here."

While I perused the items on his stall, Olen chatted away, recommending a visit to Baxter Springs, back across the state border in Kansas.

"What's a boot hunter knife?" I asked, holding up a knife in a box.

"It's styled after the old riverboat gambler knives. It's still mint in the box. The gamblers carried that style of knife as they played cards on the riverboats along the Mississippi."

"What's that?" I pointed at a black dagger with a Gothic inscription.

"That is an old German piece. I acquired a small collection of German military memorabilia from an elderly gentleman in Joplin, who brought them back from Germany during the war. This is a type of fraternal piece. We haven't identified it exactly yet."

"Can I see?"

"Absolutely."

Picking up the dagger, I shuddered as I noticed a Nazi flag draped over the front of the man's stall.

"And this old banner was from the same gentleman." Olen held up an eighteen-inch pendant. It looked like some kind of fraternal medallion on a ribbon. About the size of the palm of a hand, it had enamel inserts with various signs and insignia. The stallholder turned it over and there was a swastika on the back.

"Oh my God."

"He liberated this banner from a building in Germany during World War Two. I've had some difficulty translating it, but loosely translated it was something that was presented to the government by this particular guard corps that protected a castle in Germany, and it celebrates the hundredth anniversary of that military unit."

"Yeah." I was starting to recoil from the items on Olen's stall.

"I don't . . . I don't really keep this kind of stuff," he said. "I do buy and sell and trade it when I find it, but I'm not really a big fan of it."

"No, I'm not a fan of it myself."

"Due to the history behind it. But I've always picked up anything unusual or unique. Of course, you may not wanna film that particular bumper sticker."

I looked at the sticker and read it out loud: "Obama Sucks". Then I looked at Olen.

"It does kind of express the sentiments of a good deal of the people in this country at this time," he said.

There was another bumper sticker on the stall: "Speak To Me In English", it said. Now I knew exactly where he was coming from, but I didn't react to it.

"I like Obama," I said. "I think he's great."

"Well, I know a lot of people from other countries think he's absolutely wonderful."

"What about the killing of Osama bin Laden?"

"He's taking full credit for that, but one thing that a lot of folks don't realise is that the interrogation techniques that they started using under the previous President were responsible for gaining the intelligence that led to his ultimate capture. And Obama wanted to abolish those techniques, calling them harsh and cruel."

"What? Torture? You think torture's okay?"

"Well, no, I don't agree that torture's okay, but if someone's gonna kill a large group of people, I think you get the information out of 'em however you have to in order to prevent the death of many."

I wasn't convinced.

"He's not greatly liked at this point, but his popularity did take a bump for Osama. We'll see."

"I think you're jealous. I think if the Republicans had done it, you'd be dancing in the street."

"Absolutely not. I'm an independent. I don't follow the Republican agenda."

"Were you a George W kinda guy?"

"No, no."

"Are you a libertarian?"

"Yes. I would say you'd have to lock me into the libertarian category."

"Small government and no taxes?"

"Or low taxes, at least. I don't think we can get by without taxes, because we definitely need the services, but we're taxed too much."

"Yeah. Everybody's taxed too much."

"I would have to agree."

"Well, thanks for your time. Thanks for allowing me to rumble through your stuff."

"I don't know if you've noticed the silver and gold market in the country since you've been here?"

"It's rocketing, isn't it?"

"It plummeted last week."

"Did it? Last week?"

"Do you know who George Soros is?"

"Yes."

"He sold one of the largest hoards of silver, to my understanding, in the country. It crashed the market."

"Why would he do a thing like that?"

"That goes back to why a lot of people don't like this guy." Olen pointed at the "Obama Sucks" bumper sticker. "They're pals."

I laughed. It was all I could do in the face of such unshakeable beliefs. The Nazi banner said more to me than I felt he would have liked it to say.

It always amazes me that, in the most religious corners of this country, you often find little dark patches. You'd think that people who like Jesus would be pulled to the left politically — they should be attracted to the sharing aspect of society. But they usually seem to be deeply suspicious of it, whether it's socialist or Amish. Instead of cooperation and sharing, they want small government, small taxes and business to be left in charge of the country. They want business to tell the government what to do, not the other way round.

Ultimately, as far as I was concerned Olen was just a fat little fascist to me, so fuck him. He said he was a libertarian, but then they all say that. A lot of weird crap hides under the banners of nationalism and libertarianism. I'm not saying that nationalism is necessarily fascist — that would be ridiculous — but fascists like to hide in that independent-minded corner of things. And they do that corner a real disservice.

I moved along to some of the other stalls, which were reassuringly closer to what anyone would expect to find at a car-boot sale in Britain: people selling second-hand clothes, children's pyjamas, unwanted exercise gadgets, CDs by obscure musicians, DVDs, badges, toys, tools and rusty garden equipment. Carol and Dave Archer, a charming retired couple who spent their time travelling in a huge motor home between their various children in Florida, Massachusetts and Kansas, were selling seashell wind chimes and funky tie-dyed T-shirts. It was a pleasure to meet that kind of American. They weren't rich — they were just sauntering along, getting by. I had the time of my life chatting to them.

Mostly it was an absolute pleasure bumbling around the market, stopping to chat to people. But one guy caught me having a pee behind a tree and gave me a hard time. I wasn't going to kill the tree — I'm a healthy guy — but he insisted: "There's bathrooms over there." So I ambled over to two horrible portaloos. Have you ever looked in the hole in a portaloo? It's like gazing into the depths of hell. I couldn't help thinking that those portaloos were liable to do much more harm to the environment than me having a quick pee behind a tree.

Moving off again, riding on through the Oklahoma countryside, I caught a glimpse of the annual *Cinco de Mayo* celebrations. For reasons that nobody seems able to explain, this victory of the Mexicans over the French is a national holiday in America. Even more bizarrely, this year they were celebrating it on 7 May. I stopped for a chicken-pork pie. God, I loved it! I don't get enough chances to eat chicken — pork pie.

About a hundred miles further down Route 66, as the road widened into four lanes, crossed two huge steel bridges over the Verdigris River and approached Tulsa, a blue whale hoved into view. Given that we were more than a thousand miles from either coast, that might sound strange, but this was no ordinary blue whale. For a start, it was made out of concrete. Smiling from its pond of water, it was the creation of a man who simply wanted to bring a little joy and happiness to his son and his son's friends.

Hugh Davis was a zoologist who had travelled in Africa before settling with his wife Zelta in Catoosa, on the outskirts of Tulsa. There they opened a little zoo and reptile house beside a swimming hole on the roadside of Route 66. The local kids used to splash around quite happily in the swimming hole, but Hugh's son, Blaine, kept bugging him to build something they could dive off, because there were no rocks or trees around the pool.

In typical dad fashion, Hugh said, "Sure, sure, I'll get round to it, I'll get round to it," and did nothing for years.

But then, in 1972, when Blaine was drafted into the army and sent to Vietnam, Hugh finally fulfilled his promise. He had a friend who was a welder — the first giveaway that he might be a lunatic and could embark on something seriously stupid. (I'm a welder; I know these things.) As the welder set to work on a large steel framework, everybody's first thought was that Hugh must be building an aeroplane. But then Hugh started to cover the frame with concrete. He mixed 126 sacks of the stuff and pushed it into place with his hands. Once it had set, he painted it all light blue.

On their wedding anniversary, Hugh unveiled his concrete creation to Zelta. His lavish gift was a blue whale. In total it had cost him nearly two thousand dollars, a lot of money in the early 1970s.

When I first drew up beside the concrete cetacean, I have to admit I was a bit disappointed. Some kids were happily fishing off it, but the whole place looked a bit forlorn. This is just a park with a blue whale made of concrete, I thought. Who the hell cares? There was a wee cash desk in a wee log cabin, and a bloke came out to explain what it was all about. That happened quite often on Route 66: as soon as I stopped anywhere, someone would turn up, say hello and start chatting. They were usually very friendly, and this man was no exception. Dressed in a straw hat, Hawaiian shirt, gold watch and big glasses, he introduced himself as Blaine Davis — the fella whose badgering had prompted his dad to build the whale nearly forty years earlier.

Now about sixty years old, Blaine gave me a charming guided tour of the whale. We walked across a lawn towards the water's edge. Then, like Jonah, I entered the beast through its mouth. Inside, there was a ladder up to a space in the top of the whale's head — a huge room with a wooden floor where children could play and meet and scheme in the way that kids love to do. It was the best kids' gang hut I'd ever seen. Obviously, Blaine himself didn't play in it when he came back from Vietnam, but I'm sure the local kids had a whale of a time in it. (Sorry about that, but I couldn't resist!) Hugh also rigged up some plumbing which allowed the kids to be squirted down a slide and into the pool. And there were some diving boards —

one on the side of the whale, a high one off its tail, and three more dotted around the lake.

Hugh and Zelta opened the whale to the public, and for a couple of decades it was a popular local spot. Over the years, thousands of people visited it and had a grand old time. It was so successful that they eventually closed the zoo. But by the late 1980s, when litigation culture was starting to get a grip on America, their accident insurance premiums became prohibitive and they were forced to shut the whale, too. By then, a lot of locals had swimming pools in their backyards anyway, so they no longer wanted to come to the swimming hole.

The blue whale and the park around it fell into disrepair. Nature took over, and for a while it looked like the Catoosa Blue Whale would crumble to dust. But then some locals, people who had fond childhood memories of jumping, diving and sliding off the whale, got in touch with Blaine and asked if they could form a group to preserve it. They drummed up sponsorship from a chain of hotels on Route 66 and set to work. Nowadays, the whale even has its own Facebook page.

"We had a big sit-down dinner here last Thursday night," said Blaine. "First time we've ever had one of those. Tables, chairs, steak cooked right here on the site and everything. We had over a hundred people here."

I think it's terrific that the whale has once again become a focus and asset for the community.

"That's wonderful," I said.

"We had live music, a string quartet and everything, down here playing music."

"Really?"

"Yeah, yeah. We invited wine vendors from four different vineyards to bring their wares out here and to treat people to wine and free food. It was great."

I love the idea of millions of people driving down Route 66 over the years, glancing across at the park, and saying, "What the heck? Was that a whale?" And I was thrilled that the whale was probably having the same effect on today's passers-by, all thanks to the efforts and energy of a group of community-minded locals. The whale is nothing but a whole bunch of fun, which is what's so great about it.

But that's not what tickled me most about this wee park. Hugh also made a toilet block to serve his customers. With no architectural training, he based his design on some tribal huts he'd seen in Africa. But instead of making the toilet block from mud, he fashioned it from concrete. And, boy, has it stood the test of time. The building looks just like an African village hut, but it's as solid as a rock. Blaine told me that whenever tornadoes rip through this part of Oklahoma, which they do throughout April and May, he locks up his caravan beside the lake and barricades himself in the toilet. It's the only tornado-proof loo I've ever seen. I love the idea that Blaine shelters in there while the tornado passes by. What a tribute to his dad's skill. I was terribly impressed by it.

Incidentally, the section of Route 66 that runs through Catoosa is called the Will Rogers Memorial Highway. I'm a huge fan of Will Rogers — a cowboy, comedian, social commentator, vaudeville performer and actor who was born to a Cherokee family in Oklahoma and became known as Oklahoma's favourite son — so I was tickled that the road had adopted his name. He was a phenomenal talent, first appearing in vaudeville shortly before the First World War. I've seen films of him doing his lasso act from around that period and it's quite breathtaking. But he was also a philosopher, the type that I'd call country-wise rather than street-wise. He travelled around the world three times, made seventy-one movies (silent and talkies), wrote more than four thousand nationally syndicated newspaper columns, and became a world-famous figure. By the mid-1930s, the American public adored him. He was considered the leading political wit of the age and was the top-paid Hollywood movie star.

After the First World War, there had been plans to march the returning troops past the White House in Washington. Rows of planked seating (called bleachers in America) were erected, which sparked huge arguments over who should get the best seats for the victory parade. Someone asked Will what he thought of all the fuss about the seating arrangements.

"If you really appreciate what the soldiers did, let them sit in the seats and we'll march past," he said.

What a guy, eh? Wasn't that a splendid idea? That was Will Rogers all over. I once went to his house in Los Angeles and was really impressed. He made good use of his fame, serving as a goodwill ambassador to Mexico and briefly as Mayor of Beverly Hills. In print and on radio he poked fun at gangsters, prohibition, politicians, government policies and various other controversial topics but in a folksy, down-to-earth way that was readily appreciated and offended no one. "Lord, the money we spend on government," he said of Franklin Roosevelt's administration, of which he was a fervent supporter. "And it's not one bit better than the government we got for one-third of the money twenty years ago."

That kind of thinking was born in Oklahoma, and I can only urge you to come and experience this part of the world for yourself. I've not known friendliness and hospitality like it anywhere else, and I guarantee you'll experience it, too.

From Catoosa, I had a long ride ahead of me, and another storm was brewing. The weather had been sensational for the previous few days, and I'd hoped to be wearing fewer clothes as I continued to head southwest. But I wasn't so sure as I set off down the road towards Oklahoma City.

Before the state capital, though, I had one more stop to make. I was going to meet an oil baron.

Now, whenever I think about oil, what comes to mind is Libya, Iraq, Saudi Arabia, Texas or big plumes of flame burning on North Sea oil rigs. I've never thought of Oklahoma as an oil state. But here's the thing — less than a hundred years ago, Tulsa was the oil capital of the world. In 1859 a driller seeking salt water struck oil, and fortune-seekers immediately invaded the local Indian territory. Then, in 1901, prospectors discovered vast oil deposits at Red Fork in southwest Tulsa. Investors swarmed to the city, which in a matter of months went from a cow town to a boomtown. Four years later, an even larger oil deposit was struck and Tulsa's population grew to almost a hundred thousand people. Four hundred oil companies were based in the city. Propelling Oklahoma at breakneck speed into the twentieth century, the black gold brought two daily newspapers, four telegraph companies, more than 10,000 telephones, seven banks, 200 lawyers and more than 150 doctors, as well as numerous other businesses, to Tulsa.

Nowadays, Tulsa's big industry is gas. However, oil still has a presence, albeit in a less obvious way. It's more like a cottage industry, with "mom-and-pop" oil companies producing just two or three barrels a day.

White-haired and dressed in a light blue Lacoste polo shirt and jeans, Wiley Cox (what a great name) is a very unlikely looking oil baron. He described himself as "just about the smallest end of the oil industry you're going to get" and had agreed to show me around his oilfield. Anyone who has been to Los Angeles or some parts of Texas will have seen those nodding metal donkeys at the side of the road, steadily pumping oil out of the ground. They look like the kind of thing boys made with their Meccano sets in the fifties. Wiley had four or five of them and, with the recent escalation in oil prices, was making quite a decent living out of them.

Wiley's a perfectly pleasant man and he gave me the full guided tour, but I couldn't summon up much interest. In fact, as I listened to him talking about oil and the process of getting it out of the ground, I almost lost the will to live. That might seem ironic, given that there would be no Route 66 without oil, but it just held no fascination for me.

So I said goodbye to him, got back on my bike, and headed for Oklahoma City, which was still about ninety miles away. It was a harsh ride: long, straight roads pointing all the way to the horizon. Whenever I crested a hill, the road would stretch out in front of me again, as long and as straight as the previous stretch. The monotony and emptiness were quite extraordinary, and by the time I reached Oklahoma City I was ready for dinner, bed and a long sleep.

The next day started with the promise of a big, fat, juicy steak. It's one of those things that horrifies almost any British person — the idea of steak for breakfast — particularly if eaten the American way, which is with a Coca-Cola on the side. A *steak*? For *breakfast*? What kind of people are they? What kind of savages eat a hunk of meat dripping with blood for their first meal of the day? But actually it's fabulous. Steak and eggs set you up for the day, especially when you're going to spend that day astride a trike, and possibly even more so when you've not eaten steak for forty or fifty years.

I gave up red meat decades ago because I thought that was the healthy way to go. But in the last year I'd started eating it again. My daughter advised me to tuck in after reading a book that advocated matching your diet to your blood type. Both of us are Type "O", rhesus-negative. According to the book, red meat is good for us. So, since the beginning of the year, I'd been eating a bit of steak and quite enjoying it. Now I was really looking forward to my steak breakfast at the Cattlemen's Steakhouse. But I'd forgotten it was Mothering Sunday, and the place was jammed. There was a huge queue, so I went elsewhere and had a hamburger instead. I was disappointed to miss out on the steak, but it was a cracking good hamburger, and it set me up for the long ride out to Stan Mannshreck's cattle ranch.

Stan is a smashing guy and a really good laugh. I watched as he and his hands rounded up twenty head of cattle under the golden morning sun and drove them on to a huge trailer. Then, sitting in the cab beside Stan as we drove the cattle to market, I felt like a proper cowboy. The boys could have herded the cattle in the traditional manner all the way to the market at the edge of Oklahoma City, but Stan didn't want to do that. Oklahoma had suffered a drought for most of the last fifteen years, so his cattle were already underweight, and they would have lost even more pounds on a long drive. But there was a silver lining to this particular cloud: because of the drought, far fewer cattle were being sent to market, so each animal fetched a much higher price than a similar steer would have ten or fifteen years ago.

Travelling in Stan's big trailer with the cattle in the back, occasionally the smell wafted into the cabin. *Holy Mother of Jesus!* It was something else.

Approaching the toll gate near the end of the interstate, Stan turned to me and smiled. "Watch this girl. She's been here a while," he said. "She'll notice I've got cattle on the back. Just watch the speed with which she shuts the window as soon as she gets the money."

We pulled up at the toll booth and Stan handed over the cash.

"See you, Stan." *Va-voom*, the window shot across.

Stan told me that on a previous trip into town, one of the cattle had peed and shat itself during the stop at the toll booth and it had squirted straight through her window. After that, she wasn't taking any chances.

We dropped off the cattle at the Oklahoma City National Stock Yards, the largest feeder cattle market (dealing only in young, male calves) in the world. Twelve thousand cattle might be sold there in single a day. Since its inception, more than 102 million head of livestock had passed through the iron gates.

The National Stock Yards form part of Stockyard City, a neighbourhood of Oklahoma City that's more like a self-contained town. A bit like the Vatican, it rules itself, and it answers to the county, not the city, which dearly wants to get rid of it because of the smell and the effluent, the noise and the traffic. But it's not going anywhere. Many of the businesses in the area date back to 1910, when the Oklahoma National Stock Yards Company began its public livestock market. At its height, in the 1950s, Stockyard City's meat-packing operations employed about 10 per cent of the city's workforce. When I visited, though, it almost felt like a theme park. The fronts of many of the stores — which catered exclusively to cattlemen, selling Western clothing — were wooden and lit by gas. It was a lovely piece of period history.

Noisy and smelly, Stockyard City and the National Stock Yards are well worth a visit. I loved all the mooing and seeing the cowboys riding up and down. Anyone who went into the stockyards could see the cattle arriving and being herded into pens. Poor things, they didn't know they were destined to be hamburgers or steaks soon, although they seemed to sense that something sinister awaited them. But at least the huge abattoirs that used to be right next door to the market area had been relocated. Nowadays the cattle were transported by truck to the slaughterhouses once they'd been sold.

The stockyards hold auctions only on Mondays and Tuesdays, so I had to wait until the next day to see the auctioneer in action. In the meantime, I decided to visit the place that, tragically, most of us now associate with Oklahoma City.

On 19 April 1995, twenty-six-year-old Timothy McVeigh parked a Ryder rental truck packed with nearly three tons of ammonium nitrate fertiliser, nitromethane and diesel fuel outside the nine-storey Alfred Murrah Building. McVeigh had built a cage inside the truck so that the explosive mixture would blow towards the front of the building — he really put a lot of thought into it — and shortly after nine o'clock in the morning he detonated the bomb. The explosion decimated the building, killing 168 people and injuring another 800.

About ninety minutes later, an Oklahoma state trooper stopped McVeigh for driving without a licence plate. The trooper arrested him for that offence and for unlawful possession of a weapon. However, within days, McVeigh's old army friend Terry Nichols was arrested, and both men were charged with the bombing. McVeigh, a Gulf War veteran with extreme right-wing views, was seriously screwed up about the federal government and was a member of a militia movement. I saw him interviewed after his trial and he expressed no regret about what he'd done. He'd timed the bomb to coincide with the second anniversary of the Waco siege, in which seventy-six people (including twenty-four Brits) died when the headquarters of the Branch Davidians, a weird Protestant sect, went up in flames. That tragedy, and an earlier incident at Ruby Ridge, Idaho, in which the FBI had besieged the home of another religious fanatic called Randy Weaver, had motivated McVeigh to seek revenge. He was executed by lethal injection on 11 June 2001. Nichols was sentenced to life in prison for acting as his accomplice.

The entire front was blown off the Alfred Murrah Building, which contained the offices of the Bureau of Alcohol, Tobacco and Firearms — the body that had conducted the siege in Waco — as well as various other government departments, such as Social Security. In the aftermath of the attack, it was decided to demolish the building and replace it with a memorial to the victims. It's now a simple, quiet and understated place, which makes it all the more moving. At its centre is a large reflection pool of shallow water on black granite, at either end of which are two large bronze gates. It's quite beautiful. I spotted a bird standing in the pool and the water hardly came up to its ankles. At one end, the eastern gate is inscribed with "9:01", which represents innocence — the last moments of peace before the bomb exploded a minute later. At the other end, the western gate is inscribed with "9:03" to symbolise the first moments of recovery after the outrage.

It really is an extraordinarily powerful memorial to the 168 victims. The authorities encourage children to dip their hands in the water and then pat one of the gates to leave a handprint on the bronze. Eventually, the handprint will turn green and last for ever. I think that's a very touching idea.

To the side of the reflecting pool, 168 empty chairs, hand-crafted in bronze, glass and stone, represent each of the dead. The nine rows of chairs, each inscribed with the name of a victim, represent the nine floors of the building. They're laid out to correspond with where the victims were found, with the greatest number clustered in the most heavily damaged portion of the building. Nineteen of the chairs are smaller than the rest, representing the children who were killed in the bombing. Three unborn children also died; they are listed on their mothers' chairs, beneath their mothers' names. At the western edge of the field of chairs is a small column of five chairs representing the five people who died outside the building. At night, each chair's glass name plate illuminates the darkness. This creates a kind of life for the victims that will never go out. Like the Vietnam Memorial in Washington, the abstract nature of the memorial seems to attract people, maybe because it allows them to distance themselves from the physical image of those who suffered and to concentrate instead on their memory.

I had seen pictures of the Oklahoma City National Memorial in a magazine and had been terribly moved by it, but of course it's even more moving when you're standing within it. I was struck by how quiet all the other visitors were. It was a very hushed place. Everyone lowered their voice when they had a conversation and took the time to take it all in. When they first opened it, there was a railing along the side of the field of empty chairs, but people were constantly stepping over it in order to place things on the chairs, in the same way as they leave messages and flowers at the Vietnam Memorial and on countless war memorials in Britain. Eventually, the authorities decided to remove a section of the railing, thereby encouraging visitors to leave even more tributes. This means that everyone is now free to walk among the chairs, so I had a wander between them, reading the names and the short biographies as I went. Names like Katherine Louise Cregan, who was sixty years old and died in the Social Security offices on the first floor. Or, on one of the smaller chairs, Ashley Megan Eckles, who was only four years old. She also died on the first floor. Walking between the chairs was a deeply moving experience. It had a kind of Stonehenge feel to it. I wondered who these people were — Mary Anne Fritzler, Laura Jane Garrison, and Gabreon D.L. Bruce, who was only three months old. What lives they might have led if it hadn't been for that lunatic McVeigh.

On the north side of the memorial stands one of the most extraordinary things about the whole place. In an orchard, one tree is much older than all the others. This American elm, now known as the Survivor Tree, was the only tree that threw any shade across the parking lot outside the Alfred Murrah Building. Commuters would arrive early to secure one of the prime parking spots shaded by its branches, but otherwise it was largely taken for granted. When the bomb exploded, the tree, which is now about a hundred years old, was one of the few things left standing. However, it was heavily damaged by the bomb, with most of the branches ripped off the central trunk. Later, it was nearly chopped down as investigators recovered evidence hanging from its few remaining branches and embedded in its bark. The trunk itself was heavily scarred and blackened by the heat of the blazing cars that had been parked beneath it. Few thought it would survive.

But then, a year after the bombing, when victims' relatives, survivors and rescue workers gathered for a memorial ceremony by the tree, they noticed it was starting to bloom. The Survivor Tree became a symbol of defiance against the fools who perpetrate acts of extreme violence against society, and it is thriving again. The authorities now go to great lengths to protect it. For instance, when they were constructing the memorial and needed to build a wall close to the tree, one of its roots was placed inside a large pipe so that it could reach the soil beyond the wall without being damaged. They've even dug an underground space beneath it so that workers can monitor its health and maintain its very deep roots. On a wall around the Survivor Tree, an inscription reads, "The spirit of this city and this nation will not be defeated; our deeply rooted faith sustains us."

That tree was a lone witness to what happened on the morning of 19 April 1995, and I found it particularly moving. Every year, hundreds of its seeds are incubated, and the resultant saplings are distributed around the country and planted on the anniversary of the bombing, so there are now thousands of Survivor Trees growing all over America.

I found the memorial even more powerful than I thought it would be. It provided another example of people at their best — creating something wonderful out of something really horrific and terrible. For some reason, I felt particularly sorry for the five victims who were outside the Alfred Murrah Building that morning. There was an awful feeling of really bad luck — of just being in the wrong place at the wrong time. The other victims had no choice — they were in the building because that's where their jobs required them to be — but the five outside would have evaded the blast if they'd arrived five minutes later or left five minutes earlier.

Beside the memorial there is a small museum. One of its most extraordinary exhibits is a tape of a meeting that was taking place in a nearby building when the explosion occurred. You could listen to people doing business, then *whoomph* — the bomb went off. But I couldn't bring myself to listen to it. I didn't want to experience that.

I was very glad I made the effort to visit the memorial. I almost didn't go, because storms were forecast for that afternoon. But as soon as I arrived, the skies turned very calm. That seemed strangely appropriate.

The next morning I returned to the National Stock Yards to see Stan's cattle being auctioned. Keeping my fingers crossed that Stan's beasts would achieve the target price of about a thousand dollars apiece, I took a seat at the edge of the auction ring. Surrounded by farmers, cowboys, cattlemen and dealers in jeans, plaid shirts, boots and stetsons, I waited for the action to begin while everyone else gabbled on mobile phones to their bosses and clients.

Having been to a cattle auction in British Columbia a few years before, I wasn't particularly looking forward to repeating an experience I'd already had, but this one was brilliant. Physically, it wasn't that different from the Canadian auction. In Canada the cattle were herded behind the auctioneer's booth by cowgirls, who were extremely good at their job. In Oklahoma a couple of cowboys did the same job. But here the auctioneers' patter was something else. It was like listening to bluegrass banjo music. I've seen and heard a lot of auctioneers in the flesh and on film, but none of them could hold a candle to the Oklahoma boys. It was as if they were speaking in tongues or in some strange cow language. I couldn't understand a word, but it was absolutely smashing. The auctioneer would relate information about the cattle at such a rapid pace, yet so lyrically, that I felt I could listen to him all day.

"One twenty-six Western, one twenty-five, one twenty-six Western, one twenty-five," I thought he said, but I wouldn't have bet on it. Maybe that's what I sounded like to English audiences when I first came down from Scotland?

My only concern was that I could lose a lot of money just by twitching at the wrong moment, so after a while I left and got back on the trike.

Driving along the interstate for a short stretch, I had to pull over because I was getting scared. The wind was blowing me towards the hard shoulder and I didn't like it one little bit. So when I saw some billboards advertising the Cherokee Trading Post, I seized the opportunity to get off the road and investigate.

I mention everything that follows as a warning. If you decide to travel along Route 66, and you find yourself passing signs urging you to visit the buffalo at the Cherokee Trading Post, please take my advice. *Don't do it*. By all means fill up with their petrol or buy something from the gift shop. I bought some key rings and badges for my grandchildren, and if that's the sort of thing you're after, it's the place. But the buffalo will break your heart. And the campsite beside it will just make you feel like poor white trash.

I'd seen buffalo before and they were majestic, amazing animals with the most extraordinary eyes in huge, magnificent heads. But the pen at the Cherokee Trading Post was like a concentration camp for two miserable beasts that wandered around in their own shit, moth-eaten and ill behind double lines of barbed wire. Near the pen was a plastic buffalo with "In God We Trust" painted on the side of it. To the side were a couple of the worst totem poles I'd ever seen. I hate it when people do that kind of thing in the name of "culture". When they commercialise culture just to make a quick buck. It happens in Scotland, too, and this made me just as angry as when I see cartoons of Highlanders with kilts that are too short and big red noses. Where's the pride in that?

Buffalo are magnificent creatures, genuine Indian culture is a splendid thing, and both of them deserve much better than what was on offer at the Cherokee Trading Post. Buy your petrol there, and maybe even a key ring, but then get straight back in your car or on your bike and head on down Route 66 without a backward glance.

I wish I'd done that.

Now, though, the end of Oklahoma was in sight. And ahead lay the mighty high plains of Texas.

# CHAPTER
# TEN

# You'll See Amarillo . . .

Within a few miles of reaching the Lone Star State, the landscape started to look like Texas. I'd been rolling through the verdant hills and pastures of Oklahoma for hundreds of miles. Then, as I approached Texola — the last place in Oklahoma — the land flattened, the soil became scrubby, and I crossed the Texas state line into a lonely, empty, dusty nothingness.

Common wisdom has it that the 178 miles of Route 66 that run across the Texas Panhandle — that square block of land jutting up from the northwest corner of the state — is the most boring drive on the entire journey, if not the planet. There's some truth in that. Texas isn't a place that tolerates any deviation, and the road is as flat as a pancake and almost uniformly straight right through the state. Water towers, windmills, grain elevators, deserted towns and the whistling wind provided the only relief from the thrum of tyres on the road.

Distances between places stretched out as if Route 66 had been squeezed through a mangle, emerging flattened and with fewer interruptions. Sixteen miles into the state, I pulled into its first town, Shamrock.

Now, I always hesitate to criticise any town, as I grew up in one that most people would describe as a slum. But Shamrock, Texas, is a horrible place. Although it allegedly has a population of a couple of thousand people, it was like a ghost town when I visited. And, God help me, the hotel I stayed in was possibly the worst part of the whole place. Lying on my bed that night, I gave my current situation some thought. I didn't want to give anyone the impression that Route 66 was a glorious place where they could always get their kicks, because that patently wasn't true. The road was dying. Nevertheless, some wonderful people were trying to keep it alive, and in some places they were succeeding. In others, like Shamrock, they most certainly were not.

The next morning, I asked the waitress if I could have two fried eggs over easy and some bacon. It seemed a fairly modest request, but she just shrugged and said I could only have what was on the menu. The choice was between some soggy old thing that looked like an omelette or some wee shrivelled sausages — or both — served on a polystyrene plate with white plastic knives and forks and a polystyrene cup of coffee. Anyone who travels Route 66 needs to prepare themselves for a bit of that on the road. And if, like me, they're a bit spoiled, it gets hellish.

After breakfast, I went to look at a rather beautiful art deco building that had been restored. The U-Drop Inn — originally a restaurant and a petrol station — was one of the icons of the road. Built in the early 1930s from a design scratched in the dirt beside a nearby motel, it had a tall tower over the petrol station and a beautifully detailed café that was called "the swankiest of the swank eating places". It was also the only café for a hundred miles, so it was highly successful in its day. But like many of the establishments along Route 66, it sank into disrepair with the demise of the road. Thankfully, though, it was eventually recognised as architecturally significant and restored with the help of a local bank.

Apparently the U-Drop was best viewed at night, illuminated by its neon strips, but even in the day it was an impressive building from the outside. But it was no longer a petrol station or a restaurant. It wasn't even a museum. They had tarted it up, then shut it to the public, which confused the hell out of me.

I have a bit of a problem with art deco buildings in general. They're interesting when you drive past, but that tends to be the end of the story. Take the Hoover Building in West London. Everybody raves about it, but how many of them have been within five feet of it? They've all seen it from a car, but then *whoom*, they're past it. That's fine — no one needs to go up and lick it to like it. But art deco lovers get on my tits. They're the kind of people who read *Lord of the Rings* and like movies about little ginky punkies attacking wanky wonkies. I wouldn't let my corpse be taken to a movie like that. And I feel pretty much the same about art deco. It's for dead people. You'd be amazed at the number of funeral parlours that are art deco. That's all I have to say on the subject.

Moving on from Shamrock, I rejoined Route 66, which for most of its distance through Texas runs beside the interstate as a service road. The landscape, as flat and featureless as ever, rolled on. But the wind — *Holy Mother of Jesus* — was something else. Several times I thought I was going to be killed when side winds hit me, blowing me off course like a big hand sweeping me across the road. I was really frightened a couple of times, but after about half an hour we arrived in McLean under a very hot, blazing sun.

McLean was my mother's name, and although she had no claim on McLean, Texas, I wondered if there might be a connection. Pulling into the small town, I asked an old man in a truck if he knew where the name stemmed from, but he didn't have a clue.

"I have lived here for fifty-three years," he said. "It used to be a good town but it's pretty dead now."

I later discovered more than the old fella had learned over the previous half-century. Until 1901, the area where McLean now stands was nothing more than an unnamed cattle loading station on the Chicago Rock Island and Pacific Railroad (nicknamed the Cry and Pee, because of its initials). Then an English rancher, Alfred Row, donated some land near the loading station, thinking it might make a good site for a town. He was right — it grew quickly and within two years it had several banks, a post office, a newspaper, a wind-powered water pump, various stores and stables. By 1909, it was well established as a busy loading point for the railway, handling crops as well as animals, and requiring four telegraph operators to deal with commercial communications. Three years later, Alfred Row visited his relatives back home in England. For the return voyage, he booked a passage on a ship making its maiden voyage. That ship was the *Titanic*, and Alfred was last seen on an ice floe, frozen to death, hugging his briefcase.

McLean continued to prosper after his death, profiting from the oil boom in the 1920s and 1930s, and serving as the site of a camp for German prisoners-of-war in the 1940s. Any escapees were easily recaptured and were usually quite pleased to return after a few days on the bare plains of the Panhandle.

In 1984 McLean was the last Texan town to be bypassed by the interstate, and its sad decline began. Interstate 40 is about a mile away, but it seems like another world. Much of the town is now deserted. According to the mayor, who runs the Cactus Inn Motel, a marvellous old place, the population is significantly less than the official figure of eight hundred, although she was fully in favour of young people leaving the town to improve their prospects.

Nowadays, many of the buildings in McLean are abandoned. Petrol stations no longer pump gas, restaurants haven't served food for years, and plenty of houses have boarded-up windows and doors. On one tumbledown shop — above a fading mural featuring Elvis, a Chevy and a waitress on roller skates — a banner still proclaims McLean "the Heart of Old Route 66". I could imagine those days when the town was booming, when solid lines of cars streamed in from New Mexico to the west and Oklahoma to the east and the local petrol stations and diners were open around the clock to cater to travellers and tourists. Now it's a very different story. The main street is littered with the wreckage of the past and the concrete landscape is slowly being reclaimed by weeds. For photographers, it's a treasure trove of atmospheric pictures of urban decay, but I couldn't imagine what it must be like to live there.

Nevertheless, McLean still has several places that make it worth a visit. Next to the Cactus Inn Motel, the Red River Steakhouse serves steaks that are so juicy and tasty that many of its clientele regularly drive the hundred-mile round trip from Amarillo to eat there. It also has charming waitresses and a fantastic atmosphere, so it takes some beating. Inexpensive and mind-blowingly good, it proves that you can find good food on Route 66, even though it can be a long search sometimes.

McLean also has a lovely old art deco cinema, the Avalon, which has been restored by a Route 66 association. (Sadly, though, just like the U-Drop, it was closed when I visited.) And on Route 66 itself, McLean boasts the first Phillips 66 petrol station to be opened in Texas. Built in 1929, it served the town for more than fifty years, and it's now been beautifully restored by the Old Texas Route 66 Association. The bright colours of its freshly painted pumps were a stark contrast to the faded splendour of most of the rest of the town. It is apparently the most photographed petrol station on Route 66. It no longer pumps gas, though.

In what remains of the centre of town, McLean's main attraction is housed in a former bra factory that once gained the town the fantastic nickname "Uplift City". But it no longer specialises in lingerie; now it's a museum dedicated to barbed wire. That might sound daft, but barbed wire — or the devil's rope, as they call it — is a very important thing in Texas. I've always thought of the Colt and the Winchester as the tamers of the Wild West, but apparently barbed wire was much more important in bringing order to the wilderness.

Invented by a man called Samuel Glidden, who made millions when he became the Henry Ford of the "thorny fence", it was highly controversial at first. To the settlers of the American West, it provided security and stopped cattle barons from driving their herds across the settlers' land. But many others wished Glidden dead because his invention ended the era of free grazing on the range — which led to absolute misery out there.

This was the land of huge drovers' trails hundreds of miles in length. I'd passed a famous one the previous day, the Chisholm Trail, which led right across Texas and Oklahoma. There was also the Goodnight-Loving Trail, named after the cattlemen who used it to move longhorns from Texas all the way to Wyoming. For years, anyone could move cattle along these trails. But then people got selfish and started demanding fees, like tolls, to pass through their land. When that happened, all hell broke loose, and people started shooting each other. Anyone who put up a barbed-wire fence could stop herds in their tracks and charge for the water. This prompted countless feuds, many of which escalated into range wars, such as the Lincoln County War, which culminated in a gunfight at Blazer's Mill, a shootout that turned a young cattle guard called William McCarty into a fugitive better known as Billy the Kid.

With vigilante justice reigning supreme, much blood was shed and many communities were torn apart by the range wars. Eventually the lawmen settled the disputes, but by then the devil's rope had changed the nature of the West. So barbed wire already had a very unsavoury history, even before pictures of a corpse hanging over barbed wire and concentration camp inmates clutching barbed wire became symbols of the First and Second World Wars.

Within years of its invention, Glidden's wire spanned the nation from the Great Lakes to California, following a line very similar to that later taken by Route 66. Although Glidden ruthlessly sued anyone who infringed his patent, hundreds of rival designs were patented and many of them are now on display in McLean's museum. I'd never realised there were more than two thousand types of barbed wire, and that they even make barbed-wire jewellery and barbed-wire cocktail stirrers in Texas. The names of the different types are intriguing: Half McGlynn, Braided, Pitney, Evans, Elsie, Kitter and Ford. I'd always thought all barbed wire was the same — a series of double twists of wire around a long length of wire, seemingly designed to cut an L-shaped gash in your shorts when you were escaping from the orchard with your jumper full of apples and the farmer shouting, "Come back here yer bunch of bastards." But in the museum there were all sorts of designs on the walls, in cases and in cabinets. And people actually collect the stuff, too. They even have their own magazine, imaginatively titled *Barbed Wire Collector*.

There were lots of other novelties in the museum, like a hairy-arsed road runner with barbed wire for a tail, and a wee covered wagon made of spurred, rolled barbed wire by Sunny Mills of Amarillo. Looking at the First World War barbed wire reminded me of a song whose lyrics go something like, "If you want to see the captain, I know where he is". Then it continues for a few more lines of "I know where he is" before the refrain comes in: "He's hanging on the old barbed wire". Each verse follows the same pattern, except the person changes — "If you want to see the colonel", and so on. It's a bit of a boring song, but imagine singing it in the trenches when your friend was hanging upside down on the barbed wire. Grim times.

But by the time I'd scouted right around the museum, I had to admit it was a rather limited subject. All anyone really needs to know about barbed wire is that it can tear the arse out of your trousers, give a cow a good fright, entangle a Yorkshire terrier for life, and is nasty stuff made by greedy men.

Returning to the road and continuing my journey across the Texas Panhandle, at least there was no chance of getting lost. Route 66 closely follows the interstate, occasionally joining the freeway for a few miles at a time, and there were no other roads around to confuse me, which made a change. Quite how anyone riding solo on a motorbike through Missouri or Oklahoma manages to follow the road without getting lost is a mystery to me. In some parts, the path of Route 66 chops and changes so much that I frequently found myself lost, even with four of the production crew in a nearby car, all consulting satnavs, maps, books and all sorts of crap. Now, in the vast emptiness of Texas, at last I could relax and just follow the road.

Riding on, I passed several notable Route 66 landmarks. East of Groom, I spotted a leaning water tower that was one of the most photographed sights along the whole road — Texas's version of the Leaning Tower of Pisa. However, the Groom tower was purposely set at an angle by the owner of a local truck stop who had bought it to attract trade, so it was just another example of Route 66 tack in my book.

A mile or so further down the road stood a 190-foot-tall white crucifix that could be seen from up to twenty miles away on a good day. For a while, the crucifix, which was surrounded by life-sized statues of the Stations of the Cross, laid claim to being the tallest cross in the western hemisphere. However, the residents of Effingham, Illinois — which I'd passed nearly a thousand miles previously — put paid to Groom's boasting by erecting a cross that was eight feet taller. (Although, in the typical style of American superlatives, neither was as tall as the cross at the Valle de los Caidos in Spain, also in the western hemisphere the last time I checked.)

After about an hour, I reached Amarillo, appropriately known as "Cow Town". Near by, I passed a cattle ranch that has a larger population of cows than most towns have people in this part of America. Running alongside the road for several miles and stretching far into the distance, it is home to 28,000 beasts. The impact of the smell matched the scale of the operation, providing a succinct olfactory answer to the question: is this the way to Amarillo?

Those steers' ultimate fate was laid bare in Amarillo's temple to gluttony, the Big Texan Steak Ranch, a Western-style saloon restaurant with a twenty-five-foot neon cowboy standing by the side of the interstate. Here, the steak is free provided the diner eats it with a baked potato, salad, dinner roll and shrimp cocktail in less than sixty minutes. The catch is that the sirloin steak weighs in at seventy-two ounces, about the same as nine regular steak dinners, and you have to eat it on a raised platform under the gaze of the rest of the restaurant . . . and the world, via a live webcam. A few people, such as Klondike Bill, a professional wrestler, have managed *two* of the steak dinners in an hour. But since the Big Texan initiated its challenge, fewer than eight thousand of the fifty thousand who have attempted the single dinner have succeeded. So it's hardly surprising that the restaurant will ship in anyone wishing to accept the challenge — a small fleet of white stretch limos with longhorns on their bonnets wait outside to collect contenders free of charge from any hotel in Amarillo.

It was immediately obvious that Amarillo was in a much better state than many of the Texan towns I'd passed through earlier. It's a rather beautiful place, with a lot of impressive buildings and successful-looking people in nice shiny cars, so I reckoned it was a good place to stop.

The next day, riding through the west side of town, as Route 66 headed back into the wilds, I pulled over to have a quick look at what some people call Route 66's version of Stonehenge. Smack in the middle of miles of empty flatland, on a giant, windswept wheat farm, stands a line of ten Cadillacs that look like they have plunged from high in the sky into the earth. For reasons best known to the artist, each of the semi-submerged Caddies is arranged at a slant on an angle exactly the same as the Great Pyramid of Giza. It might sound bizarre, but I think it's an outstanding piece of art.

The site belongs to a local wheat farmer, artist and philanthropist called Stanley Marsh 3 (that's the way he writes it), who enlisted some mates who were part of an art collective called Ant Farm to build Cadillac Ranch. Stan created it in the 1970s to represent the American love of automobiles and freedom, and it has to be seen to be believed. I had seen it in many books and brochures, but when I saw the real thing with the sun shining on it, my heart missed a beat. I fell in love with it.

What's really great about Cadillac Ranch is that Stan encourages people to graffiti on it, so it changes every day. Every now and then, Stan resprays the Cadillacs in plain paint to create a blank canvas, allowing the public to start again from scratch, drawing and writing whatever they like on it. I came prepared with a spray can of black gloss, but I was quite nervous. Having seen so many pictures of it, it felt odd to be walking towards it. The closer I got, the more I thought it was a cracking thing. It's a fairly simple work of art — just a row of ten cars poking out of the ground — but it changes shape in really interesting ways, depending on how you look at it.

What really appeals to me about Cadillac Ranch is that it's a big two-fingered salute to the kind of people I really don't like — the beige-ists of the world, the kind of people who get all upset about artwork that they can't buy, hang on their walls or give to their Auntie Jeanie for Christmas. When they see something like Cadillac Ranch, they don't know what to do with it. It brings out things in them that they find disturbing. I like disturbing people like that. I grew old without growing up and I'm very proud of it. I don't give a toss what anybody thinks.

I'm so full of admiration for Stan and his creation. It was one thing to have an idea like Cadillac Ranch, but quite another to go ahead and build it.

But then, as I got within striking distance of the line of lovely, multicoloured cars, their patches and streaks of paint gleaming in the sun, I spotted something that made my eyes stick out on stalks.

"To make love to me, I know it will never be Billy Connolly," it said.

*What?*

I read it again: "To make love to me, I know it will never be Billy Connolly."

How in the name of God had that ended up on the side of a Cadillac? I thought that Stan himself must have done it. Then, looking down the line of Caddies, I saw my name repeated again and again.

"Billy + Amarillo."

"Billy C."

"Billy, see you Billy."

"Billy Dilly."

"BC."

"Welcome to the windy city, Billy C."

It was freakish. I wanted to look at them sideways, see them from different angles, just to get my head around them. That entire fantastic artwork had been prepared specially for me. What a lucky chap I was. And, God, this guy was good.

Cadillac Ranch had turned out to be the last thing on Earth I had thought it would be: a shrine to me. Well . . . I was all pleased with myself. How many people had an artwork on the Texan plains customised for their benefit? Holy Moly. It left me speechless. It wasn't just fabulous. It was amazing.

With my spray can of black paint, I added a few touches of my own. Just an exclamation mark on one set of initials and a few other bits and pieces. It was great fun, but I soon discovered that I wasn't a very good graffiti artist. It's not as easy as it looks. Ending up with dirty black fingers covered in paint, I didn't make too good a job of it.

From Cadillac Ranch, I rode round to Ant Farm's studio, where some of the artists were working on projects that Stan would later install in various parts of Amarillo. One of the wonderful things that they do is make road signs that are meaningless. They have slogans such as "I have known a slut", with the idea being that people should just stumble upon them when they're driving along or hanging out in a public place. They call this the Dynamite Museum — the "only museum in the world without walls".

When I arrived, an artist called Drew showed me around and suggested I should paint one of their rogue signs.

"What do you want to paint?" he said.

"I have no real idea," I said. "I had a thought last night and the one I came up with was, 'She kissed me once but it melted'."

"For your sign? That *is* good." He smiled. "Are you going to draw a picture or are you just going to do words?"

"I can't really draw."

"I can't either."

"You can't?"

"So what inspired you to do the Route 66?"

"I think it was just rock'n'roll. It seems to mean more to Europeans than it does to Americans. It seems to have more sort of . . . magic."

"I think you're right. I think it's one of those things we just take for granted. To Europeans, it is what they associate America with — wide-open spaces and hitting the road. In America, it is our lifestyle, but we don't really appreciate it."

In the end, I painted a cartoon of my face. Beneath it, I wrote, "I have got biscuits". It meant nothing at all, but then I started to worry that I'd done what I mentioned earlier — unwittingly absorbed another comic's material. I was so concerned that I phoned my daughter, who works in a New York art gallery. I asked her if she'd once shown me some T-shirts, one of which might have said, "I have got donuts at home". Maybe that had been floating around in the ether and I'd just adapted it a bit. But my daughter assured me that "I have got biscuits" meant nothing to her. Then I met the woman in whose garden my road sign would be placed and she seemed delighted, so I was very pleased.

I think the rogue road signs are wonderful and ought to be expanded worldwide. My original idea had been to paint a sign that said, "Beware of Route 666". I'm glad I didn't do that — it's kind of dark and strange. But I do wish I'd gone with "She kissed me once but it melted". I don't know what it means, but I like it.

As I said to Drew, I was nervous about drawing, although I am an artist. I'll say that again: I am an artist. Once you admit that, you get good. I admitted it a long time ago, and I got good. I had noticed some rappers calling themselves artists — the kind of rappers who sold stuff on the street in New York, just regular guys. They would ask, "Would you like to buy my art?" I thought that was a good stance to take. Gerry Rafferty tried to instil the same sort of thing into me when we were in the Humblebums — that what we did was art.

Everyone else did junk, he used to say, but we did art. And I believed that attitude was true.

I also really believe Lenny Bruce's theory that a comedian is a man who thinks funny things and says them, while an actor is a man who learns funny things and says them. They're as funny as each other, but only one of them is a comedian. Going to bars and learning other people's jokes then telling them in other bars does not make you a comedian — it makes you an actor . . . or a thief. It's just being a rip-off artist. But if someone thinks funny things and is brave enough to say them on stage, then they have entered the world of art. Whatever that might be.

I was mulling over all of this in the Ant Farm's studio, but I have to admit that I was starting to tie myself up in knots. I had entered that realm that we Scots call *wunnert*. "Aye, he's a wee bit *wunnert*," we say. It means lost and wondering, and it was old Uncle Willy who got wunnert: "Aye, you'll get used to him, but he's a wee bit *wunnert*, you know? He might take a piss in a frying pan, but don't worry about him. He means well."

It was clearly time to change the subject, and luckily I had the perfect thing. Somebody had told me the funniest joke a few days earlier: "Why do they give old men in old folks' homes Viagra? To stop them rolling out of bed." I thought that was the funniest thing ever!

After another fifty miles through the mind-numbingly flat and plain landscape of this flattest and plainest part of Texas, I pulled up outside a café in the town of

Adrian. I had reached a point in the journey that anyone who was fascinated by facts, figures and statistics — which I'm not at all — would regard as highly significant.

A sign by the side of the road said it all: "Los Angeles 1139 miles — Chicago 1139 miles". I'd arrived at the exact midpoint of Route 66. It was just like anywhere else along the journey, but at the same time it was a funny position to be in. I'd been on the road for longer than I had left to run. It had taken me four weeks to reach the midpoint, and I had less than three weeks remaining. Arriving at the halfway point made sense of the road and gave me a feeling of achievement.

The café — called the Midpoint Café, of course — is famous for its ugly pies. Personally, I thought they should be far uglier than they were — all big and lumpy and burned. Like a lot of things on Route 66, there was a lot of talk, a lot of bragging, but not much when you got there. Compared to many pies I'd eaten in Scotland over the years, these were very good-looking pies. I had a cup of tea and a peach cobbler, and was a wee bit disappointed that its ugliness didn't come up to scratch. Maybe they used to be properly ugly and now they were concentrating on making them nice. That would be a mistake. I was starting to like the shabby side to Route 66. Once I accepted that the road's best days were well behind it, it was much easier to accept its limitations and get on with having a good time.

My next stop was the last town in Texas and the first in New Mexico — it straddles the border. This was a particularly poignant destination because, in its heyday,

Glenrio was a thriving and hectic pit stop on Route 66. Some of the scenes in John Ford's film version of *The Grapes of Wrath* were shot there, but it has never been a highly populated place. At its peak in the 1940s, it had a population of just thirty. But its famous motel had a big neon sign that proclaimed either, "First Motel in Texas" or "Last Motel in Texas", depending on how you looked at it. And the busy post office straddled the state line, with the depot receiving mail in Texas and the office distributing it in New Mexico.

Then, one day in September 1973, Interstate 40 opened. That day, Glenrio died. The stream of tourists who had flowed through the town along Route 66 en route to California or from the Pacific coast towards the American heartland dwindled to a trickle, then stopped altogether.

By 1985, that post office was the only business left open. It served a population of two. Today, among a string of dead or dying towns along hundreds of miles of the old road, Glenrio is the deadest of all. It now has just one resident, a softly spoken mother of two, who lives among the critters and the tumbleweed.

Roxann Travis told me she was in Glenrio on the day the highway opened. Her father's petrol station became an immediate casualty. Now in her sixties, she is happy to live there alone in the house in which she was born, and she has no desire to move on.

"My dad moved house here when I was a baby and built the station and the diner," she told me. "Every summer all the traffic would be lined up the highway, both directions. It was very, very busy. He would have us go wash the windshields and check the oil so they would be ready to pump the gas and keep them moving through."

Her mum and dad used to keep horses across the road from one of their two petrol stations, but it was hard to get to them because there were so many cars. A few years later, when Roxann was raising her own kids, they could play ball on the road. Nowadays, you could take a nap on it. You'd only be disturbed when occasional tourists, like me, stopped by to gawp at the ghost town.

"It must seem very strange to you," I said, "because you must see your dad and your siblings when you look at this place."

"I do, yes. And it's real sad to watch it crumble."

"So, how long did it take for the town to die with the coming of the interstate?"

"Four or five years, I guess. The Texas Longhorn — a café, station and motel down there — was the last to go."

For a while, Roxann lived in Glenrio with her husband, Larry, who commuted to their business in Adrian — another petrol station. But in 1976 the gas station was raided and Larry was forced to his knees and shot through the back of his head. The killer went on to murder a second man the same day at another petrol station in the Texas Panhandle.

"How does it feel to live here all alone?" I said.

"I'm used to it. I'm fine with it. I like the peace and quiet."

234

Roxann has six dogs to keep her company, but they make the noise of twelve.

"Do you get visitors? Do any of the old people who used to live here ever come back?"

"Not really, no, because some are scattered out in the country. There was another house next door and they moved to Lubbock and they never looked back."

"So, where do you get your groceries?"

"I usually go to Amarillo, but for a short trip, if I don't have that much time, I'll go to Tucumcari. That's forty miles."

"Well, I really admire you. I really admire your guts. I don't know if I could do it."

Roxann showed me some pictures of Glenrio in its heyday. With a barbecue restaurant, various diners, a hamburger joint, several petrol stations and motels, it was a buzzing, vibrant place.

"They're all sitting having their dinner and they look like they're laughing," I said, looking at one of the snaps. "They all look so happy sitting eating their hamburgers. Little did they know what was going to happen. It just happened in a flash really, didn't it?"

"It went downhill fast."

"What made you decide to stay?"

"It's home!"

We both laughed at the absurdity of it. Roxann is a lovely woman, who doesn't feel at all blighted by her situation.

"But don't you need other people round you to make it a home?"

"My daughter comes every chance she gets. My son drives for a trucking company and he stops by pretty often. And I like to read, do my garden and sew and mess with the animals." Her daughter-in-law couldn't understand how she could live in Glenrio and wanted her to move to a town, which she thought would be safer. But Roxann said, "I don't think town is safe. I feel safer out here. With my dogs, no one's walked in that yard in a while without me knowing."

"Well, you certainly seem very happy."

"I like it here. I plan to stay as long as I'm able."

"Why not? You could be the mayor as well, if you like."

"People tease me about that. I'm the mayor, the sheriff and everything else."

"Postmistress . . . and, of course, you're the entire police force as well."

For a while, Roxann shared the town with a young cowboy, who was living in a deserted building, but he didn't last long. Now the only regular visitor was a cow that had broken out of a nearby ranch and was harmlessly roaming the streets.

I thought she was a wonderful, brave woman with a brilliant attitude. I'd found another friend.

As she said, this was her home. What more could anyone want?

# CHAPTER
# ELEVEN

## Albuquerque and Tucumcari, Make New Mexico Extraordinary

Glenrio took me into New Mexico, the sixth of eight states I would pass through on Route 66. Extremely beautiful and more than a little mystical, New Mexico is where Route 66's origin in the cattle tracks and wagon trails of the Wild West becomes obvious. Here, Route 66 looks more like a ribbon suspended from the vast, deep-blue sky than a road built on the ground. Now the distances were truly vast, the destinations remote and the rides long, hot and hard.

Almost perfectly square in shape, New Mexico has more history than any other state along Route 66, with Native American Pueblo dwellings dotted along the road. But it also has its fair share of the bizarre, outlandish and freaky often found along the Mother Road. South of Albuquerque, for instance, there's a town named after a 1950s radio quiz show. The programme's producers offered to rock up and record the next episode anywhere that was prepared to change its name to the title of the show. That's why some seven thousand people now live in a town called Truth or Consequences rather than Hot Springs.

From Glenrio, I rode straight through to Santa Fe, a distance of nearly 250 miles. Once again, I was buffeted by a side wind that was beyond belief. It blew me all over the damn place. Sharing the road with big rigs when there were side winds was a double-edged sword. Sometimes I thought the wind would sweep me under one of them and I'd be squashed into the tarmac. At other times, a truck would come along and shield me from the wind. But this was a finely judged thing — if a gust slipped under the truck, or between the truck and its trailer, my shield would become a lethal hazard. I had to keep my wits about me all the time.

Arriving in Santa Fe, I was booked into a hotel in which my wife and I had stayed some years previously. It hadn't changed a bit. Santa Fe is a beautiful town. It's full of tourist traps, but I don't mind that. The stores sell turquoise jewellery and all sorts of beaded things, some of them outstandingly fabulous and very expensive, but that doesn't detract from the fact that it's a lovely, relaxed and relaxing place. And the food is great — a blessed relief after all the crap I'd been eating for weeks.

Strictly speaking, Santa Fe wasn't even on Route 66 during the road's heyday. When the route was first designated in 1926, everyone expected it to go straight through the town because it was the capital of New Mexico and where the Pecos and Santa Fe trails met. And indeed, for the first eleven years of Route 66, it turned northwest at Santa Rosa, headed up to Santa Fe, then turned back down south to Albuquerque.

However, in 1937, A.T. Hannett, the Governor of New Mexico, was not re-elected and he blamed a ring of powerful lawyers and influential landowners based in Santa Fe. As an act of defiance against this cabal, he re-routed Route 66 directly to Albuquerque, bypassing Santa Fe altogether. With just a few months to go before the new governor was inaugurated, Hannett forced the road builders to work seven days a week, including Christmas, to construct a new highway through virgin landscape. The road cut across public and private land, showing complete disregard for ownership rights. By the time the new governor was installed, it was too late for him to do anything about it. Drivers welcomed the change, which shaved more than ninety miles off Route 66 between Santa Rosa and Albuquerque, but in the end Santa Fe benefited, too. The city grew on its own merits, without relying on Route 66 traffic, so when the road was decommissioned Santa Fe was unaffected, unlike most places along the route. Its isolation also meant it developed in a unique way. It's a beautiful city of adobe buildings, with none taller than three storeys. I'd strongly advise you to make the detour off Route 66 and have a look.

I'd come to Santa Fe to experience a miracle. At least, that's what I'd been told. I don't believe in miracles or the supernatural, but I don't have a problem with anyone who does. So I was quite looking forward to my visit to the Loretto Chapel, a charming former Roman Catholic church in the shadow of St

Francis Cathedral on the fringes of the downtown area. The oddest thing about the chapel is that it has no priests. Introduced to someone who was described as the owner, my immediate thought was: What do you mean, "the owner"?

It turned out that the Loretto Chapel had been decommissioned — it's now a business that charges an entrance fee. But anyone can still get married there, if they hire a priest, which seems kind of odd to me. Anyway, it's a very pretty place, built in the 1870s in the Gothic revival style for an order of nuns called the Sisters of Loretto. At the top of the church is a choir loft, a very nice and large one. But when the building was finished and the nuns looked up at the loft, they noticed a quite serious problem with it: there was no staircase, so they had no way to get up there. Apparently, the architect had died suddenly when drafting the blueprint for the building, and then the builders hadn't noticed that the staircase was missing from the plans.

Faced with a bit of a dilemma, the nuns prayed day and night for nine days. On the tenth day, a guy showed up at the chapel. Riding a donkey, he had long hair and a beard, and he offered to do the job for them. In what seemed a ridiculously short amount of time — just three months — he built a spiral staircase that led up to the choir loft. He then promptly disappeared before anyone could determine his identity or even pay him for his work. Mysterious, eh?

The staircase is certainly very beautiful. I had a close look and couldn't see a single nail mark or any trace of

240

glue. And I found it difficult even to find any joints (that is, the carpentry kind of joint: I don't want to suggest that the carpenter was smoking dope while he was making the staircase). Apparently it's all held together with dowels, but it's still a remarkable feat of construction. Unlike most spiral staircases, it has no central support and it isn't attached to a wall. That said, the owners of the church very rarely let anyone use it, so I had to wonder if it was as strong and stable as it looked.

The Catholic Church eventually declared that the creation of this staircase was a miracle, purely because some people reckoned the bearded guy was St Joseph. It was also claimed that he used only a small number of primitive tools, such as a square, a saw and some warm water — although how anyone knew that when he supposedly worked entirely alone and behind closed doors might be a miracle in itself. It's also alleged that the staircase is constructed entirely from non-native wood, yet no one saw any lumber delivered during the three months that the carpenter was in the chapel. These mysteries had kept 250,000 pilgrims a year guessing, and the entrance-fee dollars pouring into the tills. The church was so geared up for tourists it was almost silly.

As with many "miracles", there are rational explanations for several of the staircase's apparent mysteries. For instance, experts have pointed out that plenty of other spiral staircases don't have a central support; and anyway, the Loretto Chapel's staircase seems to have a concealed support that acts like a central pole. Also, its double-helix shape, like a DNA molecule, will lend it some strength — although this design probably makes it bounce like a giant spring, which might explain why the owners don't let people walk up and down it.

Even supposing that the legend is true and St Joseph did build the spiral staircase, I still have one big unanswered question: how did the builders construct the choir loft? It's a big, high platform, so how did they build it without a staircase to get up there? Did they hang upside down from the roof? That's what I wanted to know.

Seeing the crowds inside the church made me think that some people seem to be desperate for miracles. They really long for them to be true. Personally, I like Thomas Jefferson's attitude that miracles spoil religion because they are obviously tosh and go against nature. Jefferson even went to the trouble of writing an alternative Bible with no miracles or other supernatural events in it.

I left Santa Fe and headed even further away from Route 66, northwest into the mountains, through a landscape that looked like it had been built by giants. The freeway up to Los Alamos, some 7,320 feet above sea level, was one of the most extraordinary roads I'd ever seen. If European road builders were faced with a similar challenge, they would cut the road into the side of the mountain, making it wind up the incline in a series of hairpin bends. Not so in New Mexico, where they unashamedly and pragmatically built the six-lane

Los Alamos Highway straight up and through the valley.

For many years, Los Alamos was a secret town that didn't officially exist. The locals carried driving licences that had no names, addresses or signatures on them, just always the same occupation — engineer — which indicated to the police that the holder was conducting secret government work. Cut off from the outside world, this small town in the mountains was home to the Manhattan Project — America's top-secret effort, with participation from Britain and Canada, to develop the first atomic bomb during the Second World War.

When I arrived in Los Alamos, I was flabbergasted to find it was a beautiful country town — clean, well laid out, with fantastic facilities and crystal-clear mountain air. It also has the highest concentration of residents with Ph.D.s anywhere in the world, and consequently the highest per capita income of any American city (and the highest house prices).

It was a beautiful day, the kind you dream about, as I rode into the centre of town, where a string of handsome wood and stone lodges make up the Los Alamos Historical Museum. In 1942 these mountain lodges were requisitioned by the military from Los Alamos Ranch School, a private boarding school. The site was chosen for the Manhattan Project because of its isolation, access to water, and location on a table mountain that allowed all entrances to be secured. Originally referred to only as Site Y, it later became the Los Alamos Scientific Laboratory and, after the war, the Los Alamos National Laboratory. In a strip of buildings known as Bathtub Row — because they were the only houses in Los Alamos with baths — stood the school's Fuller Lodge and Big House. Both were social gathering places for Manhattan Project personnel, while other nearby buildings were used for housing.

At one of the historic lodges I met Jack Aeby, who used to be a driver for the project's scientists, many of whom had codenames in this no-questions-asked town. Sitting beside him was Frank Osvath, a machinist on the project. Both men are now in their eighties. I asked Frank what he did exactly.

"Can't you tell by looking at me?" he said. "I glow in the dark. I machined uranium for thirty-nine years."

"You did not!" I was amazed.

"I did."

"Is that a safe thing to do?"

"It was mostly depleted uranium. Enriched uranium — I just did a little bit of that."

"How did you feel about being part of manufacturing an atomic bomb? Did you know that's what you were doing?"

"They came looking for machinists at the Ford Motor Company in Detroit and about a dozen of us came out here. They told us we would build something that might end the war, but we didn't know for sure what it was."

"Really? Well, it certainly did that."

"They said they couldn't tell us how long we would be here. We would be restricted from travelling and our letters would be censored, so it was quite a restriction to come out here. Our names were changed; they gave us false names. My folks, who lived in Detroit, used to write me letters and they were censored coming in and going out. My folks came from Hungary and I wrote them in Hungarian. Those letters couldn't be censored here, so they sent them to Washington, DC, then back here, and then they delivered them to my folks. So it took a very long time."

I turned to Jack. "And you were a driver?"

"I would get the people who were coming up here," he said, "take them to 109 East Paulos, which was the headquarters in Santa Fe, and they would be met by military personnel for their induction to work up here."

"Were you allowed to speak to them about the project?"

"They all arrived with assumed names, like everybody else that worked here, and they never remembered their names, but I'd taken physics long enough to know who they really were and I'd even remind them what their codename was when I put them in the car and brought them up."

It must have been a most interesting time. I was especially fascinated by the museum's pictures of people having parties, wearing funny hats and holding drinks in their hands, and presumably falling in love in the evenings, while by day they were building the first atom bomb.

"We weren't allowed to travel, so we had to have our parties here," said Frank. "We ate our lunch here in this room. One time I came down and six men sitting around that table started to sing the Hungarian national anthem. So I joined in and sang with them.

When we got through singing I went over to talk to some of those fellows and one of them said his name was Edward Teller. He was the father of the hydrogen bomb. He played that piano over there several times to entertain us."

I found that kind of strange. There was no reason on earth why these people shouldn't have played the piano or held parties or fallen in love or got drunk, but it still seemed incongruous.

Jack took the picture of the first atom bomb test explosion at the Trinity test site, White Sands, south of Albuquerque, on 16 July 1945. It's one of the ten most published photographs in the world and I've always thought it's extraordinary — the mushroom cloud billowing in the desert — but Jack told me there's something wrong with it. He pointed to a print of the famous picture on the wall. "It's facing the wrong way. It was taken on a slide and whoever made that picture turned it over." Then he pointed at a whisp of smoke on the right of the picture. "That little plume", he said, "should be on the left. It belongs on the other side."

"It doesn't matter much, does it?" said Frank.

"I was back at base camp when I took it," said Jack, "on the south side of everything. So everybody thought that any good picture must have come from the technical staff at the bunker on the north. I'm strictly an amateur; I didn't have any technical knowledge."

The night before the explosion, Frank and a group of friends climbed a mountain called South Baldy, the highest peak of the Magdalena Mountains in central New Mexico, and slept at an altitude of ten thousand feet to ensure they would get a good view of the detonation the next morning, but when the appointed hour arrived, they thought the bomb had failed to detonate.

"We thought it didn't work," said Frank. "We knew what time it was supposed to go off in the morning and it didn't go off. They delayed it because of the weather. So all of my friends crawled back into their sleeping bags, but I was sitting up, watching the sun come up from the other direction. All of a sudden a flash went off and then I heard the sound come in later. All the others woke up and watched it; it was quite an exciting experiment. We looked down at it from above and saw the mushroom building up below us."

Their stories were extraordinary. What a privilege to have been present at such a momentous event in history, even if there was something quite horrific about it. "How did you feel?" I said. "Did it fill you with fear or joy or horror? You must be one of the few people on earth who have watched an atomic explosion for pleasure."

"Right," said Frank. "And unofficially — from a high place."

"As a matter of fact," said Jack, "there was a lottery going and people bet on the yield that it was going to give. I guessed at about twelve kilotons, which was pretty close, and it was estimated all the way from zero to infinity. There were those who thought it would set the atmosphere on fire and melt the earth."

I wondered how that person felt when the explosion took place. He probably ran off to hide under his bed somewhere.

"After the explosion, we came down the mountain to have breakfast in Socorro," said Frank. "The newspaper already had the headlines out: 'Accidental Explosion'. They thought it was an ammunition dump. We knew it was a lie, but they had to publish something because everybody around there heard that explosion and saw the big flash."

"Were they aware of radiation and fallout?" I said. "Or did it take them by surprise?"

"They knew there were going to be fission products and that they had to go someplace. The wind was blowing, so they could trace it across the country, and they interviewed people who were in that path. There were cattle that died and some people got mild exposures, but nothing serious."

Frank and Jack both looked in very good health, especially considering all their years of work on the project. A few weeks after the explosion, Jack was part of a group that dug up some of the radioactive remnants at the test site in search of new elements. In the debris they discovered a few new isotopes, including plutonium.

Then Frank told me something astonishing. "A friend of mine is the only person in the world who saw the first three atomic bombs. He not only went to Trinity, he also flew on the airplanes that dropped the bombs on Hiroshima and Nagasaki. He invented the trigger for the bomb so he was asked to go along in the airplanes to set it up when they got close. And then he dropped it. When he came back, I asked him, 'How did you feel, killing so many people?' He said at first it was a very bad feeling, but then he prayed a lot about it and realised that many of our soldiers wouldn't have to go there to continue fighting the Japanese. The war would end, so he saved a lot of lives. He was satisfied with what he did."

"Was anybody troubled with guilt?"

"A large number were," said Jack. "They circulated a petition not to use the bomb aggressively but to demonstrate its power at a deserted island someplace. There were literally hundreds of signatures on that petition, but it never reached Roosevelt. Secretary Byrnes [James F. Byrnes, the US Secretary of State in 1945] blocked it. He didn't want Roosevelt to see that."

"Really?" I was amazed.

"He had already decided with the military and all," said Jack. "They may have been correct, I'm not questioning that. But, yes, there was guilt. A lot of it."

I was very glad to hear that. Not glad that people felt guilty exactly, but it would have been deeply disturbing if no one had even cared about it.

One of the lodges had been the home of Robert Oppenheimer, who led the Manhattan Project and is widely regarded as the architect of the bomb. He apparently served the best dirty martinis in town, but he never came to terms with being the person who unleashed the horrific power of the atom bomb. Immediately after the test, he admitted that he had "become the destroyer of worlds".

Nevertheless, Jack said there "were a lot of fun sides to the pre-explosion bit. Working here was fun, a great deal of pleasure in finding things out. It was exciting looking for something very new. That question of how might it work and could we build one? And then: 'Wow, we did it!' That kind of thing. But it wasn't anybody's idea to blow up people with it. They wanted to end the war, no question about that. Certainly a demonstration would have been possible, inviting everybody in, but that suggestion didn't work. Nobody accepted that outside of the people who were concerned."

Personally, I wish the ones who drew up the petition had won. America has been left in a very weak position because it has used an atomic weapon in anger. "How could America say to Iran, 'You mustn't do it' when they've done it twice?" I asked.

"Absolutely right," said Jack. "And it's worse than that. We will not sign a non-first-use treaty with anybody."

That made me shiver.

Frank and Jack clearly had misgivings about where the world had been led by the Manhattan Project. They'd both also been involved in the development of the hydrogen bomb. Frank was sent to New York State, where they assembled the outside steel case of the new, much bigger bomb, but it was so large that it wouldn't fit under some of America's railway bridges, so it was sent by ship to the Pacific. Frank wasn't present at the detonation, but Jack took a picture of it.

"I was in a health physics group that kept people from hurting themselves with all that radiation around," said Jack. "I happened to be there at Operation Bravo. It destroyed an island completely. It's gone."

Eventually, Frank joined an outfit that cleaned up thirty-two FUAES — Formerly Utilized Atomic Energy Sites. "The big first hydrogen bomb left a great big hole in the ocean," he said. "Water filled it up right quick, but the hole was still there. All the debris from years of testing on Enewetak Atoll was dumped down that hole and covered over with concrete. I worked on that job for years. I was the garbage man."

Both Frank and Jack were intensely interested in the outcome of the latest Strategic Arms Limitation Talks that were going on at the time. "I think there are some level-headed people that realise that we've got a gadget we cannot use," said Jack. "That's what we need to realise."

Even though I didn't know much about the subject, it seemed kind of incongruous to have weapons that would wipe us all out if they were ever used.

"You use it, you're dead," said Jack. "That's why there's just no point in it."

It was fascinating to meet these two men in Los Alamos, and they were an absolute delight. I had expected them to be totally atomic, all for the atom bomb, so I was very pleasantly surprised to discover that they weren't. I had one last question: "When you were living here in the war, was there any sneaking out going on?"

"It was easy enough to do," said Jack. "Our travel outside was monitored and restricted to visits to Santa Fe. However, I had a girlfriend in Phoenix, who I managed to meet at least once. They knew about it down there because the bomb went off and she wrote me a letter and said, 'Aha, a little bigger than you thought, eh?' The censors read that and I didn't have an answer."

The next day I rode to Albuquerque, a short hop down the pre-1937 Route 66 route from Sante Fe. Again, a lot of the buildings are low-rise adobe structures, but Albuquerque lacks Santa Fe's charm. At first I thought it was a nothing kind of town, just a one-street joint with some dodgy stores, but then I visited the Rattlesnake Museum. A lot of good things were happening in the square outside the museum, and the place seemed to be buzzing, with live music and busy restaurants.

The museum itself is owned and run by Bob Myers, a self-confessed rattler fanatic. I'm not that fond of snakes myself, so I quite like the idea of one that warns you it's there. That rattling noise, which sounds like a high-pitched footballer's rattle, is a very succinct way of saying, "I'm scared! Don't come any nearer. Get lost." And, of course, it's never a good idea to go near scared animals. The old prospectors who roamed the Wild West and played guitar around camp fires at night used to keep rattlesnake tails inside their guitars. If a thief lifted the guitar, he'd hear the *tikka-tikka-tikka* of the tail, think there was a snake inside, and drop it.

Stacked to the rafters with tanks containing rattlesnakes, the museum is fascinating. Bob had a stick with which he prodded some of the snakes to make them rattle properly. There's no other noise quite like it, and anyone would recognise it instantly. If you hear it, you should stop dead in your tracks, then slowly back up the way you came and get the hell out of there. As Bob told me, rattlesnakes are not aggressive and they're much more scared of us than vice versa, but if they're cornered and unable to escape to safety, they will invariably retaliate.

Many of the snakes were beautifully camouflaged and almost impossible to spot against the rocks and sand. I was very impressed. The canebrake rattlesnake reminded me of Tom Waits, the only person I've ever known to talk about them. Then there was the mottled rock rattlesnake, the black tailed rattler, a southwestern speckled rattlesnake and a panamint rattler, which was the most difficult to spot of all. Most of them gave me the willies.

Once, in an earlier TV show, a python was placed around my neck. She was very nice, and kept whispering in my ear. I told the keeper that I thought his snake must fancy me, and he said, "It's a boy." It didn't seem quite the same once I knew it was a gay snake. And in the movie of *Lemony Snicket's A Series of Unfortunate Events* I had a snake wrapped round my wrist as I played a musical instrument. At one point in the film, I said goodbye to the snake and it kissed me. It was a magical moment, but I wasn't inclined to repeat it with any of those rattlers, just in case one of them tried to bite my face off.

Approaching the New Mexico — Arizona state line, I crossed the continental divide, the line that splits where America's rivers flow — either to the Pacific or to the

Gulf of Mexico and the Atlantic. Then I spent a night at the El Rancho Hotel in Gallup, where stars from Hollywood's golden age like John Wayne, Katharine Hepburn and Spencer Tracy stayed while making cowboy movies in the nearby mountains.

Moving on the next morning, a sign caught my eye. "Indian Ruins", it said. Hmm, I thought, that might be interesting. But, as so often on Route 66, the sign promised much more than the place delivered. Pulling in, I discovered the ruins had long since gone. Flooded or possibly blown away, only a few markings remained in the dirt. There was a trinket shop, but it had nothing different from all of the other Indian gift shops along this stretch of the road. So I got back on the trike and resumed the relentless journey west, hoping to reach Holbrook, Arizona, before too long.

Winona — which, like Gallup, is name-checked in the song — lay just beyond Holbrook and everything seemed to be going well. Then, all of a sudden, we ran out of Route 66. In itself, this was nothing new: Route 66 had stopped or disappeared plenty of times before. One moment there would be tarmac; then there would be gravel and scree, or a dead end. The crew and I would consult our maps, fire up the satnav, have a wee discussion, then go in search of Route 66. Usually this entailed doing a U-turn, retracing our steps for a few miles and then taking a different road. It happened a lot.

But this time it was different.

Carefully edging the bike around — avoiding the side of the road, which disappeared into nothingness — the revs suddenly shot up and the bike went crazy. My hand was stuck. The throttle wouldn't respond. I tried to calm the engine, but everything was moving too fast. Even now, I don't know exactly what happened.

Fighting the jammed throttle, I spun out of control. The bike wheeled around, somersaulted, then bounced off me. The big rear wheels went right over the top of me and something slammed into my ribs. My knee thumped hard into the road — a crunch of bone and flesh on tarmac. Then I was lying on my back, staring at the sky. As I lay there, I wondered just how much damage I'd done to myself.

Desperate to stand up and just get on with it — because, of course, I'm a man of steel, a real hero — I was immediately told not to move, to stay absolutely still. Mike, the director, insisted that I must continue to lie down. He wouldn't even loosen my bloody helmet, the bastard.

While I waited for an ambulance to arrive, the crew looked after me brilliantly. Then the paramedics arrived. If there's one thing at which Americans excel, it's being the good guys in a time of crisis. Three of the four ambulance crew were motorcyclists themselves, and they knew exactly what to do — and not just in terms of medical attention. They instinctively knew that they could do whatever they wanted with my T-shirt — cut it to ribbons, for all I cared — but they had to tread very carefully with my jacket. Working with painstaking precision, they sliced the jacket along the seams, cutting up the sides and around the back, and removed it in one big flappy — but easily repaired — piece.

Slipping some metal plates underneath me, they eventually lifted me on to a weird folding stretcher, then carried me off to a helicopter for one of the worst flights of my life. Clear-air turbulence and chest straps were not a pleasant combination for sore, badly bruised ribs. I was absolutely stiff and couldn't move, immobilised in case my neck had been broken in the crash. But every judder and jolt of the helicopter, every sudden drop because of the turbulence, shot like a thunderbolt through my body. With the back of my head pressed against that bloody stretcher, I gritted my teeth throughout the hour-long flight to Flagstaff.

Once inside the hospital, the doctors examined me thoroughly. After several X-rays and some tests, the verdict was that I had one broken rib and lacerations to my knee. It could have been much worse. The pain was hellish, but I was more concerned about my jacket. Someone in the crew offered to take it to a seamstress, who pronounced that the damage wasn't terminal. My jacket could be saved. Twenty-four hours later, I had it back. Both my jacket and my leather waistcoat had been magnificently reassembled. I was left marvelling at the thoughtfulness and care of the ambulance crew. That's one thing I love about America — they think about little things like that.

Unfortunately, getting my body back into shape wasn't as easy as repairing my clothes. A broken rib might sound like nothing, but there's nothing anyone can do to help the healing process. It can't be bandaged and there are no fancy creams to apply. So I just had to rest and leave the bloody thing as it was.

256

Back at the hotel, easing myself into bed, I coughed. *Christ!* I thought I'd been hit by a bolt of lightning. And when I sneezed, it felt like someone had dropped a Volkswagen on my chest. The pain was excruciating. I couldn't laugh, either. And getting in and out of bed was a nightmare. Just hellish pain.

I was prescribed some serious painkillers, but they were so strong that I was a bit scared of them and soon decided they probably weren't the best idea. I was feeling too good on them. Opiates can creep up on you like that. Opting to give the serious stuff a wide berth, I settled on some simple anti-inflammatories and had a good rest. Meanwhile, the crew and everybody else who helped me were very kind, even though I was turning into a grumpy whinge-bag. Eventually, I had to sit down and have a word with myself about my behaviour. This was real. It wasn't a game. It wasn't an act. People really were that nice, kind and pleasant. They accepted that I'd been through the mill. I'd really been kicked on Route 66.

# CHAPTER
# TWELVE

## Flagstaff, Arizona, Don't Forget Winona

After four days' recuperation, I had to face the fact that I'd have to get back on the bike the next day. My rib was still tender, my knee was still bandaged and covered in weeping scabs, but I needed to continue the journey. To be honest, I didn't give it too much thought. Like getting back on a horse, it just had to be done. Hanging around until everything had healed was not part of the deal.

The bike itself held no fear for me, but I was a wee bit apprehensive about going over bumps — simply moving around on my bed still sent sharp shocks of pain through my rib. I told myself I'd be okay. After all, the bike was a relatively comfortable vehicle with a relaxed riding position, so I ought to be fine. My main problem was that I'd now reached the part of the journey where every destination was a very long way from the previous stop. This was the big country with big distances and big, big drives.

★ ★ ★

Thanks to my emergency helicopter trip to the hospital in Flagstaff, I'd ended up further down Route 66 than I'd planned to be, so I double-backed to Payson, Arizona, where it was rodeo time. I'd never seen a rodeo in the flesh before, but I'd watched it on television and quite liked it. It was like skate-boarding or BMX biking; I hadn't realised it was a proper sport until I'd seen it on TV, but then I'd learned about it and become interested. And I'd worn cowboy boots for many years, so that had to count for something.

I was most fascinated by the clowns. For ages, I'd thought they were kind of useless, some of the worst clowns I'd ever seen. Then I discovered they aren't there to make the crowd laugh. Their real function is to protect the guy riding the horse or the bull by acting as a human decoy. I really wanted to meet one, so I turned up with high expectations in Payson, which claimed to hold the world's oldest continuous rodeo. That meant wall-to-wall ridin', ropin' and dancin' fun, and a chance for me to meet some real-life cowboys and cowgirls.

First held in August 1884, when some ranchers and cowboys got together to test their roping and riding skills and the speed of their horses, Payson's rodeo, like all the others, is based on traditional cattle-herding practices. It involves a number of sports, including racing horses around barrels, lassoing, roping and tying down various animals, but the highlight is bareback riding of horses (called broncos) and bulls. And that's when the clowns are an essential part of the action. They live their lives in terrible danger. They're not just dafties doing tricks; they distract the bull from a guy that it wants to kill. And the only way they can defend themselves is by jumping into a barrel in the arena. They wear shirts and jeans that are stitched together, teamed with stripy stockings and boots, and look absolutely ridiculous. But I suppose that's the idea — to catch the eye of the bull.

I was introduced to Rob Smeets, who told me that he and his mates didn't call themselves clowns. The guys clutching on to the backs of the bulls called themselves bull riders, so the clowns called themselves bull fighters.

"You know, I used to fight bulls," he said.

"Really?"

"Yeah, I used to fight bulls for twenty years. Three broken necks later, I had to quit. I then became a rodeo clown bull fighter. These days I just get the bulls away from the riders."

"I broke my rib last week," I said. "Now, when I think of all the people with broken ribs, there must be a high percentage among you guys."

"You bet. Especially pre-1989, when we lost Lane Frost, one of our world champion bull riders, at Cheyenne."

Frost, a professional bull rider, died in the arena as a result of injuries sustained on a bull called Takin' Care of Business. Since then, a lot of rodeo participants had worn Teflon vests.

"The vest doesn't make you Superman," said Rob, "but it does absorb a lot of the hit. So the safety factor has gotten better in the last twenty-plus years."

"And these are Braymer bulls?"

"These are all Braymer or Braymer cross. Our sport in the last twenty-plus years has really gotten into genetics, just like for years they've bred good dogs. They all of a sudden said, 'Boy, I've got a daughter out of this great bucking bull, let's cross it with this one,' and now we've got some super high-bred bucking bulls."

Next, Rob explained what happens during a competition: "When they give a marking at a rodeo, the judges mark out of twenty-five points on how well the rider performs, and it's also out of twenty-five points on how well the animal performs." So, between them, two judges will award up to a hundred points for each ride — with half the points being earned by the bull, not the rider.

"How long do you have to stay on?" I asked.

"Eight seconds, one hand. And during that eight seconds, you can't reach and slap the animal. That one arm has got to stay up as a free arm."

Unlike in the horse-riding events, bull riders are not required to shuffle their feet or spur the animal. They just have to maintain control. What amazed me was that the bulls, some of which weighed more than a ton, could arch, flex and twist like cats when they had a cowboy on their back. As I talked to Rob, though, they seemed quite docile. "How do you get them from this quiet state to that wild state?" I asked.

"It's just there. It's like pro-soccer players lying around in the locker room and then they go out there and can run and do the things that they do. The bulls are professional athletes."

"They know when it's show time."

"Exactly. When that music starts rocking'n'rolling and the noise starts going, everybody's adrenaline starts pounding, they know."

"What makes a guy want to be a bull rider?"

"The cowboy lifestyle, the mystique, being your own boss."

"It's rock'n'roll, isn't it?"

"It's man against beast. Can I ride him or am I going to get thrown off? And being able to say that I'm entered in Payson, Arizona, tonight, I'm in Reading, California, tomorrow and I'm in Hayward, California, after that. It's the road life."

"You say you fight bulls. What does that mean?"

"When those cowboys hit the ground, I step in and get that bull's attention and make him come to me."

"You do the most impressive job."

"They have what we call a freestyle contest, a lot like your Mexican matadors. They turn out a bull without a rider and they judge how well we manoeuvre around the bull."

"Just using the barrel?"

"Just my hands. No weapons, no cape."

"No barrel for protection?"

"Mainly they judge me on how well I run around him and the tricks that I perform. If I run up the fence, I lose points. If he runs me over, I lose points. I won the World Championship five times."

"*Woah.*"

"Yes, sir."

"I thought your entire job was to protect the bull rider."

"It is. But back in the day, for twenty years, Wrangler Jeans put on the Freestyle Bull Fighting Contest and they turned a bull out for seventy seconds. You were judged on how well you could manoeuvre around him, if you could jump over him, the tricks that you could do."

I thought it was extraordinary. I'd never seen anything like that. Then Rob told me something that surprised me even more.

"There's a reason in Mexico they kill those bulls the first time they fight them. They're not a dumb animal; they get very smart. After a while, if he fights you, he's seen all the tricks and it's like climbing in the ring with Muhammad Ali. They get real smart."

Rob showed me a couple of his moves. The main challenge, he said, was that "four legs are going to outrun two legs all day long". Completely outclassed by the bull for strength, power and speed, the key to surviving was to stay close to the bull's shoulder, so that he had to turn in a tight circle in order to attack. "The closer and tighter you can keep to him, the better. Hopefully, his head is right in your hip pocket and you're able to just keep circling tight and making good tight rounds. The further he pushes you out, the more he isn't bent down, then the more room he has to come and gather you. That's when they knock you as high as a telephone pole."

Speaking to Rob was a joy, but I didn't enjoy the rodeo half as much. It went on far too long and was too commercial, with a constant string of interruptions by the announcers plugging "our good friends who'll supply you with all your plumbing needs" and suchlike. "I don't have any plumbing needs," I wanted to yell. "Just get on with it. I want to see somebody being flung off a bull."

The comedy was crap, too. Seriously crap. And I know this might sound ridiculous, but I'd never previously equated rodeos with cruelty to animals. I was horrified by the shabby treatment of the animals and especially by the crowd's lackadaisical disinterest in their welfare. The bulls and horses were heaved and pulled and thrown to the ground, tied up and kicked and harassed. Nobody else seemed to mind, but I didn't like it at all.

Worst of all were the mutton busters. These are children who are too small to ride bulls. So, instead, they ride sheep. They wear crash helmets, jump on the backs of the sheep, then hang on for grim death. A lot of them were crying and limping once they'd finished their rides. It reminded me of fox hunters blooding the children after a kill. In the rodeo culture, maybe it all makes perfect sense. But, to me, it was grotesque — with the kids as well as the sheep being mistreated by the adults who arranged the whole thing. Everyone at the rodeo had been really kind to me, so I felt uneasy about criticising their way of life, but my honest opinion was that a lot of it was cruel and unnecessary.

The rodeo was an overly long, cold, unpleasant experience. By halfway through, I knew I would never attend another one in my life. But towards the end, as if

264

I needed any more convincing that I shouldn't be there, they enacted the most embarrassing patriotic gesture. Some old soldiers and sailors marched shambolically into the arena, carrying flags that signified the army, the navy, the air force, the coast guard, the marines and soldiers who were missing in action. The whole thing was a shabby, redneck affair. Very low rent. I felt embarrassed and started to get the distinct impression that I wasn't among friends. These people were the exact opposite of me politically. Then it got even colder, so I headed back to the hotel.

With the centres of population and civilisation now much further apart, I was having to get used to travelling longer distances each day. But after leaving Payson, I soon arrived at something I suspected would divide households across Britain. I suspected that every man would say, "Oh, interesting," while every woman would lose the will to live and say, "So what? It's just a hole in the ground."

I have met thousands of men — possibly millions — and I'm sure that every single one of them has, at some point in his life, taken a stick, sat on the ground and dug a hole between his legs for no reason whatsoever. Meanwhile, I've never met a single woman who has done the same thing. So, my theory is that a fascination with holes is what truly separates men from women. And now I was visiting a really interesting — some might say spectacular — hole.

It's 570 feet deep and 4,000 feet across (I also know that every man will be desperate to have these details), and those people who are good with calculators say it could hold twenty football stadiums and seat two million people if it were an arena. Quite why anyone would want to work out such meaningless statistics is a mystery to me, but at least they give an indication that this is a really vast hole in the ground. What makes it even more interesting, though, is that it was made by something really extraordinary — namely, a meteorite.

About fifty thousand years ago, a meteorite with a diameter of about 160 feet, made of nickel and iron, came flying out of the sky and belted into the Arizona desert — although in those days it was neither Arizona nor a desert, but probably open grassland dotted with woods and inhabited by woolly mammoths. Flying at a speed of maybe 45,000mph., the 300,000-ton rock hit the ground with as much force as ten million tons of TNT. That's about the same as 650 Hiroshimas. *Bosh!* Of course, it flattened everything for many miles around. The surrounding landscape is still as flat as a pancake until you come to a range of mountains in the far distance, so the shockwave must have travelled a very long way before something stopped it.

Midway between Winona and Winslow, it's at a place appropriately called Meteor Crater and the way in which it was formed plays a large part in making this such a fantastically atmospheric place. What's so great about it is that you can't see into it until the very last moment. You approach up the side and then — *boof* — there it is, revealed in front of you. Standing on the edge of the crater is like being in some kind of weird experiment. It has a magnificence and a grandeur. It's very windswept, too, which apparently has something to do with the crater's shape, the altitude and the flat environment all around it.

Before the moon landing in 1969, American astronauts trained in the crater because it was thought to resemble the lunar surface. On one of these practice sessions, one of the astronauts tore his suit as he was clambering around near the rim. If he'd done that on the moon, he would have been a dead man. So they strengthened the material and, of course, Neil Armstrong's first steps on the moon took place without incident.

Although I couldn't find much to say about the crater for the TV show, it was certainly one of my highlights of Route 66. It's well worth paying a visit . . . but only if you're a bloke. If you're a woman, there's a nice wee shop in the visitors' centre.

My rib was still agony, and the bandages on my leg needed changing twice a day, but I had to push on if I wanted to see everything before the end of Route 66 at Santa Monica. My God, sometimes it's hard being a star.

That afternoon I arrived back in Flagstaff, but this time on the trike rather than strapped to a stretcher in a helicopter. It's a lovely city that has the feel of a frontier town combined with a ski resort, mainly because that's pretty much what it is. At nearly seven thousand feet above sea level, it's a popular area for winter sports — the Arizona Snowbowl is just fifteen miles north of the city and the 12,633-foot Humphrey's Peak is even closer.

That evening, I rode up to the top of a mountain on the edge of Flagstaff. From the top, the city looked like a wee village and it was hard to believe it has a population of more than 65,000 people. In particular, it seemed very dimly lit. But there's a reason for that.

Since 1894, when Percival Lowell, an astronomer from Massachusetts, chose Flagstaff as the location for his observatory because of its high elevation, the city has been a world centre for stargazing. In the 1930s they discovered Pluto at the Lowell Observatory, which really put the place on the celestial map. People came from all over the world, and they still do to this day. When I was visiting there was a flood of anoraks in the city. There are now several other observatories, in addition to the Lowell, including a military one and a university one. To aid the astronomers, the local authorities passed laws to minimise light pollution and allow the boffins a really clear view of the night sky. Special low-intensity sodium street lights helped to make Flagstaff the world's first "dark sky" city. And it's one of the few places in America where you're not assaulted by neon signs on every block. I think this is all a rather good thing. For an amateur stargazer like me, it was almost as good as being in the far north of Scotland — where there's no artificial light at all.

I think there's something fundamental to our existence about looking at the stars, wondering what they are and what it all means. Back in the Dark Ages, they thought the black part of the sky was solid and the stars were wee holes that let through rain and the light of heaven. I've spent a lot of time looking heavenwards and wondering what it's all about, but I've never understood how the constellations got their names. Take the Great Bear — if you take away the drawing of the bear, it's just a cluster of stars that look nothing like a bear. So, as a schoolboy, I named them myself and compiled my own drawings of the night sky, creating constellations that suited my designs. I had the Great Bicycle and Uncle Harry's Ear. Have a go yourself. I can guarantee it always works.

Then, when I'd finished devising my map of the stars, I moved on to the planets, which led to my own grand unified theory of the universe — the Cup of Tea Theory.

If you look at the sun and the planets — like Mars, Venus and Jupiter — they resemble a basic atomic structure — with a nucleus and electrons spinning around it. In a way, they're almost exactly the same thing. So, I thought we'd made a big mistake over the years thinking we were the big shots in the universe. We aren't huge. In fact, we're teeny weeny — the smallest things imaginable — but we're parts of something huge, like atoms are parts of something relatively huge, like this page, or a T-shirt, or a little finger. We're all made of atoms, and the whole cosmos is like an atomic structure, so we're all part of something enormous. Our planet is like a tiny bit of gravel flying around in this gigantic thing called space that's far too big for us even to see, let alone understand, in the same way that a trout has no idea that we exist. So what is out there that we don't know about? What is so huge that we are unable to realise we are only a wee part of it? In the end, I came to the conclusion that we are swimming around in an unimaginably enormous cup of tea. That's why I loved being in Flagstaff, Arizona — it let me gaze into the heavens and think about my Cup of Tea Theory.

Standing on that hillside above the town on that very dark night, I pronounced my theory to the camera. I hope to have legions of devoted followers chanting my name before too long, with cups of tea tattooed on their chests, and wearing wee gold cups of tea around their necks, in much the same way as Christians wear crucifixes. For many years, my wife has been pushing me to publicise my Cup of Tea Theory. So I took great pleasure in writing to her to tell her that I had finally brought it into the public domain and that she should expect our first disciples to start turning up imminently.

Leaving Flagstaff the next morning, I was in the best of spirits. The mood up on the hillside had been just right, and all the crew thought we'd done a great job. And we felt proud of Flagstaff. So few places on earth would be prepared to reduce their lighting to suit the wishes of a group of astronomers. The only stain on our stay in the town had come when I'd disappeared into the bushes for a pee. It was only when I finished that I realised I'd peed right in front of a couple who were using it as a lovers' lane. Oops.

We had a long day ahead of us, so Mike rode the trike for a couple of hours while I hitched a lift in the crew's truck. I took over once we reached an easy stretch, and the painkillers dulled the twinges I was still feeling in my leg and rib. After stopping at a dodgy gas station for an equally dodgy burrito, we arrived at Monument Valley, 175 miles northeast of Flagstaff. At that point I forgot all about my injuries.

Monument Valley took my breath away. Eerie and haunting, it's hugely significant for anyone who grew up watching Westerns and John Wayne — who called this remote region the place "where God put the West". Its majestic landscape of vast, vivid-red sandstone buttes that rise to heights of up to a thousand feet is one of the most extraordinary, magnificent things I've ever seen.

Most of us have seen at least one of the seven Westerns that John Ford shot in Monument Valley, so the shadow they cast on our culture is long and pervasive. Movies like *Stagecoach*, *Fort Apache* and *The Searchers* created the image of the heroic, romantic West. I spent my childhood Saturday mornings at the local flicks watching those films, then running down the street in a cowboy suit with a gun holstered on my hip, so it was an absolute joy to see the place for myself. I just stood there, a tiny dot in that massive vista, trying to soak it all in and really appreciate it.

The place is almost impossible to describe in words. Awestruck by the red, pink and orange rocks, I immediately took pictures on my phone and emailed them to the whole family. Within minutes, the replies came flooding in, all of them saying they wanted to

271

swap lives with me. But pictures cannot do it justice. You have to stand within it to understand it and feel its full force. Suddenly, in my head, I could hear some typical Western movie music — the sort that surges to a crescendo as a line of Indians appears in silhouette on the skyline — which only added to the drama of the place. Because of its prominent place in our cultural history and its uniqueness on our planet, I think Monument Valley is something we all own. We had better look after it well.

Shortly after arriving in the valley, I met Larry, an extremely friendly Navajo man who would guide us through the entire area the next day. Monument Valley is very sacred to the Navajo, so no one is allowed to go barging through it in their four-wheel drive with the radio blaring. There's a certain protocol, and Larry was going to lead us through it. He also offered to introduce me to a medicine man, which sounded like a wonderful idea. I hoped he'd be able to sort out my sore leg and aching rib.

The medicine man was dressed in a plaid shirt and grey slacks when I met him, which didn't really fit the image I had in my head. But at least his thick, coiled turquoise necklace and silver bracelets looked authentic. He told me I looked like Kit Carson, the American frontiersman and comic-book hero. It must have been the beard and the long hair, because I wasn't wearing a fringed jacket and I've never hunted buffalo in my life. I told him about my ribs and my knee, then showed him on a map exactly where the accident had happened. He listened intently before taking me into a building called a hogan. From the outside, it looked like a large garden shed crossed with a mud hut; but once inside I could see it was actually a really sophisticated wooden building. Made from long juniper branches arranged like a wigwam, then covered with mud, it was apparently strong enough to withstand a tornado.

Sitting beside me along the wall of the hogan were the medicine man and his assistant — a kind of roadie who looked after him on his travels. They lit a little fire by removing some coals from a stove and adding some wood. Then the medicine man opened some leather and hide wallets to reveal "male" and "female" arrowheads (the females had a kind of waist; the males were a traditional diamond shape), sacred stones he'd collected over the years and crystals. Laying the arrowheads, stones and crystals on a mat, he next unpacked fragments of beech ash and threw them on the fire to make smoke. Then he prayed, blew a small whistle, and held a cup of water and some feathers in his hands. There was a lot of praying, meditating and bowing to the four points of the compass, most of which we were not allowed to film. At times, the praying intensified, becoming repetitive, like a mantra, and I found myself quite caught up in it. I'd had the same feeling listening to Tibetan and Hindu chants, and even Catholic recitations of the Psalms.

Next the medicine man consulted the map to see where I had come off my bike. He had to cool the earth where I'd landed. Muttering another prayer and fluttering the feathers, he brought peace to the earth, resettling it back to how it had been before it experienced such violence from me and the bike at the time of the crash. Having realigned the planet, he turned his attention to me. It was time for a cosmic x-ray. While I clenched a wee crystal, about the size of a cigar, in my hand, the medicine man rubbed my rib with a feather and gazed into a much larger, clear crystal — about the size of a clenched fist.

"There's a fracture in it and it's lightning shaped," he said. "It's gone along the rib in a lightning shape."

Then he picked up some hot coals from the fire with a pair of pincers, blew on them and held them near my rib, chanting all the while and waving his feather.

I loved all that stuff. It wasn't a question of whether I believed it or gave myself over to it. As far as I was concerned, it was all about being in the company of people who *did* believe it. That was the whole cheese for me, and I felt very privileged to be part of it. When I spoke to Larry afterwards, he was very open minded about it and told me he used both Navajo and Western medicine when he was sick. I thought that was a very healthy attitude.

Midway through the healing ceremony, a drummer arrived. He was a fireman, and had been delayed by a plane crash. Fortunately no one had died, he told us, although the pilot had been in a bit of a state afterwards. No kidding, I thought. Pulling out the most extraordinary drum I've ever seen, the fireman got to work, banging out a beat. His drum was actually a wee dumpy iron cooking pot with three wee legs and a skin stretched over the top. Some beads and rattles were arranged on the skin, and the pot was about a third full of water. When the drummer hit it, the beads and rattles moved and the water made the sound resonate. It was extraordinary. He said the sound would carry for several miles.

In the midst of all the chanting, singing and drumming, the medicine man's mobile phone rang . . . and he answered it. I thought that was brilliant — the clash (or possibly the merging) of the modern world of the United States and the spiritual world of the Navajo. I'd already seen an example of it when I'd handed over some money to pay for the ceremony. I was fine with that — you have to pay the doctor — and his reaction to the money had been fascinating. He'd taken the notes, straightened them out, made sure all of the heads of Thomas Jefferson on the stack of twenty-dollar bills were pointing in the same direction, then aligned all of his arrowheads and other bits and pieces in the same way.

Shortly after the phone call, the ceremony came to an end. It had all been done with a sincerity that I think is missing in Western religions, and I'm really glad I took part in it. But my rib felt no different the next day. Then again — who knows — maybe it would have felt worse if the medicine man hadn't intervened? I didn't really care either way, because he was great company. The last time I saw him, he was sitting on my trike, laughing and enjoying having his picture taken.

Larry took us back into Monument Valley just before dawn the following morning, but this time into the sacred part that the Navajo owned and controlled. They are deeply attached to the environment, and don't allow anyone to climb the buttes and mesas here. Because of their care, it's in wonderful shape — a truly moving and magnificent place.

At one point, a big beetle came over to me. I was just about to nudge it when Larry said it was a stink beetle that squirted a kind of urine if it was irritated. Apparently it's very smelly stuff, but it's used by the Navajo to treat mouth diseases in babies. Larry also told me about the huge tarantulas that come to Monument Valley from the plains each year to mate. I would have loved to see that.

His next story was about the Navajo code talkers, a band of young men recruited by the US Marine Corps in the Second World War to transmit secret messages. At a time when America's best cryptographers were searching for ways to keep ahead of the Japanese code breakers, these modest Navajo farmers and herdsmen constructed the most successful code in military history. Even now, it hasn't been broken. With a complex grammar and no written form, Navajo is the most complicated of all Native American languages, and it is spoken only on the Navajo territories in New Mexico and Arizona. In 1941, when America entered the war, fewer than thirty non-Navajos were thought to be able to understand the intricate syntax, tonal qualities and dialects of the language. So it was the perfect foundation for a code.

However, there were few Navajo equivalents for many modern military terms, so the code talkers had to be inventive. For instance, the Navajo word for tortoise was used to mean tank, and the Navajo for potato signified a grenade. Equipped with their mental dictionary of terms, the code talkers joined the marines on the battlefield and were able to encode, transmit and decode messages at lightning speed. They could pass on a three-line communiqué in just twenty seconds, while conventional coding methods took more than half an hour. Their importance was highlighted when the commanding officer of the marines' signals division at the crucial Battle of Iwo Jima said that the island would not have been taken without the Navajo's efforts.

The code talkers were also used in Korea and Vietnam, but then knowledge of the code started to die out and now many Americans are unaware of the vital role the Navajo played in so much of their country's recent history. Partly this is because the US government kept the Navajo's work secret for many years, just in case their unique abilities might be needed again. And partly it's because the Navajo are very modest, quiet, unassuming people.

Bumping around Monument Valley with Larry, I listened to more of his stories — such as how John Ford came to film in the Navajo's sacred place. Larry said it was all due to a rancher called Harry Goulding, who had been living in a tent in Monument Valley since the 1920s. In the late 1930s Goulding heard that Ford was making a big new Western called *Stagecoach*. Convinced that Monument Valley would be ideal for the film, he enlisted a photographer to take some pictures. Then this uneducated man of the wilderness packed up his bedroll, his coffee pot and some grub and made his way to California. Arriving in Hollywood, he hoped to talk to Ford in person, to try to convince him to come and film in Monument Valley. While his wife waited, knitting in their car, Goulding approached the receptionist at United Artists, where Ford was preparing to shoot his new film. Of course, he was told he couldn't see anybody without an appointment — because that's the way they work in Hollywood — so he just said, "Well, I'll make myself comfortable," and took out his bedroll. The staff at United Artists had never met anyone quite like Goulding, and eventually they realised they'd have to do something about this bloke who seemed to be setting up camp in the lobby. So they called the locations manager, who arrived with every intention of sending this lunatic packing. But as soon as he saw the photographs, he was convinced. Goulding was introduced to Ford, who thought the rancher was a great guy, and the rest is history.

Larry took me to an outlook called John Ford Point, which features in *The Searchers* — it's where John Wayne, looking for a girl who has been captured by Indians, rides out on to a spit of rock and sees the Indian village beneath him. It was one of Ford's favourite places, and I could almost smell the Duke as I looked at it. While I was standing there, soaking in the atmosphere, a red truck with a water tank on its back bounced past, a tiny speck in the distance. Larry explained that most of the Navajo people who lived in Monument Valley were elders who preferred to live in the old, traditional way. They didn't want water piped in or electricity. I thought that was kind of appealing, but it meant their water had to be delivered by truck. In a funny way, I wanted them to live in the old way, too, because that meant the place would be kept intact.

Driving around with Larry, time and again I saw vistas which I'd ridden through in my imagination when I was a child. I'd come out of the cinema and ride home on my imaginary horse, smacking my backside as I harried up Highlands Street, which was transformed into Monument Valley in my little fantasy world.

I love Monument Valley, and I felt very privileged to be standing within it. But when we were filming, part of me wanted to tell the viewers not to visit it themselves — just take my word for its beauty. Selfish, I know, but I don't want it spoiled. If anyone does come, I hope they don't come on big tourist buses with loads of other people. The way to see it is to get up early and watch the sun rise, before all the buses arrive. Of course, this is a very snobbish, elitist way of looking at things, but for a wee while now I've been saying that if anyone wants to do the world a real favour, they shouldn't come to any of the places I film for TV shows. They should just read about them or watch the programmes, and leave it at that.

After our day exploring Monument Valley, Larry helped me build a fire and prepare to sleep under the stars. He explained the problems that exist in modern Navajo families whose children get involved in drugs and alcohol. An outreach social worker, he organises *Brat Camp*-style four-day treks for Navajo teens to help them understand their sacred land, the sky and nature. An inspiring, knowledgeable and passionate character,

Larry is a very gentle man whose real passion is to help the next generation. Listening to him in such a fascinating place, I hoped he succeeded in educating the young Navajo in their culture. He deals with problems that parents and social workers face around the world, but it was still strange to hear him talking about issues that are very familiar to anyone living in Govan. Crystal meth, heroin and all that other poison are being peddled everywhere, and Larry is trying to keep Navajo youngsters away from it by making them aware of their culture. He knows it's a big step back from hard drugs to the indigenous culture, but I had to wish him the best. And I'm optimistic about what he might achieve, because he's a very inspiring man.

That night, as the sky darkened and I strummed my banjo by the camp fire, my thoughts turned to what lay ahead. For weeks now, my daily existence had been determined by the need to keep moving west. But now the end of the journey was starting to loom ahead. The next day I was due to leave for Williams, Arizona. From there, I'd go to the Grand Canyon. There were a few more destinations in Arizona to visit after that, but soon I'd be in California. And then the Pacific Ocean would be right in front of me and my great adventure would be over.

I started to wish there was more Route 66. Two and a half thousand miles suddenly didn't seem quite enough. Because one thing I had learned on this trip was that Route 66 was cut up into bits and pieces — some of it tragic, some of it inspiring, most of it fascinating and all of it interesting. All along the

Mother Road, I'd found people working very hard to bring it back to life. Something as simple as painting a few murals or making delicious pies could wind the clock back a bit. But despite all of their efforts, Route 66 didn't officially exist any more, so anyone who went in search of it had to find the fragments and piece them together to make their own Route 66. That was one of the things that made it so special.

# CHAPTER
# THIRTEEN

## You'll Wanna Own a Piece of Arizona

I had a great start to the week in Williams. A further two hundred miles down the road towards California and the coast, this was the last place on Route 66 to be bypassed. On 13 October 1984, the final stretch of Interstate 40 opened, but Williams didn't go down without a fight. It held an official day of mourning when the freeway took over. The next day newspapers in America reported the demise of Route 66; and a year later the road was officially decommissioned.

A lovely wee rural community, Williams was named after Bill Williams, a trapper and hunter. Although it was nice to name a town after a trapper, I'd hoped it was named after Hank Williams — but then I'm disappointed quite a lot. I'd come to Williams to catch a steam train to the Grand Canyon. As you can imagine, I couldn't wait to see the world's biggest hole in the ground, but I was equally excited about the steam train because there's nothing I like more than a wee choo-choo.

Bores of my age have never stopped going on about how lovely steam trains used to be back in the day, and I'm no different. They have played such an important part in my life that I have nothing but fond memories of them. Everything that I remember as being great about my childhood involves a steam train. Some of the loveliest holidays I had as a kid were spent in Rothesay, and all of them started with a steam train ride from Glasgow's Central Station. I can remember it as if it were yesterday — passing through the barrier from the public area to the ticketed platform, the engine right there in front of us, a lovely olive-green colour, hissing away. My sister, brother and I would walk with our cases, our wee bags and all our things along the platform until we came to the bit where the engineer, with his shiny cap and a blue cotton suit, was hanging out of the window, saying hello to the passengers. He had black marks on his hands and on his sweaty face, and behind him the engine was warming up with a cacophony of *whissshes*. As we passed, we would hear the fireman shovelling coal. It was magical.

Taking our places in the carriage, we'd be beside ourselves with excitement, waiting for the steam engine to start its countdown to our holiday. Like an orchestra tuning up, there would be a steady increase in random noises, culminating in a whistle, and then the engine would start pumping — *shooosh, shooosh, shooosh* — as it struggled to push the carriages out of the station. It was like a countdown from ten to one. By the time we reached one, the *shooosh, shooosh, shooosh* had become *shusssh, shusssh, shusssh* and the wheels had started to go *dickety-da dickety-dee, dickety-da dickety-dee* on the rails. We could soon see Glasgow disappearing underneath us with a *shoossssh*. Then the River Clyde: *shoossssh, shoossssh*.

We were heading west, to the seaside, miles away. The train would take us to Wemyss Bay, down on the coast in the Firth of Clyde. *Shoossssh*. On the train, there was very little to do. No connecting carriages, no tea trolley. You had to bring your own sandwiches. My dad would urge us to be quiet and not fidget while he read the paper and we'd look out of the window, getting cinders in our eyes from the smoke of the engine. Every year it was the same: "Argh, there's something in my eye!" But I couldn't resist looking out, getting a face full of smoke and steam while watching it flying across the fields of corn like a ghost, disappearing as if it were being sucked in by the crops. It was one of the loveliest things. The smoke had a funny charcoal, sulphurous smell, but to me it was eau de Cologne. I thought it was absolutely fabulous.

At Wemyss Bay, we disembarked on to paddle steamers. The first one I was ever on was the *Marchioness of Brid Albion*, which I thought was a kind of posh name. There was also a *Queen Mary II*, the *Caledonia*, the *St Columbus* and the *Waverley* (which is still operating — the last ocean-going paddle steamer in the world). Linked by a quayside bridge to the train, there was always a magical engine-room mixture of diesel and coal smoke and steam and fumes as we boarded the boat. It was fantastic.

284

So when — in Williams, Arizona — Mike asked me if I liked steam engines, I thought: Do birds sing in the morning?

From 1901, steam trains had carried passengers and supplies from Williams to the south rim of the Grand Canyon, which had become a tourist destination in the 1880s. Although hugely popular, by the 1960s most of the traffic had switched to the roads and the last train, which ran on 30 June 1968, carried only three people. That should have been the end of the Grand Canyon Railroad, but the train refused to die. Enthusiasts clubbed together and started to renovate the sixty-five miles of track, the stations and the depots, and the old locomotives and carriages. In 1989 the powerful pull of the steam engine returned to the track, exactly eighty-eight years to the day since the first train had run. Since then, they've carried more than two and a half million people to the Grand Canyon.

Unlike the steam trains of my childhood, the big locomotive I met in Williams was powered by vegetable oil — like a gigantic fish supper — which was towed in a stainless-steel tanker behind it. Donated by all the restaurants and fast-food joints in Williams, the smell of the oil was something else. One moment there might be a whiff of fish, then it was kind of meaty, then veggie. But it was always a million times better than diesel.

Looking just like Casey Jones, the train's engineer was a big man with a striped hat, overalls and gloves sticking out of his back pocket. His assistant, a thin man with glasses and a bowler hat, welcomed us on to the boiler plate of the engine and we all clambered aboard — the camera man, the sound man, Mike and me. Squashed beside the assistant, I winced as we reversed out of the station. Something seemed to be missing. Then I realised what it was: the shovelling. No *whist, whist* as the coal was shovelled and no *kerchang* as the little door to the furnace was clanked shut. Instead, there was just a wee hole with a shining flame behind it. That's progress, I suppose.

After *chuff, chuff, chuffing* out of the station, we linked up with a diesel that was hooked on to the other end of the train. Maybe a steam engine powered by vegetable oil couldn't pull such a big train on its own? I transferred to a very fancy carriage at the rear of the train, the kind of thing I'd expect the Queen to roll around in — all plush blue furniture, cinnamon rolls, cups of tea, and an open bar. Chuffing along, it took nearly two hours to reach the Grand Canyon. All the way, I couldn't help thinking about Jesse James riding through that rolling countryside. The James Gang were the first criminals ever to rob a train, so I pictured them in their dust coats with their guns out, ready to jump aboard. This was perfect terrain for an ambush — prime baddie country.

I'd never visited the Grand Canyon before, so I used the journey to try to get my head round some of the statistics. Two hundred and seventy-seven miles long (I'd thought it was about five), eighteen miles across at its widest point, more than a mile deep, and all created by the Colorado River taking four million years to cut its way through layers of rock, exposing two billion years of the earth's geological history. Unless, of course, you're a religious nut, in which case all of that erosion never happened and the fossils were placed in the ground by God, and none of the geological history counted for anything — it all just magically appeared one day about six thousand years ago.

We finally arrived at a little siding and I set off to walk up to the canyon. One of the many great things about the Grand Canyon is that it has a similar element of surprise to the one I'd experienced at Meteor Crater: you can't see it until the last few seconds before arriving at its rim. My guide — a lovely woman wearing a kind of boy scout's cap and the olive-green uniform of a National Park ranger — walked with me up about forty stairs, then steered me towards a little promontory. She promised I'd get a good view when I reached the top. I walked along a path and then got my first glimpse. I almost stopped dead in my tracks; I certainly slowed my pace. Oh my God, I thought. It was magnificent. Stunning. But then I realised I was only looking at the hills in the distance. I'd been bowled over by the beauty and grandeur of them, and I hadn't even seen the main attraction yet. I walked further forward and caught my first glimpse of the actual canyon. Of course, I'd known there was drama lurking just around the corner, but I hadn't appreciated the sheer scale of that drama until the moment when I stood at its edge. I felt the same as the first time I saw the Himalayas. But, if anything, the Grand Canyon is even better.

It's like a thousand temples of rock painted in a vast palette of colours. Sandy, pale yellows merge with cool or warm pinks and dozens of shades of red and orange. There are greens and blues, pale greys, like ash, darker blue — greys and black. It's truly awesome and almost impossible to describe — its grandeur and magnificence are just too grand and too magnificent. All I could think to say on camera was that it was so much more than I had imagined and quite unlike anything I'd ever seen in my life.

Standing back a wee bit because there was a sense of being blown by a wind whooshing up and out of the canyon, I suddenly got the frights. In the short time that I had been staring open-mouthed at it, the canyon had already changed. Even relatively small movements of the sun had quite profound effects, simply because it's so vast. There are canyons within canyons within canyons. And there are probably canyons within those canyons, but I couldn't see that far into its depths. Like an inverted mountain range, vastly more was hidden than could be seen.

With a kind of creepy silence to it, the canyon has a lovely eeriness that overwhelms and hushes the voices of all the tourists. I'm reluctant to say it has some of that old hippy "a certain kind of energy" stuff, but it does. Like the Arctic, it has a presence, a dominance, a weird kind of silencing effect that's impossible to explain to anyone who hasn't stood at its edge. It has to be seen and heard to be believed, so when you stand on the edge, it's a matter of just shutting up and sucking in the experience. As I'm sure you can tell, I loved it.

As I said earlier, I've recently started telling people not to visit the places I film for television shows. I've become concerned that these often remote, empty places will be spoiled if people rush to see them. "Go and see a good film of it," I say, "and leave the bloody thing alone." But I'm prepared to make an exception in the case of the Grand Canyon. I would urge everyone to go and see it. But, as President Teddy Roosevelt said, "Leave it as it is. You cannot improve on it. The ages have been at work on it, and man can only mar it." God bless his wee bum. What a wise guy.

Back in Williams, having returned from the canyon, I was getting ready to move on to the next destination when I heard something that piqued my interest. As one of the stops on the Chicago — Los Angeles railroad line, Williams's history had been shaped by its position on the great east — west railway that transformed a transcontinental journey from six months by covered wagon to six days by train. The railway companies recruited thousands of people for this massive construction project. Some were Civil War veterans, others were Irish immigrants, but most famously the companies also imported ten thousand Chinese labourers, fifteen hundred of whom were killed on the job. Nitroglycerine had just been invented and it was incredibly unstable — it could hardly be moved without blowing up. So the company foremen assigned the task of blowing tunnels and cuttings through the bedrock and mountains to the Chinese labourers, whom they reckoned were used to handling gunpowder and fireworks. But, of course, they had no experience with nitroglycerine. On some of the lines, one Chinese labourer died for every mile of track laid. Not that this bothered the rail companies or the government, who had a very dismissive attitude to recent immigrants.

When the railway companies reached a town like Williams that was at the end of a line, the Chinese labourers, the Irish immigrants, freed slaves, low-lifes and the poorest of the poor often wanted to settle there. However, they would only ever be offered the worst land, on the other side of the railway from the locals. Hence the phrase "on the wrong side of the tracks". When I was a boy, the tramlines in Glasgow divided the city in exactly the same way: they separated the poor from the rich.

Of all the immigrants, the Chinese were often treated worst. There was no good reason for this, as they were hard and loyal workers. It was just racial prejudice and suspicion of people who were different. But the Chinese workers came up with an ingenious way to duck out of bad treatment. In the part of Williams that was very much on the wrong side of the tracks was a brothel called the Red Garter (although I had a funny feeling that it would have been on the right side of the tracks for me). Next to it were a series of other fun palaces — mainly bars. Whenever the boozed-up locals stumbled out into the street, looking for trouble, they would usually target the Chinese workers who lived near by. But the Chinese were too smart for them. They excavated a network of tunnels underneath that part of Williams so they could slip down trapdoors, scarper down their escape routes and reappear somewhere else entirely.

Eventually, though, the constant attacks got too much for them and they moved away. Thinking about the effort that must have gone into digging all those tunnels, I was struck by how threatened they must have felt. They had done the most incredible job of building the railway, blasting paths through mountains and losing their friends, only to be attacked and vilified when the job ended. It was a rotten, shameful thing. To me, it seemed to be yet another example of the tendency among immigrant communities to seek out and persecute anyone who is socially beneath them and make their life a misery. I've seen this around the world and I wish we could get rid of it. It must have been terrifying to run like hell through those tunnels, chased by those bastards, shooting left and right to lose them.

A large fire in the 1970s destroyed much of the tunnel network, but it was still extraordinary to see the remnants. I was shown to one of the entrances by a local bar manager called Jackie. Convinced that the ghosts of two Chinese guys guarded the tunnels under her bar, she had never ventured down there herself. As you know, I'm very sceptical about that type of thing, but she was welcome to her beliefs, and she was a great sport for letting me peer through the tunnels before continuing my journey west.

After another fifty miles of sun-baked Arizona desert, I arrived in Seligman, which was immortalised as a Route 66 town in a fabulous photograph taken in 1947 by Andreas Feininger that appeared on the cover of *Life* magazine. As so often on Route 66, Seligman was later bypassed by the interstate, but unlike many other places along the Mother Road, the small town (population 456) was not prepared to take its demise lying down.

The really sad fact about Route 66 is that so many towns have been unable to put up a similar fight. For instance, the journey from Williams to Seligman took me past at least ten derelict gas stations and umpteen shutdown motels, with the wind blowing through their vandalised remains. I was often told that Route 66 was dying, but in the most derelict parts it was already dead. Many people obviously gave up the struggle a long time ago.

And yet, amid the decline, the decay, the death and destruction, little pockets along Route 66 are still thriving. This is something anyone travelling the length of the road has to get used to. You can't expect it to be like the famous song — one long, glorious highway all the way to California. It's now in bits and pieces. One place will be doing just great, with big statues in the streets, bustling businesses, everything alive and healthy. Then, just ten miles down the road, there'll be nothing but derelict houses in a ghost town.

When I visited, Seligman was certainly one of the thriving, lively places. There was a lot of tourist tat, but it was keeping the small town alive. And that survival — not to mention much of the survival along the whole length of the road — is largely due to one extraordinary man: the owner of Seligman's barber shop, Angel Delgadillo.

Born in 1927 in a house directly on Route 66, Angel has witnessed the rise and fall of the road. When the

292

interstate bypassed the town, Seligman started to die. To make matters worse, the authorities even removed the signpost that pointed to the town, so it became a secret destination. Businesses closed, people left, buildings decayed. In desperation, Angel and fifteen others called a town meeting. The result was the founding of the Historic Route 66 Association of Arizona. Elected president, Angel successfully appealed to the Arizona State Legislature to reinstate the sign. He then went on to fight in a thousand different ways to bring the town back to life. And lo and behold, his campaign worked. Next he lobbied other states to follow Arizona's lead and form their own Route 66 associations. Now, all eight states along the route have recognised the historical and social significance of the Mother Road. Eight international associations have also been formed.

Now in his eighties, Angel is Route 66's guardian angel — a role he was clearly still relishing when I visited him in his barber shop. He rarely cuts hair these days, but he continues to spend much of his time in the shop, watching the world go by on his beloved Route 66. He is a wonderfully warm, positive man, with a wicked sense of humour and a wisdom that comes from years of experience. I asked what it had been like to spend his entire life at the side of Route 66.

"I saw the dust bowl when the Okies came travelling through on Route 66, when the road was still dirt and they were going west for a better life. Then I saw all the service boys pass through during World War Two. And I saw the children of the same boys when they grew up, travelling to go see Grandma back in Oklahoma or Texas. I saw the automobile get better — from no heater and no refrigeration to heat and refrigeration. Then I saw the day that this town died for ten long years."

"Was that when the interstate came?" I said.

"September 22, 1978, at about 3p.m., the business community died. Just like that. The world forgot about us for ten long years. The travelling public took to I-40 like ducks take to water. They got their wish to just zoom. But after ten years I got angry."

I laughed. "Good on you."

"When I found out that we didn't have any signing between here and Flagstaff, I got angry. I fought the state to get those signs up and I called a meeting in Seligman to tell everyone how I thought we could get the economy back. We formed the Historic Route 66 Association of Arizona. We had a big three-day celebration with a fun run, a pageant for Miss Route 66, and we invited Bobby Troup, the man that wrote the song. We fed six hundred people at the old gym, the town was filled with news media and they begun to tell the world Route 66 is not dead."

In the summer of 1988, Angel's brother Juan, who managed a hamburger restaurant that had served almost no customers for a decade, needed to hire extra staff to cope with all the tourists who were now flocking to Seligman. Since then, the number of visitors has increased every year. Angel told me he was on his fiftieth guest book, but he'd noticed one curious wee characteristic in those books: Europeans and Asians vastly outnumbered Americans. I asked him why he thought that was.

"The United States is like the new kid on the block. We're only two hundred and thirty years old. European countries, they're centuries old and they understand the value of history. They know where they come from. They know preservation. When they read about us and see that we, the people, helped to save a piece of history, they want to come."

"That's wonderful," I said.

"And we take it for granted. We live here, right?"

"Well, you've done a grand job, Angel."

"It is beautiful to be here and witness the happy, happy people that come to travel Route 66. It's beautiful. That's a big pay for me. They don't have to spend a dime, but they are so happy that we have preserved."

He told me lots more about his life — how he followed in the footsteps of his father, who bought the barber chair in which I was sitting on 10 April 1926 for $194. In those days, Angel's father's pool hall and barber shop business was one block further south — on the path that Route 66 took through Seligman from 1926 to 1933. When the road was moved north, to its current position, Angel's dad was bypassed and went bust. He seriously considered joining the stream of Okies heading west: "We were all but loaded to go to California, a Model-T Ford pulling a trailer and eleven of us, but music stopped us," said Angel.

His brother Juan played in the Hank Becker Orchestra in Seligman. Another brother, Joe, played banjo. They'd receive five dollars each to play at a dance. "But ten dollars wasn't enough to feed eleven of us," said Angel, "so we were going to California to pick apples, pick whatever they let us." However, when Hank Becker heard the family had loaded their belongings on to a trailer, he found jobs for Juan and Joe in Santa Fe, which allowed the rest of the family to stay in Seligman. Later, Juan started his own orchestra with Joe and ten other musicians. According to an unwritten family law, each of the nine Delgadillo children joined the band when they were old enough. "I was the last one to audition and I played the drum from when I was twelve years old," said Angel. Playing at local events such as high school graduations, the band eventually became the Delgadillo Orchestra. When his brothers Juan, Joe and Augustine went to war, Angel moved on to the trombone and tenor sax, supporting the rest of the family by keeping the band going.

The remaining members of the family still play together today, rehearsing every week. One of Angel's daughters, Myrna, manages a store in Seligman, and the other, Clarissa, works in the barber shop with her husband, Maurizio, and Angel's sister-in-law. It is a proper family business, a throwback to when Route 66 ran through the real America.

Angel is a remarkable man. With an impressive talent for remembering dates, his conversation is peppered with the precise times of every key event in his life. When I listened to the way he had held his town together, and looked after his family, I wanted to be his grandson — even though he's only twenty-odd years older than me. He was named Angel for a reason.

"Billy, we have so much fun here and we make a living. Both of those things matter," he said. "But you also want to understand that the world is not what it was fifty-six years ago. The world moves so fast, we have so many distractions. I'm not against McDonald's, I'm not against Wal-Mart. We need them. But there, you're a number. Here, we greet you: 'Hello, how are you?' I guess what we're selling is service, and that is something that was lost years ago."

I agreed wholeheartedly with him.

"I've had many, many tourists over the years and still they come in and say to me: 'You people on Route 66 are like one big family. I started in Chicago, Illinois, and they all treat us so well.'"

I knew exactly what he meant. "That's what's happened to us," I said. "We were flabbergasted in Missouri, Oklahoma and other places by how nice people were to us."

"And that is what we helped to preserve. Isn't that beautiful?"

"It's lovely. Small-town America is wonderful. I'm a big fan."

"At first the travelling public that came here were mainly grown-ups. But when John Lasseter made *Cars* — I'm in it, incidentally: he interviewed me for about two hours for the extra disc with the DVD — he captured the imagination of the children, the generation that's going to inherit all of this. And now

**297**

we have children coming here from all over the world, saying, 'We saw you on the DVD.'"

Angel exuded this sort of positivity throughout our conversation. It was one of those great days, and it got even better when I walked down Seligman's Main Street and bumped into a gang of leather-clad trikers.

Ever since I'd started my journey on Route 66, I'd noticed a lot of people riding next to me on hired Harleys. Frankly, I'd grown to dislike them. Big, chrome-covered monsters, to me they had begun to look more like tourist buses with every passing day. The people who rented them were okay. Many of them were early retirement guys in search of freedom and escape after decades of hard work. But I also had a sense that they were buying into that corporate image of Route 66 that I mentioned at the start of the book. They all seemed to think that it had to be ridden on a Harley or driven in a red convertible. And that sort of corporatisation was exactly what killed the Mother Road. It had transformed the drive from Chicago to Los Angeles from a cobbled-together passage through small towns with family businesses into a sanitised procession along freeways interspersed with strip malls, fast-food chains and plastic motels.

So it was a relief to meet a bunch of fellow trike riders. They had some extraordinary custom machines, some factory ones and some home-made ones with bits and pieces of cars and other odds and ends. Like me, most of the riders refused to call their bikes trikes. Many of them were older people and had moved on from bikes to trikes, which pleased me as patron of the

British Disabled Trike Society. A lot of the guys had been injured in motorbike accidents and couldn't balance on two-wheelers any more, so they'd gone down the trike route. Anything to keep biking.

One of them had created his trike by sticking a wheel on either side of the rear wheel of his Honda motorbike (actually, I suppose it was technically a quad, because it had four wheels). It was a splendid, neat-looking machine, still powered by the original rear wheel; the extra wheels simply acted as stabilisers.

"Why did you do it?" I asked. "Why did you change your bike?"

"My left leg had given up the ghost," he said. "It would go to sleep, so I would stop at the traffic lights, put my feet down and the bike would collapse on top of my leg." He'd come up with the perfect solution to keep biking.

Another wee man was there with his wee girlfriend, who had only one leg and one arm. She had a wee trike of her own, but had come on the back of his this time. They told me they still went everywhere together, and they were bursting with positive energy. Happy-go-lucky and delightful, they would be an inspiration to anyone.

Then there was Catfish Larry, the owner of a big, beautiful, yellow trike. He told me the hilarious story of how he got his nickname, but all I can say here is that the clues were to be found in a catfish and his big bushy moustache. It was not that clean. In fact, it was downright dirty and great fun, but not wanting to offend anyone of a delicate disposition, I'll leave the rest of you to use your imaginations. Anyway, Larry came from a wee town about ten miles down the road. It had died because the stone works had been operated by illegal immigrants and the government had deported them all. Broke and trying to sell his trike, he didn't have a bad word to say against the immigrants. He thought it was ridiculous to deport them, because the economy plummeted as soon as they were forced to leave. If they'd been allowed to stick around, they could have continued to work, generating money for the town, and eventually becoming legal citizens. I thought that was a rather good idea.

After the fun of Seligman, I spent the night in possibly the weirdest hotel room in the world. At Peach Springs, Arizona, the room was in the centre of a dry cavern, 220 feet deep and 65 million years old. One of the few dry caverns in the world, there was not a drop of water in it, which made it uniquely suitable for use as the world's deepest hotel room.

Until quite recently, the cavern was a tourist attraction. People would be winched down on ropes, through holes in the rock, holding a paraffin lamp. Promised the chance to explore what was billed as a "dinosaur cave", those must have been the bravest tourists in the world, because I certainly wouldn't have done it that way. I took the newly built lift, which was scary enough, especially when I realised it was my only lifeline back to the surface.

As soon as I stepped through the lift door, I felt a huge rush of air surging up through the shaft. That air,

I was told, came from the Grand Canyon, more than sixty-five miles away. It makes its way through a series of tunnels all the way to that cavern at Peach Springs. Then, in a way that nobody really understands, it escapes from the cavern, meaning it sort of breathes. Weird . . . and a little bit scary.

Having walked down a short corridor, I entered the most unbelievable cave. It consists of two enormous rooms, with a wooden platform in the middle of one of them — my quarters for the night. With two double beds, some nice Route 66 furniture, a couch, a television and an assortment of *National Geographic* magazines to remind me what the world upstairs looked like, it was a pleasant enough place to stay. There was also a wee shower and a toilet. It was pretty much the same as any other motel room I'd stayed in on Route 66 . . . aside from the fact that the roof was about seventy-five feet above my head and made entirely of solid rock that had been hollowed out over millions of years by an ancient waterfall. I started to wonder exactly what I thought I was doing down there.

In 1962 President Kennedy decided that the cave would make a good bomb shelter. At the height of the Cuban missile crisis, when Americans felt there was a very real possibility that Soviet missiles might be launched against them, JFK had the cavern filled with enough provisions to feed two thousand people for thirty days. I suppose it was a good idea in those very dark days, but the idea of two thousand people in that cave, fighting for the food — most of it sweeties and crackers — just boggles my mind. The smell, the dark and the crush of people would have been unbelievable. And how would they get two thousand people in and out of a cavern using a lift that could carry a maximum of a dozen people at a time? And what would they do if the food ran out? And would they really have wanted to return to the world up top, which presumably would have been full of people with two heads running about, eating anything that dared to show its face, human or otherwise?

Wandering through the cave, I struggled to come to terms with the sheer size of it, but then I always get freaked out by the size and age of things like that. Talking about squillions of years confuses me. I spotted some helictites — very rare crystals that baffle geologists, who still don't understand how they are formed. Neither do I, so I moved on and found JFK's store of food and other vital supplies. It didn't look very big. Some big black plastic drums contained water that had been stagnant for years, but the provisions also included purification tablets that would make it drinkable. It would taste rotten, but that would be the least of your worries if you were confined down there for a month.

It was properly dark — not like the dark you get in your living room and to which your eyes eventually become acclimatised. Down there, my eyes never acclimatised, because there was no source of light whatsoever.

Having investigated my surroundings, I returned to my tasty little bachelor pad. About 150 feet wide and 400 feet long, the cave was quite a desirable little number, even though it reminded me of one of those rooms in which some mad bastard would hole up and plan the destruction of the world. I could imagine him sitting on one of the beds, cackling to himself and saying, "That'll show them. That'll teach them to fail me in my exams and make me a laughing stock. I'll give them something to remember."

Few people have slept down there on their own. Most guests come with their partners, but Pamela was back at home, which most of the crew seemed to find quite funny. They just skittered off and left me down there on my own. Sitting on the sofa, looking at the rocks all around me, it was hard to think that it had been like that for sixty-five million years. The thought did cross my mind that if anything went wrong, like the whole thing dropping by ten feet, they would never be able to rescue me. I would have given up the ghost long before they'd managed to drill through 220 feet of granite — no matter how many crackers and sweeties I managed to find in JFK's stash. That was a dodgy moment, but pretty soon I started to relax. Before long, it was time to go to bed, so I slipped between the sheets. That's when the one true drawback of the place struck me: maybe I was not alone.

Back in the 1920s, when these caves were first opened, they found two human skeletons. I could just about cope with that. But they also found the bones of a fifteen-foot-tall four-toed sloth — a prehistoric creature that was the ancestor of the three-toed sloth, which is ugly enough. They showed me a picture of it before they left me alone for the night, and it was kind of terrifying, especially as it was so tall. Lying in my bed, I couldn't help peering around, staring down the dark wee tunnel to check if any big hairy monsters were coming to say hello.

Eventually I overcame my fears about monsters, and after reading my book for a while I turned out the bedside lamp and fell asleep. I slept wonderfully well. With no moisture, there were no creepy crawlies. Tarantulas, lizards and snakes that could have crept around in the middle of the night and given me a bite couldn't survive down there. With nothing to tug at my bedclothes and give me the jitters, I slept the sleep of the just.

I enjoyed it so much that I decided I must come back, but next time I would try to convince Pamela to spend the night down there with me.

Emerging into the bright Arizona desert glare, I bumbled eighteen miles down Route 66 to Valentine. This section followed the path of the old Beale Wagon Road through a dusty, sandy landscape. I was a long way from the interstate again, seeing Route 66 as it had been at its inception in 1926. Although the road was very rough in parts of Arizona, lots of terrific sections were still intact, particularly the infamous Oatman Highway, which crossed the 3,550-foot Sitgreaves Pass via a series of tight hairpin bends next to sheer drops. Regarded as one of the highlights of the entire 2,278 miles of Route 66, it lay an hour or so ahead and I couldn't wait to see it. But first I had an appointment at another wildlife sanctuary.

Keepers of the Wild is a refuge for abandoned pets and showbiz animals. The vast majority of the animals are seriously dangerous and had been donated by their terrified owners. Others had been seized from people who had abused them. Compared to what they'd been through, the animals were now in heaven. One of the sanctuary's jaguars used to roam around a notorious drug dealer's back garden and was seized by the Drug Enforcement Agency in a raid. Another former resident was a cougar that used to live freely in the Los Angeles home of Slash, the former guitarist with Guns N' Roses — until it attacked his wife.

The sanctuary was founded by Jonathan Kraft, who used to have his own big cat show — like Siegfried and Roy's in Las Vegas — before he saw the light and decided to work for the animals instead of having them work for him. Grey-haired, tanned and fit in his fifties, he looked more like a movie stuntman than a conservationist, but his stories were fascinating.

"Big cats are a huge business in the United States, a fifteen-billion-dollar illegal trade," he said. "There are more animals — fifteen thousand big cats — in private hands in the United States than there are in all habitats in the rest of the world put together. It's kind of crazy."

Jonathan told me there were about seven thousand privately owned tigers in the United States, which meant there were more tigers in American back yards than there were in the whole of India. I couldn't imagine what anyone who kept a tiger at home was thinking.

"We just rescued a little baby lion that was typical," said Jonathan. "Surplus in a zoo, he was sold to a wild animal auction and some girl out of Washington bought him for eighteen hundred dollars. She thought she could keep him, but she didn't have any licence or permit, so she tried to sell him to a guy in Canada. This animal was two and a half weeks old. Crazy. So we had to intervene and we took the animal from her. His name is Anthony and he's wonderful. He's ten weeks old now, a little rascal, and so darned cute. People think they stay that way but unfortunately they end up like this guy over here."

Jonathan pointed at Sultan, an adult male lion with a huge mane of hair. Lying nonchalantly in his enclosure, Sultan was looking the other way, minding his own business, licking one of his paws, but when Jonathan called his name, he turned around, stood up and walked about four steps towards us. Then he saw the camera crew and stopped to have a think about it, until Jonathan encouraged him. With Sultan standing right in front of us, looking magnificent, Jonathan's partner, Tina, brought some meat and they threw it over the rail. This giant, beautiful animal looked straight at us, then wandered closer and started eating the meat.

"We rescued him along with a tiger and he is all right now," said Jonathan. "He's about ten years old, right in the middle of when male lions are very dangerous. They have a lot of testosterone. I used to go in and brush his mane. I don't do that any more. He'd be brushing mine, you know?"

"It just baffles me," I said. "I don't know how somebody could think they could keep a thing like that in the back yard."

"Plenty of them do. I know people, private individuals, who've got thirty or forty cats in their back yards. Of course, most of them can't provide the right habitats for them, so you've got a cage situation. Next thing, the neighbour's kid comes over and does a little touchy — feely and the kid loses their arm or their fingers. And then it's the animal's fault. It happens all the time."

Jonathan spent years interacting very closely with wild cats, but he stopped doing that because he thought it sent out the wrong message to anyone who might be watching. All food is now passed to the animals on the end of a long stick or chucked over the fence.

Jonathan pointed at a beautiful female jaguar. "Her name is Hope. She's only a little jaguar, but jaguars pound for pound have more crushing power than any other cat. Compared to a leopard, she has a very short, fat body with stocky legs. Considered the wrestler of the cat family, the jaguar is very tenacious. They're the only cat that doesn't kill by a throat bite. They take their prey, bite it in the back of the head and crush its skull."

*Skull crushers*. That sounded horrific. Yet people kept them as pets. "What kind of thing would tick her off?" I asked.

"Food, for one. And other animals. Jaguars are solitary, so she gets annoyed with other animals. I have a separation between her and the leopards. If she were to be up against their cage, she would constantly fight with them."

With about forty big cats, the sanctuary is extraordinarily expensive to run. It costs about half a million dollars a year just to keep the show on the road — not that surprising when you consider that the big cats gorge their way through four cows every week.

Quite a few of the tigers and lions had come to the sanctuary after unscrupulous photographers had abandoned them. Once they stopped being cute and fluffy at about six months old, they became surplus to requirements as far as the photographers were concerned.

"Most of them end up in a canned hunt," said Jonathan, "where you can shoot them for a fee. It's disgusting." Others had formerly been in zoos, mostly private ones. "That's the only thing I have against zoos. Why do they keep breeding these animals? We all know why: everybody wants to come and see the cubs. But what happens to the cubs when they are full grown? They end up in facilities like this. Or, worse, they go to a canned hunt where the big brave hunter can shoot one."

"Where do they do that?"

"All over the country. There are more than three hundred canned hunts in this country. It's illegal, but they move from place to place. Sometimes they let hunters shoot them in the back of a horse trailer. It's ridiculous."

"For the sheer joy of doing it? I just don't get that."

"The trophy-hunting thing is just ridiculous. And there's a couple of places in this country that actually breed lions for human consumption, to make lion hamburgers. Now, why would you want to do that? And they have licences! I would love to shut them down. Lions are now on the endangered species list."

"I've never seen it for sale."

"Some of them here in Arizona sell lion burgers for twenty-seven dollars a burger. They mix it with cow meat, but why would you?"

We moved on through the park, which had a total of about 175 animals in around forty compounds and enclosures. Jonathan introduced me to a cougar called Bam Bam that was more tame than most. "They're wonderful cats," he said. "Great survivors. This cat can take down a horse, big prey. He is a little bit shy, but if you get him one on one, he'll come and sit right in your lap. He's just a real sweetheart. I've got other cougars I wouldn't do that with, but this one is pretty safe."

"It's astonishing that in America a thing like that" — I pointed at the cougar — "is still roaming in the wild. There's something quite nice about that."

"In Arizona there are about twenty-five thousand in the wild. In the southern part of Arizona there are some jaguars in the wild. They've spotted about six of them. They've come up from South America. People always wonder what they eat. I always tell them 'slow natives'."

Later, Jonathan took me into an enclosure that housed a lioness. Standing a foot behind Jonathan, I was quaking as he tried to entice her to come out from behind a rock. Oh my God, I thought. This will be the one day when she loses the plot and rips off someone's face. But Jonathan got her out from her hiding place, put a leash on her — a *leash* — then sat her down and cuddled and kissed her.

"Come on over and see her," he said.

Very gingerly, I approached. I sat down beside the lioness, as instructed by Jonathan, who was stroking her. When my heart had stopped beating out of my chest, I gave her a bit of a stroke. I'd never stroked a lion before. It was an amazing feeling.

We moved on to look at some beautiful wolves, then Jonathan showed me some of the ways in which people have mistreated the animals that are now in his care. One monkey couldn't keep its tongue in its mouth because some bastard had removed its incisor teeth. The tongue was just hanging out, and the poor little thing was slobbering.

I thought it was wonderful that a man who had made his living from lions and tigers by making them disappear on stage had turned completely the other way and now devoted his life to their welfare. Jonathan should be celebrated and congratulated. It had been a fantastic day and I came out feeling much better, rejoicing that people like Jonathan make the world a better place.

# CHAPTER
# FOURTEEN

## Get Hip to This Timely Tip, When You Make That California Trip

Crossing the Colorado River, I entered California, the Golden State, and my home for many years. Entering the eighth and final state I would have to pass through to complete the long journey from Chicago, I had mixed feelings about the approaching end — both disappointment and relief that it would all soon be over. Shouting the battle cry of generations of westbound travellers — "California or bust!" — I eased back in my seat and pointed the bike in the direction of Barstow, some two hundred miles down the tarmac. However, when I arrived at the little town I found little worth exploring, so I just kept rolling, the miles passing easily under my tyres as I crossed the wide-open spaces of the Mojave Desert, en route to the fleshpots of Los Angeles. Then, shortly after passing through the village of Helendale, I spotted an oasis of colour in the sandy desert — an orchard made of bottles.

It was an astonishing sight. In the front yard of one of a strip of dusty properties stood row upon higgledy-piggledy row of trees constructed out of coloured bottles, most of them topped with metallic pieces of junk, like car wheels or watering cans or even a rusty old rifle. I had to meet the person who'd created this magical world of ironmongery and glass in the middle of the desert. At the back of the wonderful enchanted crystalline forest I found him — a man in a sun hat with a trailing white beard that was even longer than those sported by the guys in ZZ Top. He told me his name was Elmer Long.

Elmer is a genuine eccentric in the traditional English sense. In other words, he thinks he's completely normal; which, for my money, he is. He'd built the hundreds of trees in his front yard by welding rods on to poles bought from a scrap dealer and slipping the bottles on to the ends.

"I love it," I said to Elmer. "When did you start doing it?"

"In 2000."

"As recently as that?" Judging by the extent and intricacy of his orchard, Elmer had been working very hard.

"Yes, eleven years. But I've always collected and some of the bottles my father collected. He was a bottle collector but he had no way of displaying it."

"What was your father's idea when he collected the bottles? He just liked them?"

"He thought he was going to get rich. I mean, he found some good bottles. They're put away. But I've got photographs of him digging for his bottles. He would dig a hole in the ground maybe five foot deep and when he found an old one, he honestly thought he had a gold mine in his hand."

"Sometimes you do."

"Yes, well . . . it didn't work out that way. You've got to find someone who is willing to pay the price. You know what I found out, just by doing what I do? There's no money in it. It's all free. Yesterday, I had a couple of ladies from Mexico come here, a mother and a daughter. The daughter had an eight-year-old son with her, and before they left, the grandma gave me a hug and her daughter immediately gave me a hug. Now, if you were to compare going to a mine and excavating a vein of gold and taking it to the bank and getting rich, that's one thing. But little hugs like that coming from people from another country, that's pure gold. You don't put that in a bank, you put it in your heart, you know?"

"You've got it."

"That's the key here. I have so much fun talking to and meeting people, you never know what you are going to run into."

Just before Elmer's father died, he gave away all of his best bottles, but there were still thousands left. Around the same time, Elmer chopped down his fruit orchard. "The birds were getting all the fruit anyway," he said. "So I just pulled the orchard down and I made this."

All around us were piles of bottles, some of them sorted by colour or size, but most of them piled up randomly. "Are these ready to go up?" I said, pointing at some bottles that looked quite old.

"I found a new dump. Well, not a new dump, it's an old dump. About 1950. Somebody reached in this pile the other day and found a 1942 beer bottle. These are all old. They're better-quality glass, thicker, a lot different than the new beer bottles. And I know where there are thousands of these now. The dump continued for miles and I just gathered enough to get me by for a while. It's an hour and a half from here."

"When does the forest look at its best, in the evening or the morning?"

"It looks different every part of the day."

I asked if Elmer had a favourite bottle or tree among his collection.

"The only thing that's favourite is the things I've had since I was a kid," he said. "I've got childhood items out here. I still have my teddy bears. I don't throw nothing away. This handmade rake right here" — he struck it — "you hear this ring?"

"Oh yes."

"I found that near the town of Boron in 1960. I was a freshman in high school. I've got photographs of the trip."

"And you brought it home with you?"

"I bring everything home."

"And do people think you're nuts?"

"No. Well, in a good kind of way."

"I don't think you're nuts at all. I think you're the sanest man in the place."

Elmer's glass orchard is spectacular. I enjoyed every second of going around it with him. He's a completely non-violent man, but he'd built all sorts of bullets and empty cartridge cases into his bottle-tree sculptures. He doesn't believe in guns and bullets, but he's happy to buy old broken guns and weld them into strange shapes. They look fantastic.

Most of the items in the forest were obtained for free by sifting through rubbish dumps. Claiming to know the whereabouts of dozens of dumps, Elmer talks about them like other people talk about old churches or ruined castles — "I know where there's a beauty" — and he's marked several on his mental map that he wants to investigate in greater detail.

"I've got my eye on this rubbish dump," he said. "My wife comes with me and she sits in the car and I go and dig."

For hours or days at a time, Elmer sifts through the dumps, digging up bottles and bits of metal. One time, he found a car door with a metal detector. Then he dug a bit further, "And there was a whole car there and it's flat. So I've covered it up and I'm going back for it."

In time, he hopes to put the car on top of one of his trees. God, I'd love to see that. When I visited, there were already metal parts from at least three military Jeeps, a Model-T Ford, several tractors, a swing, a trailer, a boxing-ring bell, a shotgun, an old train, a chicken feeder and dozens of other things — all of them welded on to the tops of his trees.

Elmer's home is equally eccentric. It's made from a Bailey bridge (those portable bridges that military engineers use to cross rivers), although you would never know to look at it. And it has no taps. Instead, the pipes have on — off switches like those used on commercial pipelines. There's no television or radio, just an aquarium full of fish, and only one bed. Elmer is worried that people might ask to stay if he gets a second one. That doesn't make him unfriendly or weird. He just knows what he likes and what he wants. He'd recently held a family reunion at his house, but all the relatives had stayed overnight in nearby hotels, which was better for everyone. Elmer is actually the friendliest of men, and he spared no effort or time in showing me everything and describing every inch of his garden. He was exactly the type of person I'd expected to meet in spades on Route 66. If only there had been more dreamers like Elmer over the previous two thousand miles.

Elmer Long was by far my favourite find on the 66. He embodied everything I imagined might be on the Mother Road. I wish I'd got to know him long before I did. I wish I could call him my friend.

At San Bernardino, a few miles on from Elmer's place, the great Los Angeles sprawl began and the traffic started to build up. After weeks of empty roads and wide-open vistas, it was quite a shock. The Los Angeles basin famously has some of the most dense and aggressive traffic anywhere in the world. To get a new perspective on it, I went up in a local traffic reporter helicopter with a pilot called Chuck.

From the air, the intersecting lanes of merging freeways make Spaghetti Junction in Birmingham look like a country lane. Tens of thousands of cars mingling, going round and up and down and back and forth. It looked like a tangled fishing net. And, of course, it all started with Route 66 bringing travellers from the East who were seeking fortune or fame in the West. Although the thud of the rotors made it difficult for us to talk in anything other than broken sentences, Chuck was a terrific guide. He did a lot of swooping around, with the rotors at right angles to the ground, which I loved.

Regarded as the gateway to metropolitan Los Angeles, San Bernardino used to greet Route 66 travellers with orange groves and vineyards. But those days are long gone. In the words of that great Joni Mitchell song, paradise has been paved over and replaced by a parking lot. Nowadays, San Bernardino is a long succession of strip malls, offices and housing. But right in the middle of all that is a stunning Spanish colonial-style building — the California Theatre.

In the early years of Hollywood, filmmakers would screen test their films at the California Theatre, which in those days was regarded as being sufficiently distant from Los Angeles to escape the influence of Tinseltown. Dozens of classics, such as *The Wizard of Oz* and *King Kong*, were first seen by the public in this magnificent 1,718-seat cinema. *The Wizard of Oz* was screen tested in June 1939 and the audience adored it. But the studio executives still felt uneasy about the final song, "Over the Rainbow", and seriously discussed cutting it from the movie. They were worried that the ballad might end the film on a bit of a slow note. But Victor Fleming, the director, managed to persuade Louis B. Mayer to keep it in the final cut, and his faith was rewarded when it won an Oscar. Since then, the American Film Institute and many other polls have voted "Over the Rainbow" the greatest movie song of all time.

In addition to screening films, the theatre has presented plays, ballets, concerts and musicals, as well as stand-up comedy. Over the years, hundreds of big stars have appeared there — including my hero, Will Rogers. So when Mike suggested I should give a banjo rendition of "Over the Rainbow" on the California's stage, I knew I would be following in some very large footsteps. Slinking off to a dressing room, I sat down and had a bash at the song. I'd played it plenty of times on a guitar, but banjos are fickle wee things — some tunes just don't sound right on them. Fortunately, though, I came up with a nice, slightly melancholic arrangement — a little folky picking tune.

On the empty stage, lit by a single spotlight and with my jacket draped over a stool, I stood in front of a completely empty auditorium and had a go. I used to play the banjo in public a lot, but over the years I grew kind of nervous about it. I started making a lot of mistakes whenever I played in front of people, so eventually I cut it out of the act. Very occasionally, I'll play at a charity show or for my pals in Glasgow, but that's about it. So I was as surprised as anyone when I did "Over the Rainbow" as clean as a whistle four times with no shakes at all. Admittedly, I played a very simple version of the song, but I think it worked well. It was a bit of a breakthrough for me. Buoyed by that unexpected triumph, I got out my guitar and sang "Waiting for a Train" by Jimmie Rodgers and "We're Gonna Go Fishin'" by Hank Locklin.

Riding deeper into Los Angeles's metropolitan sprawl, after thirty miles I arrived in Pomona in the Hispanic — Latino side of town. This is probably the world capital for hot rods and low riders. To some people around here, these cars — which are fitted with amazingly complex hydraulic suspension systems so they can bob up and down — are almost a religion. Some of them are works of art, and I've always loved them. Even when I was a welder in Glasgow, I used to look at *Hot Rod* magazine and drool over the paint jobs. Now, I'd come to meet a bunch of guys who were among the best in the business.

The first thing I saw as I approached Mario De Alba's garage was a customised Harley-Davidson. It was breathtakingly impressive. As well as boasting every imaginable accessory — including knuckle-duster brakes and a skeleton side rest — it had a wonderful engraving of Benjamin Franklin on the engine block. The seat was covered in stingray leather, which was beautiful but not really to my taste. I usually prefer bikes that are stripped down rather than tarted up, but I couldn't deny that Mario had done a fantastic job.

The De Albas are a close-knit family, with Mario working alongside his three sons in the garage. They have real respect for each other's talents, and all three brothers are deeply grateful to their father for everything he's taught them. One of them — who specialises in bodywork — pointed out the artistry of his brother's paint jobs. In return, the second brother told me that the bodywork was really amazing.

"My brother's a genius," he said, while his sibling stood just three feet away.

"Oh, I don't know about that," the other brother said modestly.

It was a joy to see such love and pride within a family, especially as it was justified. They were just as talented as their siblings said they were. It was the attention to detail that really impressed me. They showed me an old Cadillac that was nice enough in itself, but then they lifted the bonnet. *Holy moly!* The firewall, between the engine and the passenger compartment — which in most cars is an oily, dirty, rusting plate of steel — had been high-gloss sprayed and lacquered. When I saw that, I thought: These guys really know what they're doing.

We went outside, where a four-wheel drive pick-up sat high above its own wheels, like a giant Tonka toy. It was amazing, but I was even more impressed by Mario's 1936 Chevrolet. A total dream car, it had red metal flake paint and an intricate pattern on the roof. Even the sun visor had been hand-painted in pinstripes. It was by far the best car I'd ever seen, which seemed fitting, as I was nearing the end of the longest road trip of my life. Inside, it was decked out like a high-class brothel, with red velvet overstuffed seats.

Mario was obviously immensely proud of it, yet he became very shy and matter of fact when I asked him about it. Standing in his overalls, he just shrugged when I praised his beautiful Chevy. Then he pulled out a photograph of a burned-out wreck and told me it was a picture of the car before he'd started to work on it. In total, the job had taken him nine years. Now it looked like a piece of fine jewellery. The paint job was so good that I had to stifle an urge to lick it.

"Show him how the hydraulics work," one of the brothers said to Mario, before going round the back of the car and opening the boot. Inside were some huge cylinders, each about the size of a fire extinguisher, but highly chromed and beautifully engraved.

Climbing into the car, Mario pushed some buttons that made the Chevy go up and down, enjoying himself immensely as the car bounced around. Whenever he took it out on the open road, he would raise it up to drive, but then drop it down whenever he came to a stop. Sitting as close to the ground as possible is a big deal in low-rider circles.

On the way to the garage, I'd worried about what I might say to a group of guys who built low riders. I thought they'd just waffle on about carburettors and pistons, which I would have found stultifying boring. Nothing could have been further from the truth. They were charming people who loved what they did, and loved and respected their family. Like so many of my good experiences along Route 66, I'd stumbled across an unexpected delight in the most unlikely of places.

As I was leaving, I thanked them for a great day, then said that I thought customising cars and bikes was like an obsession for their family. "There's no cure for you — you realise that?" I said. "You're stuck with this for ever."

"Yes," said Mario. "And I'll love to do it until I die. I guess it's special. I love to work on cars and so do my sons now. So I guess I passed it on to them."

"Do you love it as much as he does?" I asked the three brothers.

"Oh yeah, definitely," said Mario Junior, with the others nodding in agreement. "As you said, there's no cure for our illness. But it's a good illness to have."

"And I'm very happy that they learned all the skills," said Mario. "They started following me and doing everything. And they're doing it just the way I like to do it. They've got the same patience now. And I'm very, very happy that they went along with it. Because they are my good boys, my good sons."

My last destination before the end of Route 66 was strangely appropriate, given that I'd started this journey reminiscing about an encounter at Mary Shelley's graveside in Dorset. I pulled off Santa Monica Boulevard into Forever Hollywood, a grand, sixty-two-acre cemetery that boasts both Renaissance villas and palm trees. Only in Hollywood, I thought.

As I've said, I'm a taphophile — a lover of grave-yards. And with the graves and cenotaphs of Rudolph Valentino, John Huston, Jayne Mansfield and Dee Dee and Johnny Ramone, among many others, this particular graveyard was a real treasure trove for someone like me. For instance, I learned that Jayne Mansfield was only thirty-four when she died. And Douglas Fairbanks Junior's mausoleum looks like something that might have been built for the Tsar of Russia. It even has a lake in front of it. Then I saw a particularly interesting gravestone. The guy's name — DeVito — had been engraved on it, as had his date of birth — 1944. But there was no date of death. I thought he must still be alive, and had arranged his grave exactly how he wanted it while he still could. Next door was another tombstone, this time with a picture of a guy with a moustache. Again the year of birth was 1944 and again there was no year of death. I reckoned they were a couple who had seized the opportunity to invest in two prime plots in the cemetery, overlooking the lake.

Another interesting grave — belonging to a girl called Bianca — featured an angel with a broken guitar. The epitaph read: "She lived to love, She loved to rock." There was also a comment about the devil, so I guessed Bianca must have been a bit of a rocker. That pleased me.

Finally, I wandered over to the crematorium, where some big women were consoling a wee man. Everyone looked deeply sad, and it was a timely reminder of what graveyards are really all about.

Now I had to face the inevitable: it was time to bring this great, exciting, fascinating journey to an end. It was Bobby Troup's song that first prompted me to take a long ride down the Mother Road, but "Route 66" had one crucial flaw. According to the song, the road runs from Chicago to LA, but the reality is ever so slightly different. Officially, Route 66 has always ended fifteen miles beyond the City of Los Angeles boundary, in Santa Monica, so if I was going to do this properly, that had to be my final destination.

For the very last time, I swung my leg over my trusty steed — the trike that had carried me more than two thousand miles from Chicago. Then I slipped into the traffic on Santa Monica Boulevard and rode towards the setting sun. I enjoyed every second, every yard of it, but I remained very vigilant because I didn't want a repetition of an incident that had occurred a few hours earlier, when I was nearly wiped out on the Pasadena Freeway. Out of nowhere, a lunatic had veered towards me from my right-hand side and missed my front wheel by inches. Any closer and he certainly would have killed me. No doubt about it. I would have been mincemeat.

I'd had a few other hairy moments on California's freeways, too. This state clearly needed a campaign to teach people how to drive properly. They needed to learn that giving way every once in a while didn't make you any less of a man. I think the way they drive is a manifestation of a rampant selfishness among some Californians. Certain types of people are attracted to the state, and they show their true colours on the freeway.

But now, cruising along Santa Monica Boulevard, through tree-lined Beverly Hills and West Los Angeles, I managed to forget all about my near-death experience with the maniac on the Pasadena Freeway. I was approaching the last few miles of Route 66. Ahead of me I could see the warm glow of a Pacific sunset. And then, suddenly, I was there, pulling up beside the Will Rogers Highway marker in Palisades Park at the junction of Santa Monica Boulevard and Ocean Boulevard. Only a vast beach and then the Pacific now lay in front of me.

Leaning on a barrier above the beach, gazing out at the ocean, I thought back over the trip. It felt very peculiar to have come to the end. It had been a long, long way from that little signpost on Adams Street in Chicago. Officially, it was 2,278 miles, but I had ridden at least a thousand miles more than that because of all the wrong turnings, the enforced detours and the visits to interesting destinations off the beaten track. I'd covered a lot of ground, and now the sun was sinking into the ocean. It couldn't have ended better.

Route 66 means many things to many people. Everyone who travels along it experiences it in their own unique way. For the dust bowl Okies, it was a road of escape and hope. For the beatniks, it was a road of self-discovery. For many millions, it was a road of new beginnings. For countless others, it was a road of romantic adventure.

I still wasn't quite sure what it was for me. It was too soon to assess such a long and varied journey. I needed time to take it all in, sift through my memories and work out just what Route 66 was really all about. But I already knew for sure that it had been quite different from the Route 66 I'd had in my head before starting my journey in Chicago. Some parts of it had been wonderfully alive; others had been alarmingly close to death; a few had already gone for ever.

Thinking back over the many miles I'd covered, the constantly shifting landscape had certainly made a deep impression. The deserts, the prairies, the hills and the canyons were all unforgettable. But it was the people I'd met along the way who I would carry in my heart for ever: Mervin the Amish carpenter, Elmer and his bottle trees, Angel the barber, Roxann in the ghost town of Glenrio, and defiant Preston in Bronzeville.

Somebody once said that Route 66 was not for everybody; that it wasn't for people in a hurry. But I think it's for anyone and everyone. It can be whatever you want it to be. On it, you'll find whatever you're seeking and plenty more. It's about America's past, its present and probably its future. Above all, Route 66 just *is*. And it always will be.

There was a spirit and a feeling unique to the Mother Road. To understand it and to feel it, you need to drive it or ride it. So, if you're thinking of travelling from Chicago to LA — more than two thousand miles all the way — take mine and Bobby Troup's advice:

If any Joe tells you to go some other way,
Say, "Nix!" Get your kicks on Route 66.

# Appendix

# Mileages from Chicago to Santa Monica

Exactly how long is Route 66? A simple question with a complicated answer.

Anyone who travels Route 66 will at times encounter several remnants of the road between any two points on the map. In some places, travellers are faced with the choice of following the path of the original 1926 Route 66, or a mid-1930s alignment of the road, or one of two or more post-war routes.

Sometimes, such as between Santa Rosa and Albuquerque in New Mexico, one path is more than 90 miles longer than another. Consequently, there is no definitive length for Route 66. Some people say it is nearly 2,700 miles. Others claim it is 2,448 miles. The Historic Route 66 Association of Arizona states the length as 2,278 miles and that's the distance that has been used throughout this book.

**Illinois**

| | |
|---|---|
| Chicago | 0 |
| Springfield | 200 |

## Missouri

| St Louise Green | 296 |
|---|---|
| Rolla | 402 |
| Springfield | 511 |
| Joplin | 583 |

## Oklahoma

| Miami | 605 |
|---|---|
| Tulsa | 691 |
| Oklahoma City | 800 |
| Clinton | 885 |
| Elk City | 910 |
| Sayre | 926 |

## Texas

| Shamrock | 961 |
|---|---|
| McLean | 983 |
| Amarillo | 1056 |
| Vega | 1125 |
| Adrian | 1139 |

## New Mexico

| Tucumcari | 1167 |
|---|---|
| Newkirk | 1199 |
| Santa Rosa | 1222 |
| Albuquerque | 1341 |
| Grants | 1416 |

## Arizona

| Flagstaff | 1661 |
|---|---|
| Williams | 1695 |

| | |
|---|---|
| Seligman | 1737 |
| Hackberry | 1787 |
| Kingman | 1809 |
| Needles | 1870 |
| Amboy | 1943 |
| Barstow | 2107 |
| Victorville | 2157 |
| Los Angeles | 2248 |
| Santa Monica | 2278 |

(Distances according to the Historic Route 66 Association of Arizona)